A Civil War Soldier and me

Written by

Linda Zimmermann

Acknowledgements

Special thanks to: Kingfield Historical Society, Memorial Military Museum, Connecticut Museum of Culture and History, Richmond National Battlefield Park, Antietam National Battlefield, Fredericksburg and Spotsylvania National Military Park, New Bern National Cemetery, Suffolk Nansemond Historical Society, Craven-Pamlico Regional Library, Eberly Family Special Collections Library at Penn State University, John Banks, Thomas Clemens, Dan LeRoy, Kim Perlotto, Ed and Nancy Thompson, Scott Staton, Martin Willis, and Michael Worden.

To my husband, Bob Strong, who I assumed had been a willing volunteer for all my projects over the last 35 years, but has recently informed me that he had been conscripted, I owe you a trip without battlefields, cemeteries, or archives.

To contact the author, email: lindazim@optonline.net
Or write to: Linda Zimmermann, PO Box 192, Blooming Grove, NY 10914

A Civil War Soldier and Me
Copyright © 2025 Linda Zimmermann
All rights reserved. This book may not be reproduced in whole or in part without written permission.
Eagle Press, New York
ISBN: 978-1-937174-05-7

Table of Contents

1 In the Beginning	1
2 I Will Here Commence	21
3 Back to Kingfield	47
4 Matter of Faith	54
5 Albion Joins the Ranks	59
6 North Carolina Part 1: Roanoke Island	68
7 North Carolina Part 2: New Bern	84
8 North Carolina Part 3: Fort Macon	93
9 The Calm Before Antietam	109
10 Antietam: The Bloodiest Day	117
11 Two Brooks in Fredericksburg	133
12 Wrestling Mud	144
13 Siege and Surprise Attack	151
14 The Disturbing Case of James Burton	165
15 After the Siege: The Raid	173
16 Camp and Home	183
17 Wright and Wrong	193
18 The "R" Word	201
19 Absence of All That Makes Many Happy	205
20 Bermuda Hundred	216
21 The Final Days of Life	233
22 The Death of Albion Brooks	237
23 In Pursuit of my Dead Brother	243
24 Albion Goes Home	251
25 If I had a Time Machine	255
Appendix A Other Soldiers	259
Appendix B The Brooks Family	274
Appendix C The Kingman Family	298

Unless otherwise noted:

All images and Brooks-related material are courtesy of Ed and Nancy Thompson.
All contemporary photos by the author.
Images with a LOC or LC number are from the Library of Congress.
Images in the public domain with multiple online sources have no attribution.

1
In the Beginning...

History, if you are lucky, can be a very personal thing. Unless your heart is made of stone, you can't look at people's photos, read their letters, or get your hands on the Holy Grail of original source material—a diary—and not be moved in some way.

Of course, if those people are mean and petty, you can quickly grow to hate someone who lived centuries before you. At the other end of the spectrum, if those people were kind, witty, compassionate, and brave, you can come to feel as though they are great friends, or even like members of your own family—sharing their joys and sorrows, and ultimately grieving at their deaths.

Happily, it is the latter situation in which I found myself a little over 30 years ago in the early 1990s; being drawn to a very special Civil War soldier named Albion D. Brooks, through a very special collection of documents. My search for information about Albion continued over the decades, culminating in 2024 with a treasure trove of material which was not available when I first began my research.

I was then compelled to finally put pen to paper about Albion, but struggled as to how to best present the story of his brief life. Should it be a strict biography, quoting his letters and detailing the battles in which he was engaged? The historian in me said it was the standard way to do it, keeping the researcher removed from the research.

However, the story of Albion Brooks is about to be told because this historian got involved, and it became personal. The story of my travels, persistence, and emotions, are linked to his story now, thanks to chance or fate, it doesn't really matter which one.

If you are picking up this book with the expectation of reading a dispassionate account of a Civil War soldier, you are out of luck.

Fortunately for me, I was lucky enough to stumble upon Albion Brooks, and I would like to imagine that he would have felt lucky that I did.

The Trunk

In the 1980s, I worked in a medical diagnostics company in Rockland County, New York. I was a Research and Development scientist in a laboratory with lots of cool instruments and apparatus, and thought that when I retired, many years down the road, I would start writing. I was/am a science nerd, and love all things science, but writing was my passion.

When the company was sold, after working there for about 10 years, my intended career was rudely interrupted when the new owners eliminated the Research and Development department. As all my friends and coworkers scrambled to find other jobs in labs, I took a step back and asked, "What if…?"

What if I started writing now, and gave it my best shot to earn a living out of it before I starved? Very long story short, despite being very hungry for a while, I never had to put on another lab coat, and over 30 books later, I am very grateful that I took that leap of faith.

One of the topics I first enjoyed writing about was military history, in no small part because my dad was a proud Marine (there are NO ex-Marines), having served in World War II and the Korean War. When I was little, my mother worked nights and my dad would make some *Jiffy Pop* popcorn and we would stay up watching John Wayne single-handedly winning World War II. As my mother would be pulling into the driveway, my dad would say, "Hurry up and get in bed and pretend to be asleep, or a I'll get in trouble."

Walter Zimmermann
USMC April 1943

Bravely facing the Japanese Imperial Army in the Pacific was one thing. Facing my mother's wrath was, well, let's just say retreat was the most prudent option.

So, in the early 1990s, I was living in Nanuet, New York, and writing articles on a variety of topics, but with special interest in military history. Then came that fateful day when I called a local traveling salesman, who also had a side business dealing in antiques and militaria. I was working on an article on Revolutionary War and Civil War reenactors and he had connections to some military-related groups. During our conversation, he mentioned he had made an interesting purchase, and would I care to take a look at it?

In 1993, he was traveling on business in the Finger Lakes region of New York State, and decided to stop in an antiques store to see if they might have anything of interest. The store owner pointed to an old trunk across the room and said it was full of letters and papers.

"I'm tired of going through other people's junk," the store owner complained. He then offered to include all the papers with the trunk, and suggested that there may be "a few stamps worth something," on the envelopes.

Without looking at the contents, the trunk was purchased and wedged into the back seat of his car. He drove around with it for two weeks before finally dragging it into his house and thumbing through the contents. Talk about a treasure chest moment!

"Other people's junk," turned out to be over 500 original documents spanning 200 years of American history. It was a veritable *Who's Who* of United States military figures from the inception of the United States military. The letters were to and from the Thompson family; specifically, three generations of Alexander Thompsons. I spent years carefully transcribing every letter and piecing together the lives of this fascinating family. It all culminated in 1996 in my book, *Forging a Nation: From Revolution to Civil War*[1].

The following are very brief summaries of their lives.

Captain Alexander Thompson, 1759-1809. Born in New York City, his family fled when the British occupied the city. On May 31, 1779, Thompson joined Lamb's Artillery and became a lieutenant. According to his grave stone in the West Point Cemetery, he was "present at the capture of Yorktown, and other successes."

In 1794, he was promoted to captain of the newly created Corps of Artillerists and Engineers. In 1806, he became Military Storekeeper at the new military academy at West Point, NY. Among the document collection were many of Thompson's West Point receipts, including "One hundred and twelve Dollars – for Bell for the Military Academy with all the fixtures."[2] How many of America's future Army officers heard that bell ringing?

Captain Alexander Thompson
1759-1809

Colonel Alexander Thompson, 1793-1837. Captain Thompson's son grew up at West Point, and at the age of just 18, he became the 75th graduate of the Military Academy on January 3, 1812. He was First Lieutenant of the 6th Infantry, promoted to captain in 1814. He fought in the War of 1812, and at the Battle of Plattsburg, Major General Macomb

---

[1] Zimmermann, Linda. *Forging a Nation: From Revolution to Civil War.* New York: Eagle Press, 1996

[2] Zimmermann, pg. 51

wrote of Thompson that "in command of 100 men gallantly defended a bridge the enemy was endeavoring to pass."³

Colonel Alexander Thompson
1793-1837

He was to see long, hard years of service at Fort Niagara, Sackets Harbor, Fort Brady, Fort Howard, Fort Mackinac, Fort Gratiot, Fort Leavenworth, Jefferson Barracks, and Fort Jessup. Lt. Col. Thompson's final day of military service, and of his life, was Christmas Day in 1837 during the Second Seminole War, at the Battle of Okeechobee in Florida. According to the official Army dispatch describing the battle:

Although he received two balls (in the chest) *from the fire of the enemy early in the action, which wounded him severely, yet he appeared to disregard them, and continued to give his orders with the same coolness that he would have done had his regiment been under review, or any other parade duty. Advancing, he received a third ball, which at once deprived him of life; his last words were, "Keep steady, men; charge the hammock—remember the regiment to which you belong."*⁴

Lt. Col. Thompson's remains were brought to West Point, where he was buried next to his father.

The Captain's grandson and the Colonel's nephew, was Reverend Alexander Thompson, 1822-1895. His father, William, had a drugstore in New York City. Colonel Thompson had told his nephew to "let the Bible be your book of regulations,"⁵ and he followed his uncle's advice, graduating from the Princeton Theological Seminary in 1845. Rev. Thompson became the minister of several churches in New Jersey, Brooklyn, and Staten Island, New York, and eventually the South Church in Bridgeport, Connecticut in 1859. One of his favorite parishioners was young Albion Brooks.

---

³ Zimmermann, pg. 38
⁴ Zimmermann, pg. 89
⁵ Zimmermann, pg. 77

At the start of the war, Rev. Thompson helped organize the 17th CT V.I., acted as their temporary chaplain, and maintained a close connection with many of its members throughout his life. Rather than waste his time dealing with bickering parishioners, Rev. Thompson chose to move to New York City in February of 1862 to help sick and wounded soldiers, most notably with the New England Soldier's Relief Association. Known for the power of his words, Thompson was often praised for the comfort he gave to hundreds of dying men throughout the war.

On October 22, 1889, Thompson delivered the oration at the dedication of the monument to the 17th Connecticut on Cemetery Hill in Gettysburg.

Reverend Alexander Thompson
1822-1895

...Your valor, your purpose, your endurance, your privations in camp and march and field, your honorable wounds, the life devoted of your comrades were not in vain. The nation is one... Long after this memorial stone shall have crumbled, the generations to come will apprehend the results that came of this mighty struggle, in a united country, and a beneficent government, and a prosperous people...

What of the Thompson women? When Captain Thompson died in 1809, he left his wife and three daughters destitute.

Fortunately, the first Superintendent of the West Point Military Academy, Jonathan Williams, took pity, and granted them the unique privilege of giving Thompson's widow permission to board twelve cadets. The privilege of dining at the Widow Thompson's became highly sought-after; cadets "willed" their privileges to other cadets upon graduation.

The reasons why this privilege was so jealously guarded is evident; food at the mess hall was prone to mice, roaches, and decay, not to mention that the cadets were under the perpetual scrutiny of officers. Dining with the Thompsons not only meant good food, it gave the cadets a chance to unwind in a relaxed, family atmosphere.[6]

---

[6] Zimmermann, pages 55-56

The situation was supposed to be temporary—lasting as long as Mrs. Thompson lived, and until her three daughters were married. That "temporary" privilege lasted almost 70 years!

The three Thompson daughters, Amelia, Margaret, and Catherine, never married, and when their mother died (probably in the late 1830s) they retained the right to board cadets. This was a situation unique in the history of the Military Academy and it continued until 1878 when the last surviving daughter, Amelia, died at the ripe old age of eighty-eight!

It is sadly ironic that after devoting his life to his country, Captain Thompson is best remembered at West Point for his wife's and daughters' cooking!

Then there was the Colonel's widow, Mary Waldron Nexsen (1790-1858), whose pen was at least as mighty as her husband's sword. After a lifetime of service, upon his death in the line of duty, Mary was only granted a half-pay pension for five years. She fought for additional benefits for 20 years, writing to senators, congressmen, and anyone who would listen.

In a letter to her brother-in-law, William, she describes her difficulties with the government in terms which could easily be read as a reaction to any number of present-day complaints:

Dear William,   *Washington, D.C.*
                                   March 6, 1840

...I do not hesitate to Say, this is the most disgraceful Congress that ever sat - They Seem determined not to allow a Single Claim, whether just or not - and try to prevent a dollar from being appropriated - <u>except</u> to pamper their own prodigal extravagances for themselves - and they will Sit and Squander thousands of money - on their outrageous speeches to Send throughout the Country - for the purpose of Electioneering - and the <u>Small</u> sum of $100,000 is appropriated for the Stationery & printing of the House, besides $400,000 for the pay of these <u>noble liberal minded men</u> - and $25,000 for the Clerks of the House & $25,000 for the Stationery & printing of the Senate - and yet they pause and hesitate at allowing a Single farthing for the 20 or 30 years faithful Service of an officer of the Army - whose life has been yielded up for them - and they close their ears to the prayer of the widow & the orphan who ask a pittance justly due - I am sick at heart & discouraged...[7]

---

[7] Zimmermann, pg. 94

As much as I enjoyed researching and writing about the Thompsons, speaking about them was one of the highlights of my life. Being able to share the tragedies and triumphs of people long forgotten…well, it is a unique honor and deeply gratifying. I had the privilege of speaking to groups of military historians at West Point, Fort McNair, and countless Civil War Roundtables. I spoke at Gettysburg, not far from that monument to the 17th CT on Cemetery Hill. I spoke at the Smithsonian in Washington, D.C., where a direct descendant of Reverend Thompson attended, looking very much like her ancestor, and telling of her passion for being a Civil War reenactor (as a convincing-looking man with a fake beard) and training cavalry horses! Then there were the countless lectures at libraries, schools, organization's meetings, and I can't even remember where else.

Through all of those lectures over all of those years, I always added something to the story of the Thompson family; the story of Albion Brooks. It was in this document collection from that fateful trunk that I first "met" Albion. While there were many, many letters to and from many, many soldiers, the correspondence from, and about, Albion somehow stood out.

In *Forging A Nation*, was a section entitled "Brave Albion":

On August 28, 1861, Reverend Thompson recorded in his diary that he had a visit from Albion Brooks, a young man with a noble character and a pleasant manner. Brooks was also a devout Christian with a strong desire to serve his country; qualities which three generations of Thompsons had admired. Brooks acted upon his desire to serve his country by enlisting with the 8th Connecticut Regiment Volunteer Infantry on November 26, 1861.

On Thanksgiving Day, November 28, 1861, Brooks wrote the following to Reverend Thompson:

Burnside Camp Annapolis, Md
My dear Pastor
Here I am a <u>soldier</u> for my country…I have a fine lot of men in my tent…We have a fine Chaplain - he seems to be a true Christian man…Well here it is Thanksgiving & you at home eating Turkey while we poor men are in Dixie with nothing better than hard crackers & "salt horse". Well so be it…I wish I could stand in the Old South Church [Bridgeport] *next Sunday but my duty is here.*

In March of 1862, the 8th Connecticut was engaged by the enemy at New Bern, North Carolina, and again in April at Fort Macon in that state. On May 28, 1862, a mutual friend of Albion's and Thompson's wrote to the Reverend and inquired good-naturedly if he might "ask brave Albion if his knees did not shake when the shot came whistling around his head." If Albion's courage had not been tested in the first two engagements, it certainly would have been on September 17, 1862 at the battle of Antietam, where the 8th CT saw the bloodiest, single day in its history; total casualties for the regiment of about 400 reached 194 killed, wounded and missing.

In October of 1862, another mutual friend at Harper's Ferry, West Virginia, wrote to Thompson to inform him that "Albion Brooks is only about 5 miles from us. I expect a visit from him soon."

In December of 1863, Albion Brooks and about 300 other members of his regiment re-enlisted. After a well-deserved furlough in January-February, 1864, Albion and the 8th CT were back in Virginia. In June of 1864, the bloody Battle of Cold Harbor saw staggering casualties for the Union, with over 6,000 falling in the span of one hour. The loss for the 8th CT was only 8 killed and 30 wounded. But among those 8 killed, was a special friend of Reverend Thompson's—First Sergeant Albion D. Brooks.

Chaplain Moses Smith of the 8th CT Regiment wrote to Reverend Thompson, June 4, 1864:

In an engagement at Cold Harbor June 2d, your dear friend & brother A.D.B. was severely wounded. The bullet struck him in the abdomen in the left side & passed through coming out on the other side above the hip. It was supposed that the wound was mortal but we knew that it was safe & would be for his comfort to do all possible. He seemed to rally during the day (he was wounded in the morning) he rested well at night & yesterday morning thought he felt better. I left him for part of the day...on returning found him sinking...At about 1/4 of 9 of last evening, June 3 he quietly breathed his last...A little before his death he said – "I am going" & then slowly added, "So I am with You always even unto the end" & soon closed his eyes & breathed more & more slowly... [8]

Well, let me tell you the effect of reading this letter. Having come to know and like Albion a little bit, because everyone that knew him seemed to like him a lot, I was nothing short of devastated and admittedly was

---

[8] Zimmermann, pages 110-112.

crying like a baby. It was at this moment that my boyfriend (and future husband) Bob Strong called me. I was crying so hard that I could barely speak. Quite concerned, he kept asking what was wrong.

Finally, I blurted out, "Albion is dead!"

Silence.

Then, ever so slowly, he replied, "Well…yeah…"

Bob had heard all about Albion in the previous weeks, and obviously knew that someone who fought in the Civil War would not be alive in the 1990s. But that wasn't the point. At least, not to me.

"You don't get it!" I protested, still sobbing. "To me, it just happened!"

Of course, rationally, I knew that Albion was long gone. But because I had grown so fond of him, I had irrationally envisioned that Albion survived the war and lived happily ever after. And I never thought that I would learn of his death from the same heartbreaking words that Reverend Thompson had read, hold in my hands that same letter Thompson held in his hands, penned by the Chaplain who had watched Albion die.

From that moment on, I was emotionally hooked and intellectually invested in finding out everything I could about Albion Brooks. I hoped, almost to the point of prayer, to someday find a picture of this young man who was loved in life and mourned by all in death. While I was able to share what little I knew about Albion during my *Forging A Nation* lectures, my ultimate goal was to someday write a book about him—if I could possibly, miraculously, uncover enough information.

I never dreamed it would take 30 years.

Seeing Albion

As a big fan of music from the 1930s and 40s—when you could actually understand the lyrics and sing along—this chapter section reminds me of the 1937 Rodgers and Hart song *Where or When*. The lyrics have a line that goes, "But I can't remember where or when."

So it was for the moment that I first saw a picture of Albion Brooks after so many years of searching. I had even driven the four hours from my home in New York to the U.S. Army Heritage and Education Center in Carlisle, PA, to search their collection of Civil War photographs. I was like a kid in a candy store, but there were no Albion Brooks images.

Then on some website one day—I can't remember where or when—there it was! For the umpteenth time in who knows how many years that I had searched for an image of Albion Brooks, this time, there was his photo. I froze for a moment…a long moment. I was looking into his face, finally seeing the man who had caught my interest and made me cry at the news of his death.

"Bob! I found Albion's photo!" I shouted from my office.

Bob (now, my husband) came running upstairs and also stood quietly for a moment.

"Are you going to print it," he asked?

Silly question. Within minutes it was printed and framed and placed on my desk, where it remains to this day.

Perhaps it is some foolish human need, to put a face to a name, but it is a powerful thing when you can. According to a Google AI search on the psychology of needing to see faces, it stated:

The human tendency to focus on and analyze faces, a phenomenon called face perception, is rooted in our social nature and evolutionary history, allowing us to glean crucial information about others' emotions, intentions, and identities.

Okay, so psychology has a term for it, and it appears to be something programmed into our DNA. Of course, a single still image does not compare to the endless variations of human facial expressions, but it does give you the template on which your brain can imagine one's smile of joy, look of surprise, grimace of pain.

Whatever the psychological basis behind it all, it meant the world to me. *I finally saw Albion.*

Again, I hoped against hope that the day would come when I would find out even more information—although I had no idea where or when…

A Soldier's Grave

> ***I have seen what it is to die a soldier's death and be laid in a soldier's grave.***
>
> Albion referring to the losses at Antietam in a letter to home November 20, 1862

Of course, in the 1990s, after reading of Albion's death, I immediately resolved to one day find his grave and pay my respects in person. I had no idea it would take almost 30 years to get there.

I presumed he was buried in the Cold Harbor National Cemetery, and was hoping that he had a marked headstone, and was not among 1,300 unidentified remains.

When the cemetery was established in 1866, remains were recovered from battlefields and field hospitals from 22 miles around. The relatively small 1.4-acre cemetery quickly filled.

"A Burial Party, Cold Harbor, Virginia," April 1865, photo by John Reekie, print by Alexander Gardner.

When another search for fallen Union soldiers was conducted in 1867, a staggering amount of previously overlooked skeletal remains were found. While it is only to be expected that things such as weathering and seasonal vegetation might obscure a handful of shallow graves and bones, another 1,000 full and partial remains were actually discovered! Very few of these soldiers could be identified, so they were placed in the Richmond National Cemetery and marked as unknown. For many years after, bones continued to be discovered by relic hunters, farmers, and local residents. Still, to this day, remains are being found at Civil War sites.

In 1997, Bob and I took a trip to Virginia, first to visit all the sites from the Seven Days Battles, fought June 25 to July 1, 1862, as part of General McClellan's ultimately lame and ineffective Peninsula Campaign, designed to take Richmond. Also on my list was the Revolutionary War battlefield of Yorktown, not only for its historical significance, but because Captain Thompson was there. It was a very impressive site.

The focus of the trip, however, was to try to trace the movements of the 8th Connecticut at Cold Harbor, and possibly locate the field hospital where Albion breathed his last.

Unfortunately, Albion's grave was nowhere to be found and his name wasn't on any list of burials, and I feared he was one of the many unknowns. There was still a chance that his body had been shipped back to Bridgeport, Connecticut, but I had no luck there, either. Unless new information came to light—and what were the chances of that after 140 years—I would never know where Albion Brooks was laid to rest.

Years and years passed, and every once in a while, I would do an Internet search and come up empty—until one day, I can't remember when, there was suddenly a hit. I don't even remember which military history site had posted a brief mention of Albion, but my initial excitement quickly waned as I found that there wasn't anything I didn't already know. In fact, whoever had posted the information, could have gotten it from my book, *Forging a Nation*.

Then something caught my eye at the bottom of the page, under Albion's date of death; something for which I had been looking, for a very long time.

"Place of burial: Kingfield, Maine."

I was ecstatic, but immediately had two questions—"What *the hell* is he doing in Kingfield, Maine?" and "Where the hell *is* Kingfield, Maine?"

He was living in Bridgeport when he had enlisted in 1861, and he and his family had apparently been there for a while. He enlisted with a Connecticut regiment, so again, I did not have any reason to suspect he had any connections with Maine, let alone having connections deep enough for family or friends to go to all the expense and trouble to transport Albion's remains the 746 miles between Cold Harbor to Kingfield.

One of my questions was easily answered with Google Maps—Kingfield was located precisely in the middle of nowhere. You drive to Augusta, Maine, on Interstate 95, then go northwest for 60 miles. Or if you're in Quebec, Canada, you drive 55 miles from the border to the southwest. The little town sits on the Carrabassett River in a stunningly beautiful area, which in the mid-1800s must have been even further into the middle of nowhere.

My other question would take more years to answer, why was Albion's body brought to Kingfield? I finally discovered that the Brooks family was from Maine, and Albion was born in Carthage, Maine, 36 miles from Kingfield. His mother's side of the family, the Eustis', were an old New England family, which included a governor of Massachusetts, and there was a town named for them 36 miles to the northwest of Kingfield.

As the drive from my home to Kingfield, Maine is about seven hours, it wasn't somewhere I was going to go on a standalone trip. Bob's vacation time was limited, and therefore quite precious, and as I had no thoughts of a book about Albion as I had very limited information, visiting Kingfield fell into the broad and nebulous category of "one of these days."

Around 2012, an opportunity arose when we were invited to stay at a friend's vacation rental house in Ogunquit, Maine, for a few days in the summer. It was an offer we couldn't refuse, and possibly a chance to finally get to Kingfield, as well.

I absolutely love Maine! My mother's family would leave Boston every summer to spend on the Maine coast. My great-grandmother owned a small island in Bar Harbor with a cottage on it—an idyllic getaway, until the U.S. government seized it for national defense purposes at the start of World War II, and never gave it back.

But back to the Ogunquit trip. Kingfield would be about a 2-hour drive from there, not factoring in heavy summer traffic, so we planned to take an early morning trip on one of the days. The best laid plans...

The day after we arrived it began to rain. No, it poured. It poured buckets. It poured Biblical amounts of rain for days, to the point where I fully expected the locals to start building arks. Facing flooded roads, slow traffic, and just miserable conditions, we unfortunately abandoned the idea of the Kingfield excursion.

Then life got in the way for several years—or more accurately, life almost ended for both Bob and I in a series of terrible health crises, so our only thoughts of cemeteries during that time was how to avoid being buried in one.

Then Covid hit, and, well, travel just wasn't happening.

Finally in the fall of 2022, Bob was retired, we were relatively healthy, Covid had eased, and we had planned a trip to Maine and Canada. Our first stop in Maine is always the Maine Diner in Wells, for Bob's absolute favorites—award-winning, seafood chowder and lobster pie. One of the times he was very ill, I had even ordered some of that seafood chowder shipped to our home! As a vegetarian, there's not much for me to eat there, but I always get a kick out of watching Bob's eyes roll back in his head with that first spoonful of chowder. (And I admit my eyes also do some rolling with their chocolate chip cookie dough pie.) From there we drove to our hotel in Augusta for the night.

I was excited and a bit nervous the next morning as we got ready to head to the Riverside Cemetery in Kingfield. There was a photo of Albion's headstone on the *Find a Grave* website, but it didn't indicate where in the cemetery among the 665 burials it was located. Would we finally get to Kingfield, only to fail to find Albion's grave?

The drive was along beautiful and sparsely populated roads for about 60 miles. Early in the morning, there were school buses and a few cars, but we often had the roads to ourselves. My excitement grew with every passing mile, as after almost 30 years, I was going to stand by Albion's grave—I hoped. The town of Kingfield is quite small, and I knew the cemetery was facing the river, so that was our navigation guide. Without much trouble, we came upon the modern cemetery sign on white posts by the unpaved entrance at the bottom of the sloping hill. I thought that the one advantage I had in locating the grave would be that Albion's stone appeared to be made of white marble, so that should narrow it down—NOT!

We pulled in the entrance and to my shock and dismay, I saw that *almost all* the 665 graves had white marble stones! This could take a while, I thought, until something remarkable happened. You may believe the following or not, I don't really care, because it is the truth of what inexplicably occurred a moment later.

Scanning the sea of graves before me, one suddenly stood out like a beacon.

"STOP THE CAR!" I shouted to Bob like a crazy woman.

"What? Why? What's the matter?" Bob replied, somewhat flustered by my extreme reaction.

"THERE IT IS!" I shouted again, pointing to my right, diagonally across the cemetery a few hundred feet away.

Bob stopped the van, and sat in astonishment as I jumped out and literally started running, without hesitation, on an exact beeline to what appeared to me to be a glowing stone, lit up like a street light. It was <u>so</u> clear, <u>so</u> bright, and <u>so</u> obvious.

I absolutely ran the shortest, most direct line from the van, through the rows of graves, straight to the stone that beckoned me like a lighthouse—the headstone of Sergeant Albion D. Brooks!

I was overwhelmed with emotion, far more than I had anticipated. With tears welling up in my eyes, I briefly turned back toward the van and yelled, "HERE HE IS!"

Bob was freaked out, to say the least, at my bizarre behavior and seemingly supernatural knowledge of exactly where Albion was buried. But he still left the van and walked in a more sane and leisurely pace across the cemetery to join me. I was crouching down, fully swept away in the moment, when Bob tried handing me a priority mail envelope, of all things!

"What is this?" I asked in a somewhat uncivil tone, not appreciating the distraction at this intense moment.

"Just open it," Bob said with a curious smile.

"*Really? Now? I-*"

"Just open it."

With some annoyance, I opened the envelope. Then I reached in and pulled out an original photo of Albion! Bob had intended it as a Christmas present, but decided it would have more meaning at a graveside presentation. Well, *that's* an understatement!

After 30 years, I was finally standing at Albion's grave, holding Albion's picture, now fully crying my eyes out. How was it possible for a young man, who had died almost 100 years before I was born, to have such a profound effect on me? Why did I feel such intense sorrow at his tragic death and wish with all my heart and soul that I could turn back time and prevent that rebel bullet from finding its mark at Cold Harbor? And how did this one headstone, among almost 700, appear to me as a brilliant beacon, upon which I swiftly navigated with laser focus?

I have experienced enough in my long, strange life to know that the world is composed of many mysterious and wonderful levels of existence. For a few moments that day at the Riverside Cemetery, perhaps Albion and I sidestepped out of our different levels and met somewhere in the middle.

A Mere 31 Years Later

2023 and 2024, the years the dam burst, in a good way. I won't say I had given up hope of ever finding out more information about the life of Albion Brooks, but after so many years I doubted that I would find enough for a book. Also, as life had thrown all those curveballs—or more accurately beanballs—at Bob and I for over a decade, I had decided to enter semi-retirement. I gave up my insane lecture schedule which was around 60 presentations and conferences a year. I also didn't think I would write anymore books. I would just learn to relax and spend quiet leisure time with Bob.

Hah!

Or, an avalanche of information would come cascading down—everything I needed to write a book about Albion Brooks, and more, and I would devote more time and energy, and put more pressure on myself, than on any of my previous 30-plus books.

It began early in 2023, when I found that the Connecticut Museum of Culture and History in Hartford, Connecticut, had Albion Brooks' 1864 diary—a diary sadly cut short on a battlefield in Virginia. There were also some important letters in this small, but crucial collection. It was wonderful, and emotional, to read his final diary entries—the last things he would ever write. However, while it was valuable information, several months of diary entries weren't nearly enough to write a comprehensive account of his life.

I am engrossed in Albion's diary.

Then in 2024, I became aware of a new regimental history of the 8th Connecticut, written by William Liska and Kim Perlotto in 2023, *The Eighth Connecticut Volunteer Infantry in the Civil War*[9]. This would turn out to be a treasure trove of almost day-by-day descriptions of locations, events, and soldiers of the 8th CT. It would be indispensable for an Albion biography —if I could find more letters and diaries.

Almost simultaneously, before I got a copy of the book, I was astonished when one of my routine internet searches turned up the following in the archival collections of the library of Penn State University:

Albion Brooks and Kingman family Civil War letters and related materials
This collection consists of handwritten letters, diary pages and typescript transcriptions documenting the American Civil War experience of Sergeant Albion Dennis Brooks who served in the 8th Connecticut Infantry Regiment. Letters to his sister and Kingman family members comprise the bulk of the collection.

---

[9] Liska, W. and Perlotto, K, *The Eighth Connecticut Volunteer Infantry in the Civil War*. Jefferson, North Carolina: McFarland & Company, 2023

Words can't describe my elation, shock, and disbelief. Where had this been all these years? What exactly was in the collection? How the heck did the letters and diaries of a soldier born in Maine, who joined a Connecticut regiment, and died in Virginia, end up in Pennsylvania?

Further puzzlement ensued when I saw the names of donors: *Received as a gift from Edward J. and Nancy L. Thompson.*

Not another Thompson collection!? Thompson is a common name, but could they somehow be related to Reverend Thompson's family?

One thing I did know was that Albion's sister, Emily, had married Samuel Clayton Kingman, so that explained the Kingman part of the collection.

Of course, I ordered reproductions of the entire collection, and waited on pins and needles for them to arrive. In the meantime, I contacted Penn State to see if they could get me in contact with Ed and Nancy Thompson, but was told that donor information was private.

I can't recall which arrived first, the documents or the regimental history book, but I was soon happily up to my neck in the deep end of a pool of knowledge of all things Albion Brooks. As one National Park Ranger exclaimed when I described the wealth of material to which I now had access, "It's the King Tut's tomb of Civil War documents!"

Now don't get me wrong, I would dearly love some solid gold ancient Egyptian artifacts, but primary source material in the form of personal letters and diaries was just as golden in my eyes.

But wait, there's more, as those irritating infomercials always say. I didn't give up on tracking down the Thompsons, who donated the wealth of material to Penn State. I saw in the 8th CT regimental history book that there was a footnote that referenced private correspondence between author Kim Perlotto and donor Ed Thompson in 2021. I contacted Mr. Perlotto to see if he still had Mr. Thompson's contact info, and he kindly sent me an email address. Little did I ever think I would someday be emailing a Brooks' family descendant—let alone meeting one.

When I contacted Ed Thompson, he was surprised, to put it mildly, that someone had even heard of Albion Brooks, let alone had been lecturing about, and searching for, his ancestor for decades. One of my first questions was how he was connected to Albion Brooks, as Albion never had children. In brief, Albion's sister, Emily, had a daughter, Carrie, who had a daughter, Agnes, who married a man named Davis Thompson from Ohio. It was Agnes Thompson (1900-1992) who transcribed the letters, and organized and preserved the vast amount of family history which Ed Thompson eventually inherited, and in part, subsequently donated to Penn State. As far as I could determine, there was no connection to Reverend Thompson's family.

Ed graciously asked if I wanted to see the rest of the family history in person. Of course I did, but I feared he lived in New Mexico, or Oregon, or somewhere else far, far away. No, he was in eastern Pennsylvania, just an hour and a half away! We arranged for Bob and I to visit Ed and Nancy at their home in July of 2024. I was actually going to meet one of Albion's family members!

One never knows what to expect when first meeting strangers, but Ed and Nancy were warm, wonderful people who quickly felt like old friends. I also didn't know what to expect in terms of the amount of letters, photos, and documents there would be, and was astonished to see their dining room table piled with stacks of binders and boxes—and this was just part of the family archive!

I spent hours reading and photographing all things Brooks, Kingman, and every other branch of the family. Agnes Thompson must have devoted years of her life to all of this. I can honestly say I have never encountered a larger, more organized family history collection.

I was in blissful overload, and didn't think the day could get any better. Then Ed held out a couple of Albion's personal books, in which he had signed his name. He told me to take one. It didn't register in my head at first—he was actually *giving me* one of them! Books were precious to Albion, and one that he had held in his hands would be so precious to me.

I chose one and immediately clasped it with both hands over my heart. What a moment! As I write this, Albion's book sits next to my computer keyboard.

So that, in brief, was 2023 into 2024—a mere 31 years after I first discovered a young soldier named Albion D. Brooks. I now had no choice but to start that book I had been wanting to write for so long. However, this would not just be about the documents—it would now

Me with Ed and Nancy Thompson in their home, July 2024. Ed holds Albion's photo, while I hold one of Albion's books.

also necessitate 'boots on the ground,' following his footsteps from Maine to North Carolina.

It would also not just be Albion's story. It would be the story of the countless people who keep history alive with their own family genealogy, historical societies big and small, run by dedicated volunteers, little museums operating on shoestring budgets, the local experts who devote their personal time and resources to a person, a place, or an event, just because they have a passion for the past—the people in the trenches doing the soldiers' work of preserving history.

I had thousands of miles of travel ahead of me, a hundred places to go and people to meet, and countless hours of work to complete this book. I just hoped it wouldn't take another 31 years.

All the locations to which I traveled for this book.
Map by Bob Strong.

2
I Will Here Commence a History of my Life

As people grow old, they often reflect on their long lives and sometimes endeavor to put on paper the events, people, and places they recollect, now made somewhat hazy by the passage of time. Albion Brooks decided to write his autobiography at the age of 16.[1]

Perhaps autobiography is too generous a description here, as it is more of a loose chronology of his heretofore brief, but highly changeable young life. Whatever we choose to term it, we can be very thankful that the teenager gave us this information.

East Bridgeport, Conn.   August 14, 1859
I will here commence a history of my life as nearly as I can remember it from the first recollections to the present time.   A.D. Brooks

I am my father's second wife's child. I was born May 9, 1843. My father died when I was 1 or 2 years old. I had two half-sisters and brothers viz. Pamelia and Emily E., and George H. and William E. Brooks. One of my sisters, Pamelia, is now dead. She died in 1857. My brother, George, is in California, and William is in Maine. Of my sister, Emily, I shall speak.

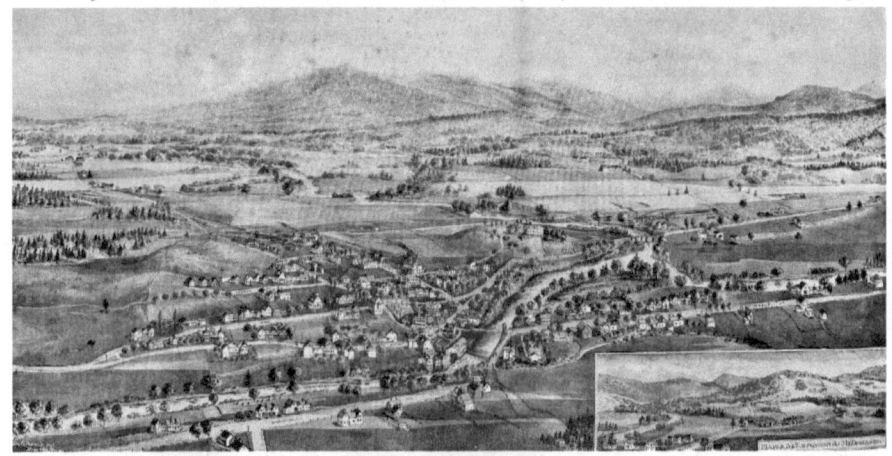

Mountains overlook the beautiful Carrabassett River Valley in Kingfield, Maine. An 1895 illustration by George Norris.

I do not recollect my father. My mother married a second time to a Mr. Landers who lives in Kingfield, Maine. We lived there about 2 years

---

[1] This was in the Thompson Collection, i.e. Ed Thompson. The Alexander Thompson papers found in the trunk will be referred to as the Trunk Collection to avoid confusion.

when my mother died which was in 1852. My sister, Emily, who came and took care of mother till she died, took me. We went to Carthage where she taught school. She then went to Jay where she had a school. I went to her school in both places.

The magnificent modern-day view from Kingfield.

I can remember an incident. Another boy and myself got in a fight (which was about the only one I ever did get into) and I had him down. The other boys came and pulled me off. They said that if it had not been for that I would have <u>killed</u> him. Very likely, a boy of 6 or 7 would do that!

My sister went from there to East Haverhill where my sister Pamelia lived. She stayed there for a few months when she was married to S.C. Kingman of South Reading, Massachusetts. We went from there to South Reading where we stayed for Thanksgiving.

The home and store of John and Pamelia Brooks Nichols at 21 River Road in Haverhill, MA, on the Merrimack River.

We then started from there and came to Watertown, Conn. We lived there for about three years and then Clayton and Emily came to Bridgeport.

Front row: Ella, Clayton, Mary, Emily. Albion Brooks is standing in the back. Circa 1859 in Bridgeport, CT.

I stayed that summer and worked for Dan Platt at $5.00 a month. I stayed there about 4 months. In the fall of 1856, I came down to Bridgeport. I went to school through the winter and in the spring. Clayton's father wanted me to come on there and stay in the office and go to school and take the place of his son who was going away.

I started for South Reading May 4, 1857, and went to school and stayed in the office. I stayed there 1 year, 11 months, and 4 days, and then I was nearly 16 years old. About the last of March, 1859, Clayton wrote and said that he could find a place in his shop for me, so I started for Bridgeport, April 8, 1859. After an absence of nearly 2 years I stood in the same place that I left 2 years before.

I then went to work in the shop where I am now.

Clayton and Emily have gone to Maine, and, should my life be spared and I am well, I mean to see it next year. But who can tell what will happen but Him who knoweth all things. Next year at this time I may be in my grave.

These are the main points although there are many that are left out, but it will do.

  A.D. Brooks

Witness
The dog   # *His seal*
Frank
The dog   # *Her seal*
Chloe

This is a fair sample of my handwriting. August 14, 1859

This is a history of my life together with the names of school teachers and places, etc.

I first went to school in Jay.

Name of Place	Name of Teacher	Year
Jay, Maine	Miss Grose	Not remembered
Jay, Maine	Mother	About 1850
Jay, Maine	Emily E. Brooks	About 1852
	And quite a number of others	
Kingfield, Maine		1851-52
Carthage, Maine	Emily E. Brooks	1853-54
Watertown, Conn.	Miss Dayton	1854
" "	Miss Lovland	1854
" "	Mr. Dayton	1855-56
Bridgeport, Conn.	Mr. Slade (gone away)	1856-57
South Reading, Mass.	Mr. Baxter (Grammar Sch.)	1857
" " "	Mr. Elston	1857
" " "	Mr. H. L. Eaton	1858
" " "	Mr. H. I. Munroe (High School)	1859

There are many teachers' names that I have forgotten. My school days are over. I should like to go about two years longer, but as I cannot, it will be of no use.

Names of Places and the Folks that I have lived with

	Name of Place	Persons	Year
Born	C		
Born	Carthage, Maine	Father and Mother	1843-44
	Jay, Maine	Mother	1845-50
	Kingfield, Maine	Mother	1850-52
	Carthage, Maine	Emily	1852-53
	Jay, Maine	Emily	1853
	Watertown, Conn.	Clayton and Emily	1854-56
	Watertown, Conn.	D. Platt	1856
	Bridgeport, Conn.	Clayton and Emily	1856-57
	South Reading, Mass.	Samuel Kingman	1857-59
	Bridgeport, Conn.	Clayton and Emily	1859

I have lived in 6 different places with 4 different persons.
Mother and Father are dead and so is D. Platt.

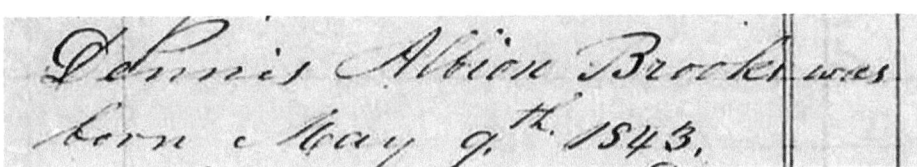

The record of his birth actually gives his name as Dennis Albion Brooks. There are a couple of occasions in the letters where his mother refers to him as Dennis.

Where to begin? Albion never knew his father, his mother died when he was 9, one of his sisters died when he was 14, his other sister took him in and they somehow managed to live on a meager school teacher's salary, he was sent away for a couple of years to work, and by age 16 his thoughts were so that he wrote, "Next year at this time I may be in my grave."

With such a tumultuous life as an orphan, who can blame him for such a morbid thought? Yet, he still retained the sense of humor to have the dogs, Frank and Chloe, "witness" his document. And, he yearned to stay in school—in no small part due to his schoolteacher sister, Emily. She was strongly influenced by their father, George E. Brooks, also a schoolteacher.

According to a fictionalized, unpublished, family history, *A Maine Family*, by Agnes Thompson, upon their father's death in 1845, the following took place in the Brooks home:

"Father wanted us to learn of all we could. He always said that knowledge is the key-stone of power, the thing that raises us above the animals," George [the son] said sadly.

"So he did. I hope that we can manage to keep you both in school," said the young widow as she left the room.

"I think I remember him best in school," murmured William, the 10-year-old. *"I can see him now sitting at his desk on the platform in the front."*

"I wonder who will get the wood for the fireplace now that father will not be there anymore," said George.

"Sometimes he would let us write on the blackboard after we had helped carry the wood in," William added.

The boys cried softly. After all, they were only 10 and 12-years-old and no one was looking at them.

"He didn't like it when we climbed on the seats to look out of the windows," said William.

"Or forgot to carry in the drinking water," added George.

"It sometimes seemed to me that when we were spelling he gave us the hardest words," William said.

"He was pleased when we spelled down the older boys, even if he would never say so," added George.

In the kitchen, the two girls were also thinking of their father and their future.

"Aunt Abigail says we will probably have to move in with grandpa and grandma Eustis in Jay," said Pamelia. Pamelia, 17, and Emily, 16, sometimes called their stepmother Aunt Abigail. She was the sister of their mother and they had known her as "Aunt Abigail" before she became their stepmother. "Perhaps we will have to go and work in the Mills."

"I don't want to work in the Mills," said Emily. "Father helped me prepare for the examinations and I have references for Carthage and Jay. I hope that one of them will take me. I want to be a teacher of like father."

"I hope that you may do so," said Abigail. "But they may already have someone else, and they may think you too young. We will have to cut our coat to fit our cloth."

"I think we can make more money working in the Mills than teaching," said Pamelia. "Besides, I don't think they will hire you at Jay or Carthage."

"Let the girl be," broke in Uncle Nathan. "It is well that she is interested in education. We will see what happens."

It was January 10, 1845, a cold blustery day. The Brooks family had just returned from burying George Brooks, the husband and father. Pamelia, Emily, George, and William were children of the first wife, Anna. Albion, the son of the second wife, Abigail, was just two years old.

George Brooks had been a teacher at Kingfield, Maine, from 1824 to 1838, when his first wife died. The family had moved to Carthage, Maine, where he was teaching at the time of his death.

The bereaved family moved to Jay and lived with the grandparents, Deacon and Mrs. William Eustis. The Eustis's had fifteen children, five of whom were still living. Five of the fifteen children died in infancy. Raising children in Maine was not easy. Abigail, the young widow, was their youngest child. And Hannah, sister of William, a blind spinster, also lived with the Eustis's.

I can say with some assurance that after studying the Brooks and generations of their descendants, education was indeed prized in their family.

In December of 1845, Abigail wrote a letter to Emily at boarding school, giving her news of her three brothers.

George is at the neighbors now and goes to school. He is well. William is here, a bed and asleep. Albion grows like a pig.

Albion would have been about two and a half years old, and apparently was a healthy boy with a big appetite! William, "a bed and asleep," was known for being rather lazy and a procrastinator, which would manifest again and again with his putting off writing letters.

Now let's take a deeper dive into the people and events which shaped Albion's childhood.

Albion's Mother, Abigail

"So if he is a mind to take me ... I think I shall let him do it."

Tragedies play out in many ways, but perhaps none are so ubiquitous as the hapless widow struggling to care for her children once her husband is gone. Abigail Eustis Brooks is no exception, and, in fact, is a classic and heartbreaking example of a tragic figure.

This idea I assumed, given what little information I had early on, when I found that her sister, Anna, passed away October 28, 1838 at age 31, leaving her husband, George E. Brooks, alone with four small children. Abigail, 25, then married her former brother-in-law on September 20, 1840, in Rutland, Massachusetts, going from aunt to stepmother of her nieces and nephews Pamelia, 12, Emily, 11, George H., 7, and William, 5. To add to that handful, she and George E. had a child together in 1843, Albion Dennis. There was little time for everyone to adjust to the new family dynamics, however, as George E. passed away in 1845, leaving young Abigail to fend for herself and five children.

Circumstances compelled them to leave their home in Carthage, Maine, and move in with her parents in Jay, Maine. Abigail's father, Deacon William Eustis, age 77, would die just two years later. Her mother, Anna, age 72, was often in poor health, so Abigail had to care for her, too. Added to this family unit was Abigail's Aunt Hannah, age 62, who, in addition to having her own frequent health problems, was described as being a "blind spinster," so Abigail would have needed to care for her, as well.

For seven years after her husband's death, Abigail struggled; her own physical health slowly eroding, and falling deeper into both poverty and despair.

Then, at the end of 1851, she heard of a widowed farmer looking for a wife, Abisha Lander, in Kingfield, 21-years-older than her, and married him. It was not a love match, but a business arrangement—he needed someone to keep house and care for his 9-year-old granddaughter, and she needed a comfortable home for herself and Albion, after the other children went off to work and boarding schools.

Any hopes of a stable life in the Lander household were soon dashed, however, as Abigail, only 38-years-old, worn out by the burdens of life, died February 16, 1853, just a little more than a year later. She was buried in the frozen ground of the Riverside Cemetery in Kingfield, as her now orphaned son, Albion, 9-years-old, looked on with "bitter tears" in his eyes; yet one more loss in his brief life.

It all made for a poignant story, much of which I inferred due to the circumstances. It wasn't until the July 2024 meeting at Ed Thompson's house to photograph letters that the truth of Abigail's story was confirmed—and it turned out that the truth was even more tragic than I thought. It was with a heavy heart that I read the following letter from Abigail to her niece/stepdaughter, Emily, describing her impending marriage to Mr. Landers.

Jay, October 26th, 1851
Dear Emily,

I attempt to address you once more by the silent language of the pen, probably the last time under the paternal roof. Don't faint, for I must tell you the whole story. Perhaps you may think that I am cruel. Don't be hasty forming your judgment upon the subject. Perhaps when I come to tell you of the situation you may think that I have taken the wisest course.

There is one thing about it. I have got tired working out and Albion wants a master. It is not a fit place for him here and that is not all. I feel the need of a home. I once had a home but for seven years past I have felt that I had none. Although it has been a great privilege to me having a place that I could call home and have Albion and have it where I could see him, I have thought that I would not unite myself with anyone as long as your Grandma there remained alive, but I have got to look out for myself. If I can better myself by changing my situation I think it is my duty to do it.

I will give you a description of the one I am about to unite my destiny for life, for better or worse. In the first place, he is a man of good standing in society. His family is very respectable. He is called a very pleasant man and I foresee that you would be received pleasantly if you should make us the visit. As far as property, he is what you call independent. He is a farmer; has a good house, barn and shed, and carriage house, horse and carriage. So if he is a mind to take me and Albion with my poverty, I think I shall let him do it. All the family he has at home is a little Grand Daughter, the same age as Albion. Her mother is dead. The most I'm afraid of is I'm not good enough for him.

I shall go as poor as ever. I don't know, Aunt Hannah thinks I have not done much towards living. I don't know as I have spent my money foolishly. I have tried to keep my way clear but she is not satisfied. It is because I am going to leave. I do feel bad to leave mother, but I must commit her in the hands of the All Wise Being who cares for the widow. There's one thing about it, Emily, that I have tried not to disgrace myself or the family. The course that I am about to take I do for the best whether it will prove so or not is more than I can tell.

Probably you would like to know where my anticipated home is. I will tell you. It is in the town of Kingfield, the land of your birth, about two miles from where you used to live. I was up there a week ago. It looks about as it did. I wish your Father could be carried up there. If I had had the time I would have visited your Mother's grave.

I presume you would like to know what name I'm going to change for. I will tell you if I can spell it. It is Lander, Mr. Abisha Lander. Will that do? I should be glad to know what you think about my plans and how Uncle's mind stands about it. I presume he has an interest in my welfare and prosperity.

Now, Emily, if you wish to make me a present, it will come very acceptable. I wish you to not [?] yourself about it. Those spools of silk, I'm very much obliged to you indeed. Perhaps it may be in my power to do something for you. It is best to live in hopes.

I must begin to draw to a close by telling the health of the family which is not very good, Aunt Hannah in particular. She has been more unwell than usual. Mother has not been very well but is better. All well Uncle Nathan and Aunt Sarah are here. Aunt L. has sold her farm. We do not know where she is going. George has gone up to Carthage. I some expect he will get a school. He will see William I suppose. Albion has gone over to Uncle Nathan's. He trains him like a young colt.

I had a letter from Mrs. Nichols [Note: Pamelia's married name]. *I suppose you know who I mean. I would like to have you tell me something about her settlement in the world.*

Please give my love to Uncle and Aunt and all the rest. Accept a good share for yourself. Mother and Aunt Hannah send their love. I wrote you sometime ago but have not heard from you since. Now, if you don't take any more notice of this, I shall not trouble you again very soon. Perhaps you would like to know when I leave. I expect to go about the 10th of November.

What do you think about it?

A.E. Brooks

Where to begin unpacking this letter?

"So if he is a mind to take me and Albion with my poverty, I think I shall let him do it."

To our modern sensibilities this seems almost barbaric, practically medieval—a young widow giving herself to a much older man she doesn't love in order for her to give her young son, and herself, a home. While that all speaks for itself, I am compelled to highlight certain points.

- Abigail starts the letter by emphasizing how tired she is, but perhaps this fatigue was from more than overworking? Given the fact that she would be dead and buried in less than 16 months, perhaps her health had already started to deteriorate?
- "Albion wants a master." Not 'Albion needs the love and guidance of a father figure.' Not 'Abisha Lander looks forward to raising Albion like his own son.' Not 'Albion is fond of Abisha and is happy to start his new life in a new home.' From the general tone of the letter, it doesn't appear as if Albion had ever even met Abisha, so even if he was in need "of a master," he wouldn't have chosen Abisha.
- "…not unite myself…"—unite myself? Please, Abigail, do try to suppress your passionate expression of love and affection, and reverence for the sanctity of holy matrimony!
- Then there's the rather cold admission that Abigail knows her mother needs help, but sorry, she's on her own now because Abigail needs to look out for herself. I may be sounding a bit harsh, but I really am not passing judgment on her here—Abigail had been taking care of stepchildren, Albion, her mother, her aunt, and she had reached a breaking point. We probably have all been there, done that, when your mind and body have had enough—an exhausted, lonely, poverty-stricken widow about to face another long, brutal, dark, and cold Maine winter. It was too much.
- In the next paragraph, she dispassionately enumerates the positive aspects "of the one I am about to unite my destiny for life, for better or worse" as if she was listing the assets of a business—and make no mistake, for Abigail this *was* a business decision.
- As shocking and painful as this part was to read, the truly stunning line was, "He is called a very pleasant man." What!? It's obvious she doesn't love Abisha, there's not even any indication she likes him, but this line makes me wonder if she

even knows him! Have they ever met, or has this all been arranged by a third party? Abigail does later mention she had been to Kingfield "a week ago," so perhaps a meeting between the future husband and wife had taken place. However, to say what other people think of her fiancé with no personal opinion does not give one a warm and fuzzy feeling about the relationship.
- And then there's Aunt Hannah, who was obviously nagging Abigail about, well, everything! Perhaps Hannah played no small part in motivating Abigail to leave the Eustis' family home.
- Speaking of Kingfield, Abigail tells Emily "I wish your father could be carried up there." Is this another instance of one of the Brooks being buried in the place of death, in this case, Carthage, only to have his body moved to the Riverside Cemetery at a later date? It would appear to be the case.
- Perhaps Abigail was trying to inject a little humor into what must have been a shocking letter when she tells Emily, "I presume you would like to know what name I'm going to change for. I will tell you if I can spell it."
- Finally, if there was any doubt as to whether this marriage was for love or a business arrangement, Abigail writes the following: "So if he is of a mind to take me and Albion with my poverty, I think that I shall let him do it." No glorious, romantic triumph of love, just resignation to defeat in a cold, cruel world that has beaten her down.

What of Albion in all this? Did Abisha form a fond paternal bond with his stepson? Did Abigail's passing draw them closer together?

Sadly, no, and I don't need to delve into much speculation on this account.

1. Immediately following Abigail's death, Emily wrote to Clayton saying she wanted to take Albion as her own—even though this meant taking the boy from the security of "a good house" back to the relative poverty of a single woman on a meager teacher's salary, but at least there was love and affection in the relationship.
2. In all of Albion's many writings, the man who had so much praise for the people in his life, and often saw the good in others, had only ten plain words regarding his stepfather. In

the family history he wrote in 1859, he simply recorded, "My mother married a second time to a Mr. Lander."

No need to read between the lines, especially with only one line! For Albion, this must have been an unsettling and unpleasant time in his life, when his beloved mother gave herself to a much older man in a loveless marriage, and all too soon sickened and died.

In this letter, Abigail also wrote, "The course that I am about to take, I do for the best, whether it will prove so is more than I can tell."

Abigail Eustis Brooks is indeed a classic and heartbreaking example of a young widow trying to provide for herself and children in an age where few opportunities were available to women. Such arrangements are often called 'marriages of convenience,' but in the end, did anyone benefit from this?

Abisha lost another wife, Abigail died, and Albion became an orphan. Yes, we can still hope that perhaps for a year, Abisha and Abigail weren't so lonely, Albion wasn't cold and hungry, and there was some glimmer of hope for a happy future.

Or, perhaps, we, too, should resign ourselves to the inevitability and finality of this tragedy.

Emily Steps in and Steps Up

When Abigail became sick and helpless, Emily left work at the fabric mills in Massachusetts and rushed to her side to care for her. She wrote to her brother, William, but no one else came to Kingfield and she cared for Abigail alone.

> *Kingfield, Maine, January 10, 1853*
> *Dear Brother,*
>
> *I am sorry to write you that Mother is very sick and cannot live but a short time unless relieved. The Doctor has given her up. She has no reason or sense only at times.*
>
> *If you would like to see her, you had better come up as soon as you can. You can come on the stage from Saturday or Wednesday. Come as soon as Saturday.*
>
> *I want to see you very much.*
> *Goodbye, Emily*

Thanks to a large collection of letters between Emily and Clayton[2], who were not yet married, we have a glimpse into Abigail's suffering, and

---

[2] Thompson Collection.

Emily's desire to become more than Albion's sister—perhaps to Clayton's dismay.

> *Kingfield, Me., January 23, 1852*
> *My dearest friend,*
> *It seems a long time since I sat down to write you a letter. Mother has been, and still is, very sick and my time is all taken up. So please pardon my negligence. I am truly grateful to know that you still think of me when I am so unworthy of anybody's love. My heart is very wicked, deep as the unfathomable gulf of dark despair. The old year has fled and with that many a happy dream. The new year will soon be past and so our years will soon be all gone and the places which now know us will know us know more.*
>
> *I am more discouraged about mother then I have been before. She has not been as well for two or three days. I do not think she will ever be any better. She appears to have a stroke of the palsy in her left side. She cannot use her left hand or arm. She has an entire prostration of all her faculties, of mind as well as body. Nobody knows what the matter is. Not even the physician can give any account of it, only what they guess at. But while there is life there is hope. She is in the hands of one "who is too wise to err." But if she cannot be spared, can we not have at least one friend, next to a parent? I am all discouraged,-hope you will write to me soon even if my letter is not worth answering.*
>
> *Good-bye, E.E. Brooks*

> *Dear Clayton, since writing the above, I have received your long and welcome letters. Many thanks for your kindness. Mother is sick and it is impossible for me to return at present. I would urge you to come and see us were it not that the people here might not like it to have me bring company as they have all they can do just now, but if I stay much longer I hope you will come.*
>
> *It is snowing hard today and it is dark and lonesome. I love to think that I have one friend who loves me. Please write soon if you can and forgive my neglect. I cannot tell how many times I have tried to write to you and have not made out.*
>
> *Yours truly*
> *Emily*
> *I received a letter from Lucie Ellen[3] a short time after coming here. My love to all.*
> *Good-bye.*

---

[3] Clayton's younger sister.

I mean to send for some paper soon that I can write you a longer letter. We live some ways from the stores and I have not thought to send when I had a chance.

- Emily's despair is palpable. She had lost her father, mother, and now her stepmother/aunt was dying. It was a dark, snowy, Maine winter, and they obviously didn't live close to town.
- "I would urge you to come and see us were it not that the people here might not like it to have me bring company." Well, that speaks volumes about the Lander family.

To Miss Emily E. Brooks   *Watertown, January 25, 1853*

Dear Emily, Again I am permitted to write a few lines to you, the dearest image that is reflected in my heart, and it seems to me that each succeeding time I write to you, you are nearer and dearer to me than ever before, and I long for the time to come when you will give me all your affection and confidence.

...I was not expecting a letter from you at the house of your mother, and find you over the sick couch of her, patiently watching to relieve every want, watching every motion, and ready to tender a hand, administer relief and soothe every pain. I should want you for my nurse in case I should ever be sick.

I was happy to know that you obeyed the dictates and impulses of your true womanly heart and hastened to your mother's bedside at this time, when you of all others, was the one needed and wished for. I have seen several instances of your goodness,-I do not flatter you by saying the same,-and of pure love to God, to me, and to your friends.

...Hoping to hear good news from you, your good health etc..

I am your own S. Clayton Kingman

All hopes that the 38-year-old Abigail Eustis Brooks Lander would recover from her stroke were soon dashed.

Kingfield, March 12, 1853
Ever Dear Friend,
I have the sad intelligence to write you that our much loved mother is dead. Yes, and that is a mournful event for every one of us. I have a great deal that I want to say to you that I cannot write.

I shall return in a few weeks. I think that I shall be to my sisters in Haverhill two weeks from next Saturday. I should like to see you there if possible. I thank you for your letters. Mother's little boy is almost 10 years

old. I want to take him for my own. What do you think about it? Are you willing? Would it be too much for you? Please write me what you think about it as I should like to know before I start.
Emily

Well, that must have been a bombshell to the anxious prospective bridegroom, yearning to start a cozy love nest with his prospective bride—Can she bring along her little brother!? While it is perfectly natural for a compassionate and caring woman like Emily to want the best for her brother, Albion, it is also perfectly understandable that this must have been quite a shock to Clayton. A 10-year-old "son" was probably not in his dreams of newlywed bliss.

To Miss Emily E. Brooks
Kingfield, Maine *Watertown, March 20th, 1853*
My Dearest Emily,
You have no mother now, they are both gone. As I reflect on all the blessings attendant on a mother's love, I think of your losses and I sympathize with and pity you. My heart yearns for your love, trust and affection.
...I now come to a subject that will be of interest to us both I presume, that of taking a boy for your own. I hardly know what to say. You have been with him, taken care of him, you are in or have been in this situation, motherless, but what shall I say to your question?
You wish for him, and I would acquiesce in your desires. I would love to have him with you as ours. What shall we do? To board him in Lawrence would be some expense and we have no home now to take him to with us, though I do hope we shall have in the fall. Would you not be willing to begin in a humble way or manner that will wait longer, say? Your judgment will be better than mine in respect to that.
If you could find a good place to place your (son) brother that way, and then take him when we could be with him, but dear Emily, do you find circumstances may dictate to you?

A prime example of a man walking on eggshells. Eggshells covering a minefield. Of course, Clayton will "acquiesce" to Emily's desire to raise Albion as her son, because if he protests too much—as in, "Emily, it's either Albion or me!"—he may lose Emily. And, of course, Clayton would *just love* to have her little brother with them as soon as they're married, but couldn't they maybe find "a good place to place him" instead?

My heart goes out to poor orphaned Albion, obviously not wanted at the Lander's house, and most likely not wanting to be a burden to Emily, especially as she is about to become a bride. However, I can also sympathize with Clayton, as no man in the history of dating has welcomed the kid brother tagging along.

In a subsequent letter, Clayton asks about Albion, and as they had never met, requests a description of him. Emily's response is priceless.

> *North Jay, June 6, 1853*
> *...Albion is fast asleep as it is only six o'clock and I have not called him yet. He is very homely like myself so you will need no more description.*

It will come as no surprise to any man who has ever had any kind of a relationship with a woman that Emily would get her way and step up and take responsibility for Albion. It would be a great leap of faith that she would be able to support them both, and they would have some very lean times the remainder of 1852 and most of 1853, when Emily taught school in Carthage and Jay, Maine. However, the important thing was that they were together and provided each other the love and affection of family in an often-unforgiving world.

The image of a 19th Century 'School Marm' is often one of a stern old spinster with no sense of humor. Emily Brooks was anything but that. She was kind, compassionate, caring, with an apparently offbeat sense of humor, which shows itself in this wonderful Valentine she sent to her brother William when he was away at boarding school. I have no idea what it means, but it must have been an inside joke.

You're very WIDE AWAKE, I see,
And so am I, old chap, you'll find;
I've got both my eyes open tight,
And shan't take you and go it blind. Emily

It was a long, long, three-year courtship between Emily and Clayton—which was almost permanently derailed when he took a job at the Tredegar Iron Works[4] in Richmond, Virginia. While there, he wrote the following to Emily on November 15, 1852:

This forenoon I went to a Slave Auction and saw a young woman sold for $500.00. There were several sold before I got there. Two young mothers with babes 2 and 4 months old were sold: too bad! They are stood on a platform and examined by anyone and sometimes they are, when young and blooming, deprived of clothing for a spell and set up for to increase the price of them. What is a virtue worth when it is bought and sold at a price? Oh, God forbid!! There are several places of Auction every day from 9 until 1 o'clock.

Clayton makes other mentions of the deplorable sales of "men, women, and children" which take place frequently. In addition to the Southerners' lack of Christian values and morals, he was also disgusted with the "dirty" Tredegar factory and the "very low" society of the population in general. He was also paying an exorbitant amount for his rented rooms, which didn't live up to his expectations, either. On December 2, 1852, he wrote to Emily:

I pay $16.00 for board per month and am not so well cared for.
...the shop is not so good and the work is different from what I agreed for, and dirty. The principles of the employers I shall not mention. Society is very low and 50 or 75 years behind the North.

Whether lack of morals, the low society, or the dirty shop—or all of the above—caused Clayton to return to the more civilized North, we get a different perspective of the situation in a letter dated February 9, 1853, from George to his sister, Emily, in what appears to be some criticism of his future brother-in-law. Perhaps the real reason Clayton left was that his ego was bruised:

I was very sorry to hear that Clayton was disappointed in his expectations of southern greatness. I should suppose that he must command good pay to be able to pay sixteen dollars a month for board, and moreover, think that a person who pays that much ought to live pretty well.

---

[4] Tredegar would make half the cannons used by the Confederacy, including those that that started the Civil War when they fired at Fort Sumter. Tredegar also made the armor plating that turned the Merrimack into the ironclad CSS Virginia, made famous for its battle with the Monitor.

Whatever the situation, Clayton returned, but Emily seemed to have a case of cold feet for a while, attempting to politely delay the marriage. Finally, they were married at Pamelia's house in Haverhill, MA on November 17, 1853. The newlyweds and their "son" Albion spent Thanksgiving at the Kingman house in South Reading, MA, then went to live in Watertown, Connecticut, where Clayton had gotten a position with the Wheeler & Wilson Manufacturing Co., who produced that wonderful new invention—the sewing machine.

Clayton most likely feared that this new son of his would turn out to be a 19th Century *Albion Dennis the Menace*, but in an undated letter[5] written from Clayton to one of his brothers sometime before September of 1857, he wrote:

Albion is well and quite a boy he is now. I do not know how I should get along if it were not for him. I was fortunate to have a boy so soon, and so truthful, kind and honest as he is. 'Twas a real pleasure and blessing to me to have him with me. I trust he will always be such as he grows older.

Indeed, Albion would always be "truthful, kind and honest," in the seven short years left in his life.

However, as much of a help as Albion supposedly was to Clayton, it didn't prevent him from being sent to work and live with others for years. Albion wrote that at age 13, he worked for Dan Platt in 1856. That is all the information there was in the Thompson Collection, but with some persistent digging I found the following.

Uncovering the Sad Story of Dan Platt

No man is an island—like it or not, we are directly connected to dozens of people, and tangentially to hundreds. Obviously, while doing this research there were many names that came up, and while I would like to have an extensive family tree and *curriculum vitae* on each and every one of them, in both a hard copy and a digital file, the harsh reality is that some people are lost in the sands of time. Which doesn't mean I didn't keep trying, and trying, to pry some kernels of information from the records on people in Albion's life—if I could figure out the spelling of their names from his handwriting, that is!

One warm and sunny afternoon on vacation in Florida, in February of 2025, when I could have been floating in the pool on an inflatable chaise lounge, I instead was on my laptop—next to the pool, at least—searching for Dan Platt. Albion gave us a name, a location, Watertown, CT, and the

---

[5] Thompson Collection. Clayton writes that they are thinking of going to Pamelia's for Thanksgiving. Pamelia died on September 3, 1857.

Instead of being in the pool, I am writing and researching.

fact that at age 13, he worked for Platt for four months in 1856 at the wage of $5 per month. Unfortunately, he didn't mention what that work entailed, or any personal information about Platt, other than at the time he wrote the brief history of his life in 1859, Platt was dead.

I quickly found Watertown census records for 1820, 1830, and 1840, but unfortunately, they did not list occupations. They also did not provide exact ages, only ranges. For example, the categories were "Under Age five," and "Of ten under fifteen," for both males and females. In the 1830 census, Dan Platt and his wife were in their thirties, and they had two young boys, and two young girls. By the 1840 census, one of the boys had passed away, and another young female had been added. Interesting, but not particularly helpful.

The real breakthrough came from a newspaper search, which provided the following from the *Litchfield Enquirer*, November 1, 1849, page 3:

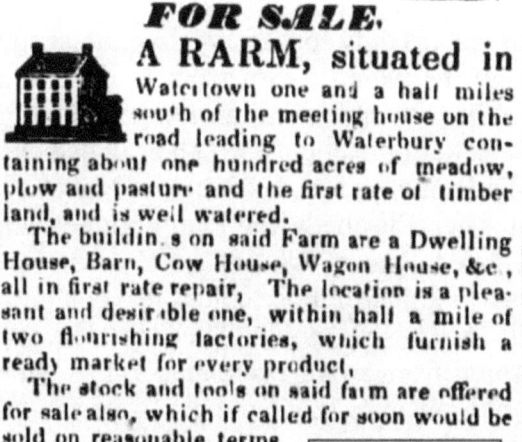

First, I assume "RARM" is a big, fat typo, and not an obscure 19th century term for some type of farm. The big question was this, why on earth would Dan Platt want to sell a large farm that seemed to have everything a man could want, something to pass on to his son, and someday his grandsons? I considered illness, financial difficulties, etc.

Then my historic 'spidey sense' kicked in as I looked at the date again—1849.

Perhaps a certain 20-year-old son dashed his father's hopes and dreams for the future of the family farm, because he had been bitten by Gold Rush Fever? Perhaps his son ran off to California like countless other gold-crazed people—like both of Albion's brothers—seeking their fortune at the end of a sluice and the bottom of a gold pan? Great theory, but could I find the documented evidence to back it up?

Sitting by that enticing pool that warm and sunny afternoon, I did find evidence—sad, heartbreaking evidence.

Litchfield Enquirer, August 29, 1850, page 3:

Death Notices: In Auburn, California on the 30th of April, Henry Dwight Platt, son of Dam Platt at Watertown, age 22.

It took about two more seconds to confirm that Auburn, in Placer County, California, just 18 miles from Sutter's Mill where the Gold Rush began, had indeed been a hub of gold mining activity, and now is home to the Gold Rush Museum. As an historic marker in town reads:

City of Auburn - Gold discovered near here by Claude Chana May 16, 1848. Area first known as North Fork or Woods Dry Diggings. Settlement given name of Auburn in fall of 1849. Soon became important mining town, trading post, and stage terminal. County seat of Sutter County 1850 and Placer County 1851. Destroyed by fire 1855, 1859, and 1863.

So, Dan Platt lost his only son, Henry Dwight, at age 22, crushing any hopes that someday he would return from California and take over the farm. The *Find a Grave* website has an image of the Platt gravestone in the Milford Cemetery (Connecticut), which provided even more sad news. Just two years after losing his son, his daughter Mary, would die. In a letter from Mary to her sister, Elisabeth Ann Platt[6], both of whom were working as seamstresses, dated January 18, 1852, "You ask how is my cough. I must tell you I have another of those colds. As yet it has not made me sick and I hope it will not."[7] Nine months later, on November 5, 1852, Mary passed away, perhaps from an illness related to that chronic cough?

Dan would pass away in 1856, and his 14-year-old daughter, Martha, would follow him to the grave the next year. Poor Emily Ford Platt, Dan's wife, who probably once thought herself to be very fortunate, giving birth to five children, with a husband who ran a large farm, only to lose all of

---

[6] Eliza Ann Platt Merwin, Aug 24, 1825-Jun 7, 1898, is also buried in the Milford Cemetery.
[7] www.sparedshared3.wordpress.com

them, save Elisabeth. Emily, at least, lived to the relatively ripe old age of 77, passing away in 1869.

Speaking of death, Albion simply recorded he worked for Platt for four months, and returned to school in Bridgeport in the fall of 1856. What he didn't write was that the reason he most likely went back to school was that Platt had died on September 10, 1856.

It was with mixed emotions that I uncovered these pieces of the story of Dan Platt. Of course, I was pleased to find out what I did, but it was yet another tragic tale of the fragility of 19th century life. And for 13-year-old Albion, it was losing one more person to whom he may have grown fond—perhaps even viewed as a much-needed father figure—and forcing him to move yet again.

Another thought about the Platt family's possible influence on Albion occurred to me as I was writing this. Young Henry Platt died in far-off California and was buried there. The gravestone in the Milford Cemetery records Henry's name, but his body is not with his family. Albion must have heard the story of Dan's son, and of how his remains were not brought home. This may have weighed on Albion's thoughts, and influenced his subsequent explicit directions to be brought back to Kingfield to be buried by his mother, as well as the several mentions of the poor soldiers dying in the south whose bodies would never be returned to their loved ones in New England.

Dan Platt was only a name on a sheet of paper when I began, but with just a few pieces of information, his story grew into a wide picture of life and death, which all became pieces of the puzzle of Albion Brooks.

Albion returned to the home of Emily and Clayton, who now lived in Bridgeport, CT, where the Wheeler & Wilson Manufacturing Co. had moved its operations. But he didn't stay for long, as he was shipped off to work for Clayton's father, Samuel, in South Reading, MA.

While more of the story of Albion's brother's adventures during the California Gold Rush will be covered in the Appendices, this story was too good to not include here, as it shows that while gold mining was dangerous business, it was equally dangerous to travel back and forth to California at that time. According to family history, William Brooks only intended to mine until he earned enough to pay for college, but a friend had strongly urged him to remain just a few months longer so they could return together:

But young Brooks adhered steadily to his purpose. He embarked on a vessel bound for Panama and once more passed through a perilous adventure on the trip back. He crossed the isthmus without mishap, but the vessel which was to take him to New York was wrecked on the coast of Cuba. But Mr. Brooks escaped with the money he had made in California, and on his arrival in Maine entered Waterville College.

However, before you think that if William Brooks had only listened to his friend and stayed longer, he would have avoided the dangerous shipwreck, the story continues:

His partner, however, who left on a later boat, was drowned when his vessel went down with all on board.

Two Years in a Post Office

Samuel Kingman was born in Hingham, MA in 1802. He went to school in Boston and learned the trade of tailoring, which he began practicing in 1824 in his own 12'x14' shop on Salem Street in South Reading, MA, which was renamed Wakefield in 1868. According to family history, Kingman may have moved his shop to the corner of Albion and Main Streets. Regardless, a tragedy struck his business in 1851. On October 11, 1851, the *Boston Evening Transcript* printed the following:

WHOLESALE ROBBERY. At South Reading last night, the tailoring establishment of Samuel Kingman was robbed of all it contained—a stock worth $1000, or more. It is suspected that the plunder has been taken to New York.

Family records claim the theft was about $5,000 and "was such a heavy loss at this time, that he never resumed the tailoring business again." That's probably not true, as he most likely continued tailoring for a few more years, at least, but the robbery did prompt him to pursue a new career. On May 19, 1853, Kingman was appointed postmaster of South Reading, a position which he held until 1874.

In 1827, Samuel had married Sarah Ring Pope, of a "respectable South Reading family," and they had 9 children. Family history said:

"Sarah Ring Pope was of a sweet and kindly disposition, and a true and earnest Christian...She was one of those genuine 'New England Mothers,' whose love for

MRS. KINGMAN.

right and duty is the predominant feature of their lives,—a mother in the truest sense of the word.

"Her daughter says of her,--'she was a quiet, patient soul, always cheery,--not given to much talk. Her children always knew what she meant was what she said,—and they all loved and respected her the more for it. She was the 'Master Mind' in the home, but she and father never differed in bringing up the children."

Family accounts of their Golden Wedding Anniversary in 1877 stated that remarkably after 50 years, "all the 'Wedding party' were there but the minister, Mr. Ruben Emerson." The date of the celebration was delayed from the actual anniversary day so that 8 of their 9 children had time to travel for the big event.

Samuel Kingman

In addition to love of family, Samuel loved gardening, keeping very impressive flowering plants and fruit trees at his Eaton Street home. He was also a member of the local militia, the "Washington Rifle Grays," which perhaps inspired three of his sons, William, Orlando, and Charles to enlist during the Civil War, as well as the marksmanship of his son, Samuel Clayton.

Family history also says about Samuel Kingman:

"He was small in stature, yet commanding in presence, and even when he was advanced in years, was more sprightly than many much younger. He had a warm heart, a kind and genial disposition, a kind word for all, and a smile which is so expressive of the feelings within, greeted every one with whom he came into contact with. He was an "Old school gentleman," little, smart, and sprightly. He would touch his tall silk hat to all his friends in such a courtly style, and he was a friend to every one, -- rich or poor.

"About a year before he died, he was trimming one of his apple trees, when he fell. He never really recovered from his fall. He died very suddenly of 'Apoplexy' Nov 25, 1880."

Both Samuel and his wife, Sarah (who died in 1890), are buried in the Lakeside Cemetery in Wakefield.

What influence did Mr. and Mrs. Kingman have on young Albion during his almost two years in South Reading? Other than the few lines Albion wrote about his stay, there is no other evidence to indicate his thoughts and feelings of the Kingman family, although he did later continue to enquire about William, Orlando, and Lucy.

The Kingman home on Eaton Street
in South Reading, MA, c.1870.

The fact that Albion did not live with the Kingman family in their Eaton Street house, but instead "stayed in the office"—presumably the post office—is incredibly sad, and rather inexplicable. Samuel and Sarah are described in such glowing terms as being kind, compassionate, and wonderful people and parents, so why didn't they let a 14-year-old orphan stay under their roof? With so many children, did they simply have no room? Even so, couldn't a room have been rented in a house, so the poor kid didn't have *to live all alone in a post office for two years*?

Perhaps Albion did nothing more than record his time spent in South Reading, as well as the teachers he had during that time, as he did not have fond memories of it, and he rarely wrote a bad word about anyone.

Finally, just before his 16th birthday, "Clayton wrote and said he could find a place in his shop for me," and Albion returned to Bridgeport. I suspect Emily had something to do—like everything!—with Clayton's offer to bring her brother/son back to her.

In the Thompson Collection was also a somewhat rare letter from William at college in Waterville, Maine, October 2, 1860, to his brother Albion in Bridgeport. It was full of brotherly advice, not the least was to be sure to "Wash yourself thoroughly once a week."

It has been some time since I received your last letter and I presume you have begun to think that I have forgotten you entirely—but such is not the case and though I have not written still it has not been from forgetting you but from a bad habit which I have of putting off-off-off what I ought to do.

October 12

And even now. Well you see that I have put off again but I will do so no longer. I was very glad to hear from you and to receive your ambrotype and I thank you so much and I will send you mine as soon as I have it taken. I should have had it taken yesterday but for some reason or other failed to, but I will try to have it by the next time I write.

I'm glad the way has opened for you to study and I pray God that you may be prospered and be enabled to do much good in the world. Strive to keep your heart warm and well filled with God's love. Keep very near to the mercy seat, have Christ dwelling in you richly and then it will be well with you and your labors will not be in vain in the Lord!

But be sure and keep your health good. Wash yourself thoroughly once a week and take a good amount of exercise. I have been to see Emily at Carthage. Clayton came here and I went up with him. I had a very pleasant time, found the folks all well. They spoke of you and expressed a strong desire to see you. I could not help having peculiar emotions aroused as I saw again our old house at Carthage. Many things looked so natural,-the house,-the brook,-the pasture and the whole lay of the land. I noticed some apple trees that we planted from the seeds.

But this will not please you so much as it will to hear about Jay at which place I made no call as I was in a great hurry. But Grandmother's place looks as usual save the old shed, the one between the woodshed and the barn, is no more. It has been taken away.

But Emily will tell you all about things so that I will not attempt to do with the pen what she can do so much better with her tongue. My studies are pretty hard, more so I think, than any terms since I have been in college, but still I have time to write if I were not so careless, which I hope I may cease to be.

Be frank and confidential with Emily and Clayton. They will feel free, I think, to assist you.

Be kind enough to write soon and let me know all about you and your studies. My respects to all my friends and

Yours affectionately

William E. Brooks

So, this was Albion's turbulent childhood and the people who shaped it. His brothers George and William (see Appendix for more information) went off to boarding schools, then to California to find their fortunes in gold, so Albion did not have much contact with them in the 1850s, and few letters. William did come back, but George stayed and had quite the adventurous life in the 'Old West.'

Albion went to school as much as he was able, while working on farms, in a post office, and in the sewing machine factory. Religion played a huge part of his life, and he became good friends with Reverend Thompson of the South Church in Bridgeport, CT.

Speaking of religion, the Thompson Collection has several essays Albion wrote in 1861 on "New England Homes" and several pieces with strong moral content. He showed a knowledge of world history and an extensive knowledge of the Bible, as well as an ongoing sense of his own mortality. On his 18th birthday in Bridgeport, a landmark which most boys celebrate—well, like 18-year-old boys—Albion chose to write an essay.

Thoughts on my 18th birthday May 9, 1861

Another year has gone, another milestone has been passed and I am so much nearer to eternity. My desire is to become a minister. My prayer to God is that He will allow me to be a Shepherd of his flock....

And what have I to overcome—tis my evil passions, the <u>lusts</u> of the flesh. Grant oh Lord that I may trust in thee and take all evil desires from me.

Imagine that—a teenaged boy having sexual desires, God forbid! Clearly, prudish Victorian morals and repressive religious restrictions were alive and well in young Albion, who, for all the many places he lived, led a sheltered life of church, work, and school.

He was only two when his father died—too young to remember the stable, happy homelife with his father, mother, and four step-siblings. From that age, he was always on the move from place to place, never staying more than a couple of years in any one town, with any one person. He worked hard throughout his childhood. He loved learning and he loved the church. He was very fortunate to have a sister like Emily, but while she was family, he most likely hoped to someday have a family of his own, in his own stable, happy home. Given a chance, he would fulfill his dream of being a minister and learn something about life along the way—maybe even live a little and have some fun.

Unfortunately, there was a war brewing that would prevent the hopes and dreams of millions.

3
Back to Kingfield...and on to Carthage and Jay

As the previous chapter may have engendered a sense of melancholy, I thought it best to take a slight sightseeing journey before delving into the war years. With just about every new piece of information I learned, there were new places to visit. Although I had already been to Albion's grave, there was so much more to find.

It was hot and humid weather when we arrived back in Maine in August, 2024. Part of the trip was to Eastport, a stunningly beautiful coastal town where my 3rd great-grandfather Handasyd "Handyside" Edgett (1802-1856) is buried. He was the captain of a ship called *Ruby*, and navigated the treacherous waters of the Bay of Fundy, where a couple of other of my ancestors drowned—including Handyside's own brother. By the 1830s, Eastport was one of the largest U.S. ports, second only to New York City. However, rather than continuing to thrive into the 21st century, according to the 2020 census, the population of Eastport was just 1,288, making it the lowest populated city in Maine.

And speaking of the Bay of Fundy, another 3rd great-grandfather, David Cook, left Hull, England on the ship *Trafalgar*, alone, at the age of just 18 in 1817 to come to Canada for the promise of 100 acres of land and a year's supplies. He almost didn't make it. On July 25, in a thick fog—for which the Bay of Fundy is notorious—the *Trafalgar* was dashed against the rocks of Brier Island, Nova Scotia. While the ship was lost, fortunately, the 159 passengers and crew were saved. David Cook would go on to found the town of Cookville, where he met my 3rd great-grandmother, Charlotte Towse of Garton-on-the-Wolds, Yorkshire, England, and the rest is Linda Zimmermann family history. (So as you can see, I don't just track down the lives of people to whom I have no relation.)

After a few days of being tourists, it was finally time to return to Kingfield, then visit Carthage, Albion's birthplace, and then on to Jay, where he lived with his grandparents when his father died, and then later with Emily after his mother died. I felt anxious and excited when I awoke in our hotel in Waterville that morning. Would I find the information I wanted? Would I find the grave of Albion's mother? Would the weather cooperate so I could get some good photographs of the majestic mountains—the image of which had been etched in Albion's young mind as a child?

I opened the curtains in our hotel room and my heart sank. Fog! Thick, pea soup, no-way-in-hell you're going to see the mountains, let alone photograph them, fog. It was Bay of Fundy-style fog.

We had breakfast, packed up and headed toward Kingfield, which was about an hour away. About ten minutes in, Bob said it looked like there was some sunlight peeking through up ahead. He was trying to be encouraging, saying that perhaps the fog would burn off by the time we arrived. While I appreciated his optimism, it was hard to believe that such fog would dissipate anytime soon. However, occasionally—just very occasionally—I enjoy being proved wrong.

Like some great cosmic defroster switch being flipped on, the sky suddenly cleared, revealing picture-perfect blue skies and photogenic, puffy white clouds! In fact, it turned out to be the absolute perfect weather day in terms of temperature and humidity and clear skies. While it would be a great dramatic and poetic opportunity to claim this weather shift was an act of divine intervention, it was no more than a prosaic high-pressure system moving in. (But the reader should feel free to go with a divine intervention idea if it makes you feel better.)

Approaching Kingfield from the east, with the majestic Longfellow Mountains framing the region to the west, and the Carrabassett River flowing through town, it's easy to see how this place would have spectacular scenery in every season—although apparently winter here can be quite long and hard, with an average yearly snowfall of 107 inches, which is almost 9 feet! Such deep snow must be a challenge for modern snow removal equipment, and one can only imagine what it was like when Albion was a boy.

After arriving at the Riverside Cemetery and taking a few wide-angle photos, I went to Albion's grave and was pleased to see a new American flag in the GAR holder in front of his stone. Then Bob and I started searching through the other 664 grave sites for his mother, Abigail, and it wasn't long, or far, when I found it.

About 75 feet away, Abigail rests between her brief husband Abisha Landers[1], and his first wife, Kezia[2] (1794-1850). Albion's wish was to be

---

[1] The name is spelled both Lander and Landers in documents.

[2] While her gravestone reads "Kezia" many records spell it Keziah, and some even Kesiah. Also, given the fact that Landers is just as often spelled Lander in the records, and you can get a confusing number of name combinations. For example, the 1850 census has Abisha and Kesiah Lander. Her maiden name was Mills

buried next to his mother, but I suspect the Landers' family didn't want that—or perhaps it was Emily who didn't want him to be with the Landers?—so he ended up by his father, whom he never knew, and his aunt and stepsisters, whom he also never knew. It's a shame that after transporting Albion's body the 746 miles from Cold Harbor to Kingfield, they couldn't move it another 75 feet, but this was what was ultimately worked out by all the concerned parties at the time, and the machinations of family politics are lost in the sands of time.

I felt a wave of sadness by Abigail's grave, knowing what she had gone through after George's death, how she struggled to take care of everyone with very little money, finally giving up and marrying a much older man she didn't even know, then soon suffered some type of stroke and died at the age of just 38.

I also thought of 10-year-old Albion standing by his mother's grave the cold day of her burial, "crying bitter, bitter tears." And could he have ever imagined that not much more than 10 years later he, too, would be lowered into the ground of that same Riverside Cemetery?

Abigail and Abisha's graves. That's me in the background at Albion's grave to show where he is in relation to his mother.

I no doubt could have spent quite a while brooding in the cemetery, but we had an appointment with the Kingfield Historical Society. The Historical Society is fortunate to have a beautiful old house on High Street, and they have done a terrific job of filling it with all manner of artifacts which give a wonderful picture of life in times gone by.

Their archives provided a newspaper article from 1930, describing a trip to Kingfield undertaken by Albion's two nieces to research family records. It drove me up a wall that only their husband's full names are used! Mrs. Loomis was Carrie Emily Kingman (1861-1939), and Mrs.

West was Evelyn Clayton Kingman (1873-1968). Carrie was one of the children to whom Albion referred in his letters home during the war when he almost always ended the letters "Kiss the children for me." Carrie was instrumental in preserving the family history.

Kingfield newspaper May 27, 1930

Mrs. Hiram Benjamin Loomis, wife of the President of Hyde Park School of Chicago, Ill., and Mrs. Joseph I. West of Washington, Conn., sisters, were in Kingfield Wednesday night and Thursday, looking up records of ancestors, who were early residents of Kingfield. These ladies are granddaughters of George and Anna Eustis Brooks and daughters of Emily Eustis Brooks and Samuel Clayton Kingman. George Brooks was a schoolteacher in Kingfield for a number of years and here his children were born: George Brooks, William Eustis Brooks, the latter a minister preaching in various towns in this section. Emily Eustis Brooks, born September 22nd, 1829, Pamelia, Albion Dennis Brooks, son of George Brooks and Abigail Eustis, second wife, was killed at battle of Cold Harbor and body sent to Kingfield and buried in Brooks plot in old cemetery by his sister, Mrs. Kingman. Abigail's second husband was Abisha Lander of Kingfield and she is buried in the Lander plot here. George Brooks and the wife, Anna Eustis, are also buried here. Through the Eustis family Mrs. Loomis and Mrs. West are related to the Websters, Benjamin and John C., the father, Benjamin Webster having married Mahitable Eustis. Some of the older people of the town among home are Hiram Hutchins, recall Albion and William Brooks as schoolmates here. Mrs. West and Mrs. Loomis were much interested in the Webster bequests to the town and made a copy of the will. They expressed the hope that the town will erect buildings that will be self-sustaining, near the center of the village, accessible and suitable for all civic and municipal purposes. This was their first visit to Maine and they thought this particular section the most beautiful of any they had seen. On their return they are stopping at Jay to look up family records.

Also, there was an article from a centennial publication in 1916 that described the Landers' family, and mentioned that the location of Abisha's farm was where Oscar Record lived at present. That, coupled with an old map from 1861 on which we discovered family farm names, seemed to indicate that Abisha's place was along the modern Route 142, otherwise known as Salem Road, to the south and west of the downtown area. There are a couple of old farm houses and barns still standing there, and hopefully more research will determine just where Abigail and Albion spent those 14 months under the Landers' roof before Abigail died.

I'm also hoping further research will reveal where George and Anna Brooks lived between 1824-1839, when George was a schoolteacher, and where they had their four children, Pamelia, Emily, George, and William. Abigail wrote to Emily that Abisha's farm was about two miles from the former Brooks' home, and assuming their home was not far from the school where George taught, it may be possible to narrow down the location.

Our next objective was the place of Albion's birth, Carthage. It was a nice 35-mile drive to the south through even more beautiful scenery. I knew it was a small town, but was hoping for at least an attractive "Welcome to Carthage" sign to photograph, and some quaint, old main street. No such luck. There was an interesting older structure for the Carthage Historical Society, but that organization doesn't seem to be active at present. Other than that, there was a tiny town hall that was closed, and a transfer station for the approximately 500 residents to bring their garbage. And that was it for Carthage.

After a quick lunch in Mexico, Maine, which is a small town on the Androscoggin River, in the shadow of a very large and smelly paper mill across the river in Rumford, we headed for the North Jay Cemetery where several members of the Eustis family are buried. At the risk of sounding like a broken record, the drive was 20 miles of yet more beautiful scenery.

Yet another picture postcard-view, this one from Jay, Maine.

The cemetery is not large, and is well maintained. I knew from photos on *Find a Grave*—as well as those taken by Carrie and Evelyn in 1930—that Albion's grandparents, Deacon William Eustis and his wife, Anna's gravestones were rectangular, dark, slate gray, so it only took a minute to locate them. Again, I pictured little 4-year-old Albion and his siblings standing here watching their grandfather being buried.

Next to them, was the grave of the probably disagreeable "blind spinster" Hannah, who was so critical of Abigail. There was also Albion's

Aunt Sarah and Uncle Nathan, who "worked him like a colt," but otherwise seemed to be a kind and caring man. Many of the cast of Eustis characters were here; influences, for better or for worse, in Albion's youth.

Finally, we entered Jay, which was a bigger town, big enough to have a library, so I asked Bob to keep his eyes open. As we were about to cross over the river, he saw a sign for "Library Parking" and quickly turned in. I went in to see if perhaps they had an historical reference section, or could at least direct me to an historical society. The woman at the desk was very helpful with names and phone numbers.

I told her and another woman working there some of Albion's story and about my book project. I was then stunned when one of the women said she was from Kingfield, her great-grandparents were buried in the same cemetery as Albion, she had gone to school with Eustis children, and she had had a baby sitter named Landers! What were the chances!?

Reeling from our busy day and history overload, we headed south, checked into a hotel, and tried to process all that had happened. We quickly gave up and went to bed early. Processing could wait.

From Carrie Kingman Loomis' scrapbook from her 1930 trip to Maine.

4
A Matter of Faith

Albion Brooks was religious, but more importantly, he was a man of faith, a faith that was genuine, unyielding, and was literally expressed with his dying breath.

Perhaps my distinction between religion and faith needs some further explanation. The 19th century—and indeed, just about every century in modern times—had an abundance of church-going, ultrareligious people. They would put on their Sunday best, dutifully sit through a long sermon, sing a hymn or two, and drop some coins in the collection plate. Once they fulfilled their religious duties for the week, they went back to their regular lives, which did not always reflect the principles of their chosen denomination, to say the least.

They spoke the words, sang the songs, followed the rituals, but did they have true faith? Did they believe the words and songs and rituals?

Albion did. From everything others said about him, to his private letters, to his most personal and intimate diaries, he had faith that God was with him. However, it must also be pointed out that while unshakable, that faith did shift over the course of the war. Initially, he clearly believed that God would protect him from harm.

After years of the hardships and privations of army life, and watching men die by the thousands from disease and battle casualties—with some being blown to pieces before his eyes, Albion's youthful and innocent optimism turned to a decidedly darker resignation—that even if he was to die, which appeared increasingly likely, he firmly believed it was all part of God's plan and he "trusted in Him."

This all-pervasive faith and the endless bible quotations in his letters and diaries was something I personally found to be…well, to be perfectly honest, at first, I found it to be a bit irritating.

I suppose a biographer should not say something like that. I suppose I should just relate his words and let his faith speak for itself. But all biographers have a bias toward their subjects, for better or for worse. It's just that I am being honest about mine.

I was irritated because of my personal bias, because at first, I believed he was one of those Christians in name only, spouting scripture for every occasion.

I was wrong. Not that Albion's words converted me to his point of view, but the more I read, the more I realized he was a genuine man of faith to his core. His faith was at the center of his heart, soul, and perhaps most importantly, his actions.

Before delving into his faith, I should explain the root of my bias—distinctly negative lessons I learned as a child.

I was not yet in kindergarten, so probably four years old. My mother had lost her job and had to report to the unemployment office in Spring Valley, New York. I vaguely recall crowds of unhappy people waiting and waiting to speak with unhappy staff. My mother quickly realized that she didn't need to make the situation even more stressful by having a very impatient four-year-old in tow, so she hired a babysitter to watch me for that hour or two.

The sitter was a religious Hispanic woman who would meet us in Spring Valley. We would walk around town and always end up in a local Catholic church, where she would say prayers in Spanish—which sounded very exotic to me—and light a candle. I must say that the ornate church made quite an impression on me, especially the dark recess with all the glowing candles. I thought that there must be something good and true about this thing called religion.

Until the day of the Great Lollipop Scandal.

We were a typical, middle-class, suburban family, not rich and not poor. We never went hungry, but we also weren't lavished with treats all the time. So, when on this particular day, my mother gave the sitter a quarter to buy me not one, but a bunch of lollipops—one of those bundles of about 6 to 8 held together with a little rubber band—it was a special day, indeed.

I wasn't to eat any of them until after lunch, but I still vividly remember walking around town holding them proudly like a bouquet of sweet, artificially flavored goodness on a stick. My favorites were orange and cherry, and I planned to save them, and ration them to one a day to make the treats last.

So, there I was, standing in the dark recess of flickering flames, in the sacred and solemn church, as the sitter lit her candle, crossed herself, and silently said another prayer. She then turned, walked over to me, bent down, and started pulling lollipops out of my bundle, including the orange and cherry flavors.

"What are you doing!?" I protested, in the type of shock and horror that only an innocent four-year-old can feel when confronted by an unjust adult.

"I'm going to give these to my daughter," she calmly replied, pulling out another lollipop, as the rubber band continued to contract on my diminishing bundle.

"But these are mine! My mother paid for them!" I emphatically stated.

"*YOU have to learn to share*," she scolded me, as if *I* was the one doing something wrong.

Had she asked for a couple of lollipops for her daughter, I would like to think I would have reluctantly parted with them—but not the orange or cherry. I have no illusions that I was that selfless and noble.

Of course, I was never given the option. Instead, I stood helpless in this holy shrine, with this supposedly religious woman, as she literally was stealing candy from a baby.

The hypocrisy did not escape me, even if I may not have then known the word. At that moment, I realized that people could pretend to be good with their religious trappings one second, and then literally turn around and immediately be so petty and uncaring as to upset a child by stealing her lollipops! In a church! Then try to make that child feel guilty for complaining about being robbed!

I must have told my mother about the Catholic Candy Caper as we drove home, as I never saw that sitter again, and it was back to the unemployment office for me the next week. It would be long and boring, but at least I could keep my lollipops!

The next major disillusionment came around the fourth grade, when I was attending Sunday school at the Good Shepherd Lutheran Church in Pearl River, New York. The Zimmermanns had been protestants since the time of Martin Luther. In fact, in recent years, I traced 400 years of Zimmermann christenings, marriages, and funerals, to the same little church in the small town of Oberöwisheim, Germany.

As a family, we would go to church every Sunday when I was very young, but that eventually diminished to just Easter and Christmas. I still enjoyed weekly Sunday school, as I embraced any chance to learn something. Until the day the Sunday school teacher gave me a note to take home to my mother.

Apparently, the teacher did not approve of the fact that I asked questions. In a nutshell, she told my mother that I was too young to be thinking for myself. I was not to question the stories from the Bible. I was to be an obedient child, believe everything I was told, and keep my mouth shut.

I'm sorry lady, I have a brain and I enjoy using it.

Needless to say, thus ended my church life, and I never went back, despite a couple of letters mailed from the Sunday school teacher begging me to return.

That is how my cynicism was born, and over the years it was constantly reinforced by more hypocrites, and people around the world doing horrible things to one another in the name of their god.

So, when I kept reading the endless "Blessed be Thy Name," "Praise ye Him," and "He will take care of us. He will never leave us nor forsake us" entries in Albion Brooks' diaries and letters and essays, I thought it was just window dressing. I fully expected to eventually discover the real Albion—the petty, hateful, deceitful, hypocritical Albion, questioning his faith when the going got tough, but I didn't, because that was *not* who he was. Albion Brooks talked the talk, he walked the walk, and my irritation gradually turned to admiration and respect for his deep, genuine, unflinching faith.

But you needn't take my word for it.

From Captain William Hawley[1], Head Quarters, 3rd Brigade, 2nd Division, 2nd Army Corps, 14th Connecticut Regiment, to Reverend A.R. Thompson in Bridgeport, CT, June 7, 1864:

> *... I found that poor Albion had met a soldiers death, that I should see him no more on Earth again - He was one of the few, who though under so much of the evil influence of army life, did not fall into <u>one</u> bad habit of the army - On the other hand his Captain told me he was a <u>better</u> boy than when he left home - His life is an example of a Christian patriot that is truly noble - Not many have rendered such faithful service to their country as a soldier as he, not many Christians have been so devoted & true to God, as this noble boy has been. Under all the trying circumstances of his life as a soldier - It is sweet to know that he is now far from all the sounds of war & at peace with the Savior, whom he loved so well...*

Connecticut War Record, July 1864[2], From the Eight Regiment
Camp of the 8th Regiment, Conn. Vols.
Chesterfield Co., VA., June 20, 1864

Of these last I must say a few words respecting one, whose loss is felt by us all. I refer to Albion D. Brooks, Orderly Sergeant of Company A. In early life he gave himself to Jesus Christ, and hoped to become a minister of His Gospel. At the commencement of this war, he was studying to prepare for that work. But the call of his country seemed to him the call of God. Like many a noble youth he left the school for the camp—Classics for the Tactics and Manual of Arms.

---

[1] See Chapter 22 for more of Captain Hawley's letter.
[2] See Chapter 22 for complete article.

Unlike too many in our army, he did not leave his piety at home. He entered the army to serve God, and he did serve God. In the tent, on the march, in the trenches, in the fight, in the hour of death, he manifested a power controlling his heart and life.

"He has fought the good fight, he has kept the faith."

Regardless of your religion, faith, spirituality, or complete lack thereof, before you read the letters and diaries of Albion Brooks during the Civil War, know that *what he said was what he meant*. He truly "fought the good fight," and "kept the faith" to his dying breath.

5
Albion Joins the Ranks

It is astonishing to the point of being incomprehensible that the predominant belief in early 1861 was that the war would only last a couple of months. Despite generations of pent-up tensions and animosity, Union regiments were initially mustered in for a mere three months of service. Reality soon set in, however, and three-year regiments began forming.

The prevailing sentiments in the North in the early months of the war were encapsulated in the diary entries of Reverend Thompson in Bridgeport, CT[1]:

April 13, 1861... We are all greatly agitated by the news of the bombardment of Fort Sumter today and tonight God grant that what we hear may be exaggerated. God help their beleaguered men for Christ's sake!

April 16, 1861... Fort Sumter has been bombarded and compelled to surrender. The President has acknowledged it in a proclamation declaring the Southern states in rebellion and calling for 75,000 men. Volunteers are flying to arms. The war spirit flames like the burst of a volcano.

The humiliating Union defeat at the Battle of Manassas on July 21, 1861, quenched that "war spirit" considerably, as the misconceptions of a brief and relatively bloodless conflict were dispelled. A shocked and devastated Rev. Thompson wrote:

July 22, 1861 ...word had come of a great battle and Wo for us! A defeat & rout. It seemed impossible to believe it. I rushed up to the newspaper office, and found alas every bulletin full of the fearful tidings. I feel as if my heart had frozen dead in me.[2]

According to family history, Clayton Kingman tried to enlist with the 8th Connecticut Volunteer Infantry sometime after its formation was authorized on August 15, 1861, but he was rejected for being too small. Also, according to family history, Albion "begged to go in his place." Was this true, or family lore?

Clayton's father, Samuel, was described as being a very small man, and photos of Clayton certainly show him to be of a diminutive size, but I haven't found any record of his exact height. However, as Army Regulations required a minimum height of 5 feet and 3 inches, we can

---

[1] Zimmermann, p. 105
[2] Zimmermann, p. 108

assume he was shorter than that—if he had truly been rejected trying to enlist. If so, this must have been a blow to his patriotism and ego. Especially as two of his brothers, William (50th and 8th MA) and Orlando (2nd Co. MA Sharpshooters), would successfully enlist.[3]

As for Albion begging to take Clayton's place, it just didn't work that way. Albion was free to enlist on his own, and didn't need his brother-in-law's rejection to do it.

Whatever the actual circumstances, Clayton stayed at home while Albion joined the army in November of 1861 at Age: 18, Height: 5 feet 6 inches[4], Complexion: Light, Eyes; Grey, Hair: Light, and Occupation: Student.[5]

Several months before the war began, Albion received a curious piece of advice in a letter from his brother George in Horsetown, California, January 3, 1861, to Emily:

And tell him should his country call, there is a time to fight as well as a time to pray, and that the safest way in the hour of danger is to keep your eye on the enemy, and then you won't be shot in the back. I tell him this as one who has known some dangers.

No doubt with his big brother's words of wisdom on his mind, Albion enlisted, but not soon enough to travel with the 8th CT from Hartford, CT to their camp in Annapolis, Maryland, so he had to travel from Bridgeport to Annapolis on his own—for which he submitted receipts for the travel expenses totaling $8.00.

Burnside Camp, Annapolis, Maryland
November 7, 1861
Dear Brother and Sister[6],
I arrived here last evening safe and sound. Found Lieut. Hoyt and am now in the camp, armed and equipped, a soldier of Uncle Sam but I have not been sworn in yet though most likely I shall before 6 comes on.

So far the soldier's (ahem) life seems quite pleasant, though I miss the pleasant beverage and evening meal, but then we must expect to suffer worse things than that.

They do not seem to like the Captain very well, though they seem to like Hoyt very much. The men in my tent are as good a set as can be found in any Regiment. There are 9 of us, of which 2 or 3 of the oldest beside

---

[3] See Appendix for their letters.
[4] Subsequent documents indicated he grew to 5 feet 7 inches in two years.
[5] From Albion Brooks' military records from the National Archives.
[6] "Brother and Sister" always refer to Clayton and Emily.

myself are members of some church and, what is better, they are not Christians in name but in deed. We have prayers every night and if we can we shall have it in every morning, but we have to get up at 6 o'clock, drill till about 9 or 1/2 past, then we have breakfast of one cup of coffee, meat and potatoes; for dinner we have soup; for supper we have coffee, bread, though some of the crackers are invented to do good service and I think that to take a few of them they would answer for a piece of tin which Brother was so afraid I would be without.

Tell Mr. Brown that Mr. King, Williams, and Tomlinson are in the same tent with me. Two of them were members of the same church as he in the Navy. They are fine men.

The chaplain of the Regiment is a fine man though I have not had a chance to get acquainted with him as yet. He is the son of one of the members of the South Church.

I arrived in New York about 1/2 past 1, left New York for Baltimore at 6; arrived in Baltimore about 4 in the morning; left Baltimore at 1/2 past 7 for Annapolis and arrived in Annapolis about 10 or 1/2 past. There is, I believe, a train which leaves New York about 8 in the morning, so you could travel the longest part, if not the whole, in daylight.

There were from Baltimore all along the way, within speaking distance, sentinels. There were any number of soldiers on the train. There were quite a number of encampments along the road.

I saw Governor Hicks of Maryland the afternoon that I came here; he is a pretty good natured sort of man. Lieut. Hoyt went with me over to the State House.

I saw some of the greatest locomotives coming in which I ever saw. They agreed with every other thing which they have or have done here. If the Southerners keep growing shiftless as you go South, by the time anyone has reached New Orleans it must be shocking to behold. I can compare one of those locomotives to nothing than a dead horse who has been picked by the crows.

But I must close. Be sure to come up next Monday. There are about 16 or 17,000 men here. There are 1 or 2000 cavalry. There is a Regiment of Zouaves which number I have been told 1700.

Give my love to all inquiring friends. My love to you and the children.

Good night
Your affectionate brother
Albion
P.S. We do not know when we shall move from here. Probably not before 2 or 3 weeks.

Excitement and optimism for an 18-year-old who has never had a place of his own and never really belonged anywhere, but now having his first taste of a "soldier's (ahem) life." There is obvious pride in that little "ahem," and deservedly so, as what a leap of courage it was for any man to leave home and join the army.

Albion's rather dry wit and sarcasm also are in full display as he takes a swipe at the "shiftless" Southerners whose inferior locomotives are like "a dead horse who has been picked by the crows." Over the course of the war, he would make reference to the rather shabby state of Southern towns and houses, being very unlike his beloved "New England Homes."

Henry Morris Hoyt was a printer in Bridgeport at the start of the war, and served with the 1st CT V.I. for its term of three months. He then joined the 8th CT as a lieutenant of Company A. Albion mentions that the men "did not seem to like the Captain very well, though they seem to like Hoyt very much." The first captain was Henry Loomis Burpee (1821-1864), who resigned on December 24, 1861. Hoyt became the new Captain of Co. A on the following day.

Burpee was a dentist before the war. His widow's pension request indicated that while he had resigned from the 8th CT, he was with the 7th U.S. Colored Infantry at his death on February 9, 1864. Just four months later, his brother, 34-year-old Colonel Thomas Francis Burpee of the 21st CT, was wounded at Cold Harbor on June 9, 1864, and died at White House, VA, two days later.

Albion also wrote that he and Hoyt did some sightseeing at the State House together, which in general might seem odd for a lieutenant and a new recruit to do, but Hoyt had been a family friend back in Bridgeport, and as I've stated before, everyone liked Albion. After the war, Hoyt became the publisher of the *Morning News* newspaper in Bridgeport. He died at home of heart disease on April 2, 1885, and age 50, and his funeral was attended by many veterans of the 8th CT.

A charming present-day street in Annapolis with the State House in the background.

The first chaplain of the 8th CT was Reverend Joseph Judah Woolley, born in Bridgeport in 1832. He was with the 8th CT during Burnside's North Carolina campaign, but had to resign due to illness on March 13, 1862. During the Spanish American War thirty-six years later, he again became a regimental chaplain, this time with the 1st Rhode Island Regiment. In 1906, and the age of 73, he had a severe attack of appendicitis. A doctor told him not to get surgery as he could recover without it. The beloved reverend died within days of the doctor's advice.

Albion also mentions three of the soldiers of Company A, 8th CT, with whom he was sharing a tent:

- Lewis D. King of Naugatuck, CT. In the September 26, 1862 edition of the *Hartford Courant*, King was listed as missing in the Battle of Antietam. King had been captured, but was paroled on October 6, 1861. He reenlisted at the end of 1863, and was discharged on September 18, 1865. A pension was filed on April 2, 1879.
- Horace N. Williams (1825-1909) of Naugatuck, CT. Discharged for disability on January 8, 1863. Reenlisted as a corporal with the 2nd CT Heavy Artillery, wounded at Petersburg March 25, 1865, discharged for disability on August 7, 1865. After the war, Williams, a farmer, was living in Litchfield County, CT, with his wife and three children. He was 84-years-old when he died in 1909, and was buried at the Calhoun Cemetery in Cornwall, CT.
- John B. Tomlinson (1830-1903) of Monroe, CT. He was discharged September 1, 1866. The 1880 census shows he was a bricklayer in Naugatuck, with a wife and daughter. In the 1900 census, the 69-year-old was still employed as a stone mason.

Albion and these three men all started out together full of optimism. One would be captured, two of them wounded, one of them would be killed. The three survivors probably carried the physical and emotional scars of the war with them throughout their lives.

Then there was the letter from Albion Brooks to Reverend Thompson on Thanksgiving Day, which was in Chapter 1:

November 28, 1861, Burnside Camp Annapolis, Md
My dear Pastor
Here I am a <u>soldier</u> for my country...I have a fine lot of men in my tent...We have a fine Chaplain - he seems to be a true Christian man...Well

here it is Thanksgiving & you at home eating Turkey while we poor men are in Dixie with nothing better than hard crackers & "salt horse". Well so be it...I wish I could stand in the Old South Church [Bridgeport] *next Sunday but my duty is here.*

"Camp Burnside, Annapolis, December 25, 1861 by E. Sachse & Co. from a sketch by A. I. Richards of Company K." Alonzo Richards was killed in action at Antietam on September 17, 1862.

In anticipation of a grand review by General Burnside, members of the regiment decorated the camp with evergreen branches and red berries. Note the arches and company letters (close up of Company A below). Also note the skyline which depicts the Naval Academy Chapel dome on the left, and the State House steeple on the right, with the harbor in the background, which helps triangulate the location of the 8th CT camp.

This print is in the collection of the Memorial Military Museum in Bristol, CT, founded in 1975 by retired school teacher Jack Denehy, who was a Marine during the Korean War, then served with the CT Air National Guard and the U.S. Coast Guard. He passed away in 2010, and his wife, Carol, has been tirelessly managing the museum ever since. It is a gem of a museum—one of the finest small museums I've ever seen.

Carol was very gracious in extending an invitation to view the museum and photograph the print. It was a genuine pleasure to meet with her as she is one of those dedicated individuals keeping history alive and making it available to the public.

After my visit, she was able to obtain more information on the owner of the print, who at first glance appeared to be Charlotte Perry. Upon closer examination of the inscription, it was Charlotte Jones, wife of Julius C. Jones, the "Wagoner" of Co. C of the 8th CT. His obituary in the *New Haven Daily Morning Journal and Courier*, May 12, 1881, said he was one of the "best teamsters" and had "many thrilling experiences" in his 22 months in the army. He received a pension for injuries during the war, which supposedly contributed to his death from "typhoid pneumonia."

Carol Denehy and I at the museum.

Tragically, his son, Charles A. Jones, also a teamster, died in a bizarre accident just two years later, as *The New Hartford Tribune* reported on June 6, 1883: "an axle broke, when the horses shied and ran, the load was overturned and he was found dead under the logs. In his pocket was found a tract entitled, *Is the End Near?*"

Albion's Diary Entries

The whereabouts of Albion's 1861-63 diaries are unknown, so at present, all that exists are the transcripts of Agnes Thompson. Obviously, she had some trouble transcribing the following, and without the original diaries, we may never know the missing words—although perhaps we can assume Albion saw a "very pretty" lady?

December 13, 1861 Friday Evening
On patrol, the most interesting case was a man from ? ? that it ? the Guard House ? that most likely ?. I hope that ? be ?. I do not have picket. Saw a very pretty ? at a store where I went to buy coffee.

December 14 Saturday Evening, 1861
Saturday night has come. This week has gone, never to return. God, make me Thine, take ? of ?. Was stationed at the commissary, but shall go at 12 out in the street. Received a letter from Clayton. He sent me a box yesterday.

The following is chilling, and one of several near-misses that Albion would experience throughout his service. Life or death was a game of inches.

December 15th, 1861 Sunday Evening
I think one of us had a narrow escape. About 4 in the morning, 4 of us were on patrol and a pistol was snapped at us from the cellar window of a house. I was the last one and next to the window. Perhaps someone got up at 4 o'clock at night to snap a cap so as to scare us, but I don't believe it. But He has saved us. Lord, I am with you. Lord - my thanks.

The "cap" to which he refers is a copper or brass percussion cap containing mercury fulminate, which when struck by the hammer of a muzzle loader firearm detonates, sending a spark to the gunpowder, thus firing the weapon. One could just "snap a cap," or fire an unloaded gun to frighten the soldiers, but Albion believed it was a loaded weapon fired close to them, and he narrowly escaped being wounded, or worse.

December 16th, 1861 Monday Evening
I received a box from Clayton with a turkey and lots of good things. I was in ? H.

December 17th, 1861 Tuesday Evening
We have got to go up to camp tomorrow so most surely we shall not stay here this winter. O thou God, I thank you for the ?. Sent a letter to ? Day. Bless me.

December 22nd, 1861 In camp
Received a letter from Fannie Day.

December 28th, 1861
Received a letter from Reverend Day. He sent a dollar which had been given on the subscription paper. Most likely we shall leave here in two weeks. I have a very bad cold but if I take care of myself I shall get well.

Reverend Day was most likely Reverend Guy Bigelow Day (1818-1891) of Bridgeport, CT. There was no Fannie Day in the family, so it is not known who this was. Perhaps the nickname of his wife?

Also, Albion reports having "a very bad cold," but as measles and typhus were killing other soldiers in camp, he could consider himself lucky it was only a cold. It would be good that he took care of himself and got better, because the army would soon be on the move.

Perhaps it was a street such as this in Annapolis where someone fired a shot at Albion and the other men while on patrol.

6
"One of the Most Desolate Places"
Burnside's North Carolina Expedition: Roanoke Island
January-February 1862

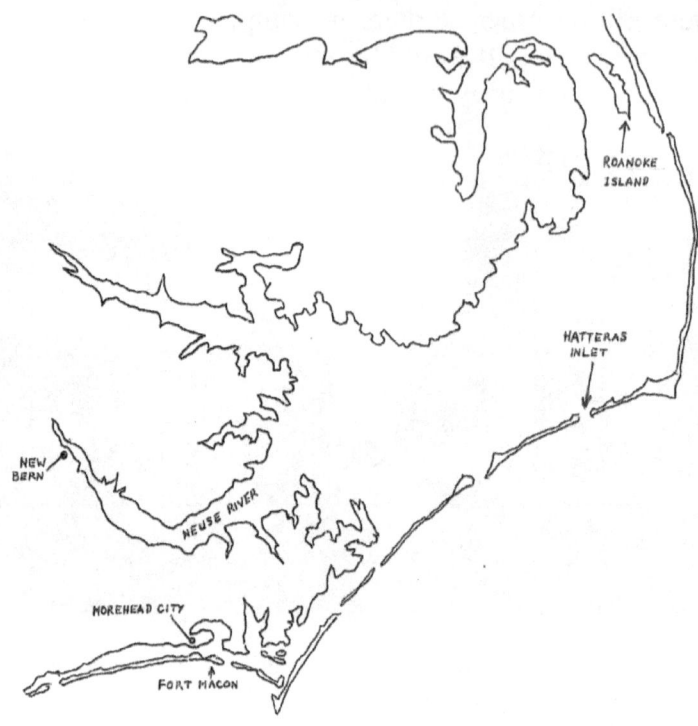

The North Carolina campaign.
Map by Bob Strong

In his book, *The Burnside Expedition*[1], Union General Ambrose Burnside described his North Carolina campaign of 1862—in which the young 18-year-old volunteer, Albion Brooks, would get his first taste of war and experience firsthand the hardships, suffering, and ever-present specter of death.

On page 6, Burnside states:

> *One evening in the following October, General McClellan and I were chatting together over the affairs of the war, when I mentioned to him a plan that I had given some thought to for the formation of a coast division.*

---

[1] *The Burnside Expedition*, Burnside, Ambrose, N.B. Williams & Co., Providence, 1882

After giving him a somewhat detailed account of the plan, he asked me to put it in writing as soon as possible, which was done. The next day it was presented to him, and it met with his approval. He laid it before the Secretary of War, by whom it was also approved.

I am compelled to pause at this point as I have to say that when I first read this, it seemed a remarkably casual account of a major operation that would result in thousands of casualties due to disease and battle. I was immediately reminded of the countless Mickey Rooney and Judy Garland movies where the two kids would be sitting around the farmyard and one would suddenly say, "Hey, let's put on a show!"

While I recognize a musical comedy movie may not be the most appropriate analogy for a bloody civil war, I think it is nonetheless oddly similar that two people are sitting around "chatting," and suddenly say, "Hey, let's put on a coastal invasion!" I guess that when you are two powerful generals who, with the swipe of a pen, can control the destinies of thousands of men, it's just another day at the office.

Burnside then described his plan in more detail:

The general details of the plan were briefly as follows: To organize a division from twelve to fifteen thousand men, mainly from states bordering on the northern sea coast, many of whom would be familiar with the coasting trade, and among whom would be found a goodly number of mechanics, to fit out a fleet of light-draught steamers, sailing vessels and barges, large enough to transport the division, its armament and supplies, so that it could be rapidly thrown from point to point on the coast with a view to establishing lodgments on the southern coast, landing troops, and penetrating into the interior, thereby threatening the lines of transportation in the rear of the main army then concentrating in Virginia, and hold possession of the inland waters on the Atlantic Coast.

Hmmm, great idea, but why does that sound so familiar? It is just like…wait, it's on the tip of my tongue…the United States Marine Corps!

On the www.usmcu.edu website, they state: *On November 10, 1775, the Second Continental Congress meeting in Philadelphia passed a resolution stating that "two Battalions of Marines be raised" for service as landing forces with the fleet. This resolution established the Continental Marines and marked the birth date of the United States Marine Corps. Serving on land and at sea, these first Marines distinguished themselves in a number of important operations, including their first amphibious raid into the Bahamas in March 1776…*

While I can't say if Burnside thought this was an original idea, as the daughter of a proud Marine, I would have appreciated if he had said to McClellan, "Hey, let's put on a coastal invasion with a division of Marines!"

While most plans look good on paper, putting them into action is something else entirely. Burnside explained:

There was great difficulty in procuring the vessels of a light draught, almost everything of that sort having been already called into service; but after much difficulty I was enabled to report to General McClellan on the twelfth of September that a sufficient amount of transportation and armament had been secured for the division. It was a motley fleet.

This "motley fleet" needed considerable alterations to make it seaworthy and ready for battle.

North river barges and propellers had been strengthened from deck to keel by heavy oak planks, and water-tight compartments were built in them. They were so arranged that parapets of sand-bags or bales of hay could be built upon their decks, and each one carried from four to six guns. Sailing vessels, formally belonging to the coasting trade, had been fitted up in the same manner. Several large passenger steamers, which were guaranteed to draw less than eight feet of water, together with tug and ferry-boats, served to make up the fleet which gave a capacity to transport fifteen thousand troops, with baggage, camp equipage, rations, etc. Light-draft sailing vessels were also added to the fleet, on which were stored building materials for bridges, rafts, scows, entrenching implements, quartermaster's stores, tools, extra ordnance, stores, etc., all of which were ordered to rendezvous at Fortress Monroe. Coal and water vessels were chartered in Baltimore, and ordered to rendezvous at the same place.

A remarkable amount of work fortifying vessels, procuring supplies, and coordinating everyone and everything before a single infantry soldier is involved! Had all gone smoothly, the expedition would set sail before the winter of 1862, but what were the chances of that? In reality, zero.

The transports were ordered to Annapolis Harbor, at which point, after most mortifying and vexatious delays, they all arrived by the fourth of January, 1862, and on this day, orders were promulgated for embarkation, which were received from one end of the camp to the other with most enthusiastic cheers.

While arguably, the terms "mortifying and vexatious delays" could be used to describe General McClellan's overall command of the army until

Lincoln removed him once and for all on November 5, 1862[2], following his latest failure to pursue Lee, after the Battle of Antietam, but that is fodder for another book.

For Albion Brooks, life was about to change in ways he could never have imagined. While the same could be said for the rest of the country, the frontline soldier changed the most, suffered the most, and inevitably died most often. Just days before embarking on the North Carolina campaign, Albion, very sick with a cold, commented in his 1862 diary:

January 1, 1862: Another year has commenced, another year is coming and we know not what it will bring to us. To many that Happy New Year will be spent for the last time. They will lay down in their tents to die, or the bullet will lay them low. God grant but few may die. I will try to keep the page each day after today.

Albion's cold grew worse, and the following days he wrote:

January 2, Thursday Evening. Captain Hoyt excused me from duty till my cold is cured. Hoyt is the best man we could have. Lord, grant me Thy spirit. I thank Thee that Thou has kept me so far.

January 3, Friday Evening. Was in my tent all day. My cold is some better.

Burnside had written that the transports arrived in Annapolis on January 4 and the camp of the 8th CT must have been abuzz with gossip and activity. While there was undoubtedly excitement amongst the new recruits as to the possibility of seeing their first action, no rational man could have escaped thoughts of what might be ahead. Albion wrote:

January 5, Sunday Evening. We were paid last evening. I sent home $21.00. We are to leave here tomorrow. Most likely we shall have a hard time. Those that are sick will have a hard time.

Albion also wrote a letter home to Clayton and Emily.

12 o'clock noon, Annapolis, Maryland January 5, 1862
Dear Brother and Sister,
We have orders to join the vessels tomorrow morning. Most likely we should if nothing happens.

---

[2] Lincoln initially relieved McClellan of overall command on March 11, 1862, but reinstated him on September 2 for the Maryland Campaign.

We were paid yesterday. I send $21.00.

Give my love to all who enquire. If I had time I would write a great deal more.

I will try and do my duty. When you hear of anything that makes you ashamed of me, then you may be sorry that I enlisted. All I ask is your prayers and I will try to keep my powder dry.

My love to Orlando. Kiss the children for me. My love to you one and all. My next will be from [just a line drawn] *where Hurrah for Dixie.*

While Albion spent his early years in Maine, it was in the interior, not the coast, so he did not have the seafaring experience that some of the other New England boys may have had, so there must have been some trepidation amongst the 'landlubbers.' For those who had grown up along the coast and had been employed on ships out at sea before the war, one look at the "motley fleet" was probably also enough to strike some fear in their hearts. Albion accurately predicted they would all have a "hard time," although no one could have known how hard, and for how long.

January 9, Thursday Evening. *We came on board the Chasseur Tuesday afternoon. We struck our tents Monday morning, then marched to the (illegible) where we stopped all night. We started from Annapolis about 11 o'clock, probably we shall (illegible) not, but we shall be kept and I believe that God will bless this expedition and this is my prayer. I sent a letter this morning to Clate and to Mrs. Thompson.*

January 11, Saturday morning. *One of the transports went aground. There was heavy fog and we stopped there all day. We arrived this morning about 1 o'clock A.M. Now we are going under sail about the rate of 7 miles per hour. Thank ye the Lord.*

January 12, Sunday morning. *We arrived at Fortress Monroe Saturday at ½ past 3 A.M. At 15 minutes of 1P.M.*

The Burnside Expedition fleet at Fortress Monroe, *Harper's Weekly,* January 25, 1862, page 53.

we are just passing Cape Henry. There is a schooner ashore. The weather is splendid. We are going for where?

½ past 5 P.M. we are passing down the North Carolina coast at about the rate of 6 or 7 knots. Most likely we go to Hatteras Inlet. So passed nearly one Sabbath. I have never passed one like it before. God grant that we shall not have to spend many away from home.

Sunday at ½ past 12. After a splendid sail we arrived here at Hatteras Inlet. It is one of the most desolate places I have been. I hope that they will send us south where it is warmer. The last part of the sail was rather rough and windy. The vessel rolled considerably. I was not in the least sick. Where we stop next I know not, but God will be with us. We need not fear evil.

To the countless people who spend small fortunes to buy and rent houses on what is now a popular vacationing area along North Carolina's Outer Banks, it is somewhat amusing to hear Albion's assessment that, "It is one of the most desolate places I have been." He certainly wasn't alone in his opinion of this being a desolate and inhospitable place, made all the worse by the awful conditions on board ships that were not seaworthy and in constant danger of sinking.

It is also remarkable that Albion did not get seasick, as so many others did. Hundreds, if not thousands suffered the constant misery of seasickness, vomiting overboard—when they could reach the railings in time—in rough conditions that stretched on for weeks. Many no doubt preferred to be on land in battle than spend one more day on these rocking and rolling vessels.

The storms were relentless, and not only sickening, they were deadly. The fleet off Hatteras, *Illustrated London News*, Feb. 22, 1862, page 40.

January 14, Tuesday P.M. *The wind blows quite hard and there are a number of vessels outside of the bay. One large ocean steamer is aground and they think she is going to pieces. It is well for us that we got in as we did. But he has said: "Lo, I am with you, even into the end of the World."*

January 18, Sunday morning *we are yet at Hatteras. My health is very good, better than it has been since I enlisted. Two or three schooners have sunk. We do not know where the expedition is going though those that live have faith. God alone knows how many will be called from time to eternity.*

On the front page of *Frank Leslie's Illustrated Newspaper*, February 15, 1862, there was a description and illustration of the tragedies befalling this "motley fleet," blaming both the "fury of the elements" and "villainy of the contractors" who didn't fortify the vessels as they had been paid to do. The paper suggests that hanging the dishonest contractors would be an end to such crimes:

TRAGIC INCIDENTS OF the Burnside Expedition.

It seems now to be generally conceded that, deeply as is to be deplored the untimely fate of such gallant men as Col. Allen and Surgeon Weller, no expedition of equal magnitude has ever passed through the ordeal of so terrible a storm as that of the 13th January with so little loss as that whose arrival in Pamlico Sound we recorded and illustrated in our last number, and some of whose tragic incidents we portray in the present number. And when it is borne in mind that, in addition to the fury of the elements, there was the villainy of the contractors, who purposely deceived the Government for the sake of gain, the event almost reaches the regions of the miraculous. It is currently reported that, when Gen. Burnside saw so many of his vessels ashore, he turned round to one of his aids and said, "Those villainous contractors have ruined me." The Tribune, *in quoting the words, significantly reminds Gen. McClellan that Wellington, an Irishman of considerable military genius, very efficiently put a stop to the career of army villainy by hanging half a dozen rascally contractors one fine morning before breakfast. But we are afraid that no such summary action will be taken by our Government, whose forbearance is fast exhausting the patience of the great American people. The three incidents our Artist has sent us have been so well described by the Correspondent of the New York* Times, *that we quote him:*

Melancholy Death of Col. Allen, Surgeon Weller, &c.

The most lamentable occurrence, however, which I have to mention is the drowning of Col. J. W. Allen, of the 9th New Jersey, and of Surgeon F.

S. Weller, of the same regiment, caused by the swamping of a boat in which they, with other officers, were returning on board the ship Ann E. Thompson. During the gale of Monday and Tuesday, this ship, with five other ships and barques, were compelled to remain at anchor outside, and at a distance of from two to five miles north of the inlet.

On Wednesday (this morning), several boats left their respective ships to go on shore, among them one from the Ann E. Thompson, for the purpose, as they said, of reporting to the Commanding-General, and to solicit a steamtug to tow them in. It was one of the ship's quarter boats, and was imprudently loaded down with twelve persons. Imprudently, I say, because there was a heavy line of breakers running on the beach, and on each side of the Inlet. There were in the boat Capt. Merriman, of the ship; his second mate, Mr. William Taylor; three seamen, two privates of the 9th New Jersey, Col. Allen, the Lieutenant-Colonel, the Adjutant, the Quartermaster and Surgeon Weller—twelve in all. They entered the inlet, and after calling on Gen. Reno, they spent some time wandering on the beach collecting shells, surveying the forts, &c.

They then started to return to the ship, but in attempting to pass through the breakers, near the east side of the inlet, the boat was filled by a roller and capsized. Being a long distance from any vessel, their perilous situation was not noticed, and they were over half an hour in the water, clinging by turns to the boat and struggling unsupported in the breakers. By this time our vessel, the Highlander, in tow of a steamtug, came up to them. Capt. Dayton instantly lowered away two boats, one of which was manned by his second officer, Mr. Higgins, and the other by the officers of the 23d Massachusetts, who were on board. Nine persons were rescued alive; two lifeless bodies—those of Col. Allen and Surgeon Weller—were taken into the-officers' boat, and one, the second mate, had sunk to the bottom. The bodies of the unfortunate officers were carefully lifted on to the quarter-deck of the Highlander, where Dr. George Derby, the able surgeon of the Massachusetts 23d, assisted by twenty willing hands, began their efforts to restore them to life. Artificial

respiration, and every expedient known to medical science, were resorted to for the purpose, and these exertions were continued without intermission for two hours. These humane efforts, however, proved unavailing—the vital spark had fled.

Shipwreck of the Transport New York. [sic, was the "City of New York"]

One ship, the screw steamer New York [sic], went ashore on Monday, on the south end of Hatteras Inlet, with a cargo of Government stores valued at $200,000, and is now totally lost. To add to the misfortune, the greater part was ammunition, ordnance, etc.

A Soldier's Funeral.

The two officers of the 9th New Jersey who lost their lives on Wednesday, and whose remains had been deposited in a small building on shore, under guard, were to-day prepared for burial under the supervision of Quartermaster Keys. The only ceremony observed was the lowering of the flag at half-mast on the brig Dragoon, and a dirge played by the band. The bodies were tightly sewed in canvas, and covered with a coating of tar to exclude the air. They were then deposited in strong boxes and conveyed in a boat to the high sand ridge two miles east of the fort, where they were buried, and the spot marked by a wooden slab containing their names. Persons who may be sent to recover their remains can have the spot pointed out by inquiring of Capt. Clark, Commissary, or of Capt. Morris, Commandant of the post. The Chaplain of the regiment being still on board of the ship, outside, accounts, probably, for the omission of the usual religious ceremonies, or of anything to characterize the burial as a funeral. There are a great many Chaplains hereabout, but I notice there is little attention paid to the decencies which mark these and events in civilized life.

The Drowning of the Horses.

The steamer Pocahontas, well known as a Baltimore and Chesapeake boat, which was chartered to convey horses to this point, and which had on board 113 horses, mostly belonging to the Rhode Island 4th regiment, went ashore in a storm on Friday night last, about 12 miles north of Hatteras, and all the horses, except 24, which swam ashore, were lost. No lives of the crew were lost. The steamer is a total wreck.

During the gale she first blew out some portion of her worthless boiler, and the grates fell down. The boiler was plugged or patched, and then the steering gear gave way. This was mended, when the smoke-pipe blew down, and as the vessel, from laboring in the sea, had sprung a leak, she was run ashore. The sending to sea of this worthless old hulk, after it was known how utterly unsafe she was, with a full deck load of valuable *horses and a crew of men, was most inexcusable. There was drunkenness and disorder on board. The boat is said to have been built in 1829!*

Valuable horses were thrown overboard 10 miles at sea, and when the vessel struck, or was near the beach, the teamsters who had charge of the horses were so careful of their own worthless carcasses that they refused to go down on the lower deck and cut the halters of the animals, thus leaving the poor brutes to perish on the wreck, when they might nearly all have been saved. The Government ought to sift this case to the bottom, and call as witnesses the pilot of the Spaulding, *and* George Brown, *an intelligent surfman of Long Branch, both of whom were on board. They found oats and hay on the beach, thrown ashore from the wreck of the* Grapeshot.

There were, besides the crew, five carpenters on board, who lost all their tools and clothing. They were hospitably received and entertained by the people near Hatteras, and arrived at Hatteras Inlet on Saturday, bringing with them the horses which had so courageously struggled through the surf and reached the shore, despite the neglect of their keepers.

What a horrific loss of men, horses, and supplies! At least some of the men had a chance of survival, the poor horses tied up below decks had none. It is clear that the "villainous contractors" should have been brought to trial and punished—with a suitable punishment perhaps being that they would be sent out to sea in one of their own shoddy vessels. It is also clear that as the author of this article states, the fact that more ships were not lost was nothing short of "miraculous" given the circumstances.

Word of these tragedies spread through the fleet, but Albion tried to remain hopeful, as conditions aboard the *Chasseur*, as unpleasant as they were, were much better than many of the other ships:

January 20, Monday morning. *This morning is quite pleasant. We do not know when we may leave here. There have been quite a few vessels wrecked here. May God grant that this expedition may be successful. We fare quite well. None of the letters will go, they say, until after we strike. God grant the strength to resist all evil.*

January 26 Sunday. *Here we are at Hatteras, have been on board almost two weeks. We do not know when we will move from here. I should like to be in the church in Bridgeport this evening. I have not been to a church or gone to a prayer meeting in almost 3 weeks. Blessed be thy name, Great Father.*

It has been one of the most cloudy days today of any since we have been here. We had preaching this afternoon by Rev. Eaton of the 56th. God enable us to do more for Thee, give me strength.

January 27, Monday evening. On guard. The weather was cold and cloudy. We have coffee and hard bread at 7 A.M., eat "salt horse" about 4 P.M. We must pray that God will bring us safely through.

January 31, Friday. Another month has passed. Another month of privileges has gone, gone forever. We are yet at Hatteras. I hope that we may soon go and do whatever is our duty.

An undated letter from Albion written while still on board the ship:

On board the transport Chasseur, Hatteras
Dear Brother and Sister:
Here we are in the same cold stormy place we have been for two weeks.

Likely, ere you receive this, we'll have moved from here. The blow will be struck and the Union cause will rejoice or sorrow, but I Trust that this expedition will not be in vain.

My health is very good in spite of three weeks on board the ship, three weeks in which I have eaten an enormous quantity of "hard bread" and "salt horse" or rather salt beef. They are very modest in the price of anything good to eat here. Whiskey sells for $3.00 a quart,--I have not touched a drop--and horrible stuff at that. Cheese is from 50 to 75 cents a pound, a pie only $1.00

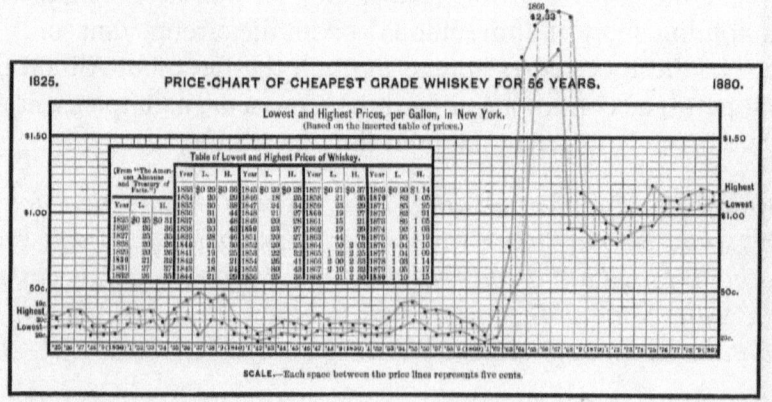

War is hell--especially on whiskey prices. The spike hit in 1862, and took until 1870 to stabilize.[3]

---

[3]OEN,https://manifold.open.umn.edu/projects/accessible-appalachia/resource/table-9-1-price-chart-of-cheapest-grade-whiskey-for-56-years

Oh, ye men at home "City Guard," I think you would not think it so much fun to try "serving" for a month or so on shipboard. I like it "first rate" even so.—

Where we are to go, you know more and better than we do. I hope that we may soon move.

Hatteras Inlet is a mean place. It is nothing but a sand bank and that is more than half covered with water at high tide.

Many a poor fellow has been laid to rest here in the sand. God grant that if I am to die it may not be here. They are laid in the grave with nothing to mark the place of their burial but a board at their head and feet. The water and storms will soon remove even those marks, and careless feet will tread on their graves, but they will sleep in peace till that great morn when we shall all rise and stand before the judgment of Christ.

But we are all full of hope,--we're hoping soon to return,--though I expect to be gone a year and I think we all will stay that time.

I did not expect to write again until we were landed,--but I will send this,--but shall not write again till we have had a battle. When you write, please do that right off, direct to

8th Regiment Company A, Connecticut Volunteers
Burnside Division, Fortress Monroe

Kiss the children for me, give my love to all who may feel any interest in the youth who is in the "Army" and my love to you all.

February 1, Saturday. *Another month has arrived. Help me, O God, to do my duty, help me in every hour of trial, give me strength in the hour of need. We fare rather hard, nothing but coffee and hard bread in the morning and fat pork at 3 or 4 P.M. We shall be off this vessel soon I hope, by the help of God, to do my duty.*

February 2, Sunday morning. *Quite windy but pleasant. Another Sabbath on shipboard, another Sabbath away from home. A man in Company C died this morning. A great many more have perhaps died from disease than by the bullet.*

Albion was correct—It is estimated that about 66% of all soldier's deaths during the Civil War were the result of disease, not wounds from battle. He was also correct that Hatteras was a "mean place" for soldiers, and for the families of those soldiers who died and had no hope of ever recovering their loved ones remains—something that haunted Albion.

Two men from Company C had recently died: Thomas C. Clark on January 28, 1862, and John Bulkley on January 31.

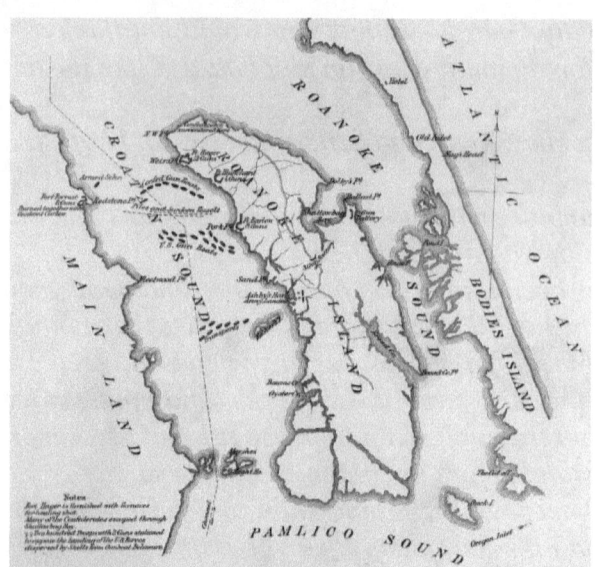

Roanoke Island Battlefield Feb. 8th 1862
Library of Congress, G3902.R6S5 1862.A5

February 4, 1862 Tuesday. We expect to move very soon. We leave our knapsacks so perhaps before I shall write in this album we may have received our orders. This may be the last I shall write here, but I trust in him who is my Rock and my High Tower. The Lord will hear us in the hour of trouble. He will take care of us. He will never leave us nor forsake us, even into the end of the world. Amen.

February 5 Wednesday 2 P.M. We started from Hatteras about 8 o'clock. Rather windy and cold. We have just received our cartridges.

February 6, 12 o'clock noon. We anchored last night. We started about 8 A.M. There was a heavy fog and it began to rain. We have anchored but there is no fog now. One sweetly solemn thought comes to me over and over, the thought of home today more than ever before.

February 7 We slept on deck last night. There is a big fog now. Very likely we shall not land today.

We arrived at Roanoke Island about 11 A.M. and at that time we commenced firing. The whistle of the cannon ball is in the air. Some troops are landed. I do not know whether we shall be or not. Great Master, into Thy hands I commit the keeping of my soul. If I die, receive me onto Thyself for Christ's sake. Amen.

5 P.M. the fog cleared away and we started in about 8.

Landing troops on Roanoke Island, *Frank Leslie*, Vol. 8, No. 328, p. 245.

February 8 Saturday evening 6 P.M. *We had our first battle today and we were victorious. The 8th was held as a reserve, but was not called for. We landed last night.*

This "first battle" for Albion and the 8th CT was on Roanoke Island, North Carolina—best known today for Sir Walter Raleigh's ill-fated colony, founded in 1585. By 1590 it had vanished, and the "Lost Colony" is now subject to countless theories and television shows.

It is doubtful anyone was pondering the fate of those approximately 120 colonists shortly after 11 am on Friday, February 7, when the Union fleet's artillery opened up on the Confederate Fort Bartow—they had their own fates to worry about. Bands played patriotic songs, and to add to the fuss and bluster, Lord Nelson's famous message at the Battle of Trafalgar went out, "This country expects every man to do his duty." There must have been a great swell of pride felt in every new soldier's heart who is about to overwhelm a smaller, poorly-equipped enemy.

However, all glorious illusions melted away as the troops were towed to shore in little boats, right up to large swamps of chilly, knee-deep muck. Once they trudged to camp, which was no more than a blanket on the ground, the cold, miserable troops got rained on all night—but at least they were finally off those damn boats, and at least they were finally going *to do* something.

It was still raining lightly when the attack commenced the morning of Saturday, February 8, but Albion and the 8th CT would not be storming the fort. According to Burnside's official report:

Soon after the attack was commenced, I ordered General Parke to place a regiment in the woods to the north of Hammond's house and extending up to the main road, to prevent the possibility of the enemy's turning our left. The Eighth Connecticut, Colonel Harland, was detailed for this service.

Which was not to say there wasn't some danger, as bullets were flying through the air even in their set-back position. There was naturally controversy over which regiment acted the bravest and took the fort, but the end result was that the fort was taken, thanks to everyone's efforts—not to mention the thousands of artillery shells the day before. The Confederate forces all ran out of the fort and headed north to Forts Blanchard and Huger, but later that night the white flag went up and 2,488 rebels surrendered.

This battle was tiny considering the mass slaughters to come, but it was certainly not inconsequential, especially for the family, friends, and comrades of the 24 Confederates and 41 Union soldiers who lost their lives. Anyone who had enlisted because they thought it would be a fun adventure was quickly being disavowed of those opinions.

However, a victory is still a victory, and as they say, to the victor goes the spoils—in this case, in the form of 2,488 prisoners that Burnside didn't know what to do with. He couldn't spare the ships to bring them north, he would have had to feed them, care for them, and guard them, so he decided to parole them.

Parole was a bizarre practice born out of necessity of the situation—the same men who were just trying to kill you, were asked to pinky swear that they would not fight you again, unless, of course, they were exchanged with some of your Union parolees who had also pledged the same pinky swear oath. Once exchanged, everyone was free to start trying to kill each other again.

If you were one of the Union soldiers whose best buddy got a rebel musket ball between the eyes at the Battle of Roanoke Island, you were none too happy to see these prisoners being set free. It is one of the peculiar and ridiculous 'rules' of war, which otherwise sees men tearing each other apart with their bare hands if they have to, to kill and survive.

For Albion, all this death and carnage must have affected him deeply, but no soldier could dwell long upon yesterday, when he had to keep warm today.

February 9 Sunday evening *I have worked some today, cutting wood. Good Lord, I think I was right for I worked so as to have a fire to keep me warm in the night.*

There is a note in the family records of interest with this diary entry:

Note: it worried him that he had worked on Sunday.

To those of us in the modern world, the division of days is mostly work week and weekends, but to many people of the 1800s, and especially to Albion, the Sabbath was a sacred day of prayer, not work. While we don't have the written words of Albion expressing his conflict about working—and God forbid, fighting—on the Sabbath, this notation, along with Albion writing, "I think I was right," indicates a huge shift in something he never would have considered doing a year earlier. But as Albion stated, war changes a man in ways he couldn't imagine.

In the weeks following the battle, Albion and the 8th CT fell into the routine of camp life, without any particular concerns, other than the rainy, cold weather. As a prime example of the soldier being the last person to find out what was going on, he even speculates that they might remain in camp on Roanoke Island "all summer." However, the North Carolina Expedition was just getting started.

Roanoke Island is a beautiful place, and there is considerable emphasis on the Lost Colony and their Elizabethan history. It isn't easy finding any traces of their Civil War history, however, which basically consists of signs that aren't always easy to find, or in the best condition.

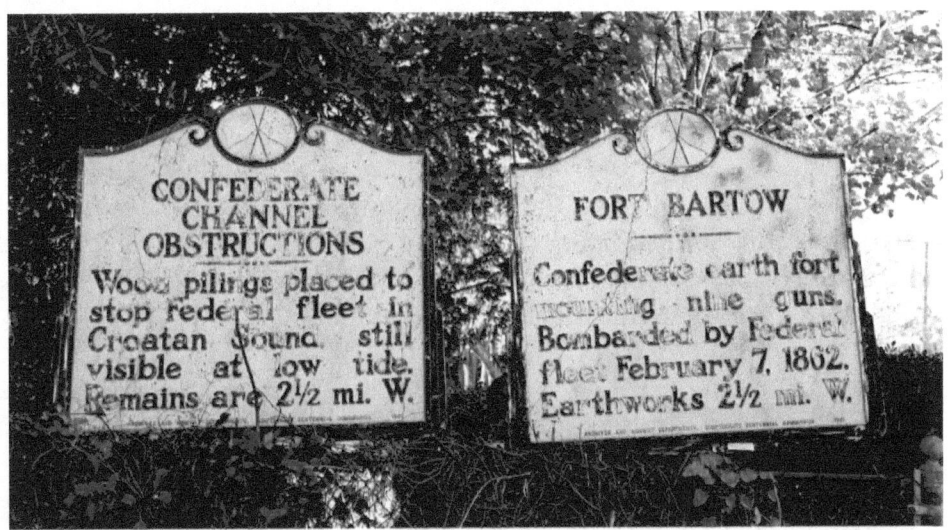

Chapter 7
"We are going now, I suppose, to take New Bern"
Burnside's North Carolina Expedition: New Bern to Carolina City
February-April 1862

Before continuing with the North Carolina campaign, I had quite the campaign of my own to trace Albion's footsteps and take a lot of photos for this book. I could have completed this entire project without traveling further than a library archive, but as I stated at the beginning of this book, this project became personal so I *needed* to go where Albion went and see what Albion saw, wherever I could.

In addition, and arguably even more importantly, for as long as I have been writing, I have steadfastly believed that the best way to write about something is to experience it. Obviously, I can't recreate the Civil War, but I can walk a battlefield, see the terrain, understand who was where and when, and try to envision past events in my mind's eye. So, what that all translates to, is a hell of a lot of driving and running around, questionable hotel rooms, and sketchy road food. But who am I kidding, I love every historical moment of it.

In November, 2024, I planned an epic road trip—27 sites to photograph across Virginia and North Carolina, all in under a week, as a huge coastal storm was forecast to hit. Thank god Bob loves to drive!

After seven hours of driving from New York to across the Chesapeake Bay Bridge and Tunnel, the list of objectives commenced: Fortress Monroe, Newport News, Portsmouth, Suffolk, Hills' Point Battery, Deep Creek, Dismal Swamp, South Mills, Roanoke Island, Hatteras Inlet, New Bern, Morehead City, and Fort Macon. Then heading back a different way several days later, we stopped in Cold Harbor, White House Landing, Aquia Creek, and Fredericksburg. And that doesn't take into account the unscheduled stops.

I hope these efforts and photos are appreciated by the casual readers who may be inspired to get up out of their chairs and see a place with their own eyes. There's *nothing* like it.

Speaking of fatiguing travels, we now resume our regularly scheduled coastal invasion, Albion writes:

February 11 Tuesday evening *I am very tired having taken quite a tramp up to the batteries. Most likely we shall stay here for the present. Lord, I thank Christ and feel that He has kept me from fear and harm.*

February 13 Thursday evening Received a paper from Clayton today. We came up to the fort today. We may stay here all summer. God help me to live as I should.

February 14 Friday evening We came in camp today. It seems like home after sleeping in rain and cold for a week or so.

February 16 Sunday evening We did not have any preaching. Wrote a long letter to Clayton. Praise Him.

February 17 Monday it has rained more or less all day. The ground is damp.

February 19 Wednesday I was detailed all day.

February 21 We do not have much to do. Received a pair of mittens from Clayton.

February 22 Saturday evening Thirty-six of us were detailed for extra duty. We came to Hatteras and loaded the vessel with provisions.

Saturday night. Another week has gone, gone to eternity. Lord, grant that I may love Thee more serve Thee better.

February 23 Sunday We left here about 9 A.M. Arrived at Roanoke at 8 P.M. Had a pleasant time.

February 25 Tuesday evening We came ashore. Received a letter from Emily.

February 26 Wednesday evening We did not drill any today. Give me strength to do as I should, O Father.

February 27 Thursday evening Went out on drill.

February 28 Friday The last day of February gone, gone to eternity. We are to be paid in a few days most likely.

March 2 Sunday We had preaching and a very good meeting in the evening. Lord, help me to obey Thee in all things.

Not a lot going on, but relative peace and quiet is never a bad thing in war. Finally, in early March, word spread that they would soon be on the move again, although like everything else in the army, it was hurry up and wait. And wait.

March 3 Monday There is a report that we leave here tomorrow, tents and all. Received some papers from Clayton, but no letters. God, I am with you always, even into the end of the world.

March 5 Wednesday morning The tents are all ready to be struck.

March 6 Thursday morning We are on board the Chasseur.

March 8 Saturday evening. We are ordered to be ready to leave at an hour's notice. There are as many men, I should think, as there were when we left Hatteras. We are to carry [illegible] pounds of cartridges. Be Thou with us, O god, and give us the victory.

March 9 Sunday We have had a lovely day. It seemed like a Sabbath in our old New England.

March 10 Monday. We have not made any move yet.

Leave it to the Army to rush everyone from their comfortable camps, back to the crowded ships where accommodations were not at all accommodating, and then sit there for five, long days and nights.

March 11 Tuesday. *We started from Rodanthe at 10 A.M. Our engine was stopped by a rope wound around the screw. A brave fellow of my Company from* [several words illegible] *the ball going in the* [illegible] *inflicting such a dangerous wound.*

Once they were finally underway after a week of delays, they promptly ground to a halt when Albion's ship, the *Chasseur*, which had been towing a schooner, became stuck on a shoal. In an attempt to get free, the tow line was cut, but then the "rope wound around the screw," i.e., tangled in the propellor so the ship became both unable to use its engine and stuck. Tugboats finally helped free the *Chasseur*, and the next day the rope was removed from the propeller.

However, Albion's description of "A brave fellow of my Company" somehow sustaining a "dangerous wound," is a mystery. Was the injury somehow related to the tangled rope? Was the "ball" a musket ball, or part of some machinery? It is moments like this that it is so frustrating not to have the original diary, only transcripts with words "lost to eternity," as Albion would say.

The motley fleet, fresh off its first victory, now headed for New Bern, North Carolina. As Albion was to experience more and more fellow soldiers' deaths throughout the war, it's clear his thoughts often turned to the terrible cost.

March 12 Wednesday. *We anchored off Hatteras last night. It's a splendid day. We are going now, I suppose, to take New Bern. How many now so full of life will, in a few hours, will be cold and stiff in death, God above knows. ½ past 5. By the grace of God we have met with no enemy position as yet. Along the banks are quite pretty houses in among the pines.*

March 13 *We landed and marched quite late.*

What Albion doesn't write, is that their long march beginning along the Neuse River, was on very muddy roads and the soldiers slept very little in the heavy rain that night. Burnside wrote:

On the night of the twelfth, orders were given for landing, and on the morning of the thirteenth the troops were put ashore, in very much the same way that they were at Roanoke. By one o'clock the debarkation was finished, and the troops were put in line of march. About this time the rain began to fall, and the roads became almost impassable. No ammunition could be carried except what the men could carry themselves. No artillery could be taken except the small howitzers, which were hauled by troops with drag ropes. This was one of the most disagreeable and difficult marches that I witnessed during the war. We came in contact with the enemy's pickets just before dark, when it was decided to delay the attack until morning. A most dreary bivouac followed that night[1].

March 14 Friday. *Up front 6 A.M. We have not brought up very heavy firing, but the bullets whistled considerably. Two were wounded. A bullet struck my finger just enough to draw blood. God has kept us and given also victory.*

This was the second near miss for Albion with a bullet grazing his "finger enough to draw blood" (the first being when someone shot at him in Annapolis). Obviously, a fraction of an inch difference could have had very different consequences.

The Confederate line which the Union soldiers had to assault was facing an open area beyond some woods where the rebels had cut down all the trees. They had a fortified line with rifle pits, logs, and artillery, with their right flank bent back along some railroad tracks. The 8th CT was on the left of the Union line, between the 4th and 5th Rhode Island, under command of General Parke. Union skirmishers were driven back, and initial attempts to storm the Confederate fortifications were repulsed by artillery and heavy musket fire—with one of those shots just barely

---

[1] *The Burnside Expedition*, p.27

missing seriously wounding Albion. The Union men were ordered to lie down, and for over two hours they were stuck in position.

The railroad tracks and earthworks at the New Bern Civil War Battlefield Park trail.

Finally, the defenses were breached on the Confederate right flank by the railroad tracks, and the rebel forces ran. It was reported by more than one member of the 8th CT, that their colors were the first to be raised on the ramparts. While that helps to build regimental morale, it came at the cost of 90 killed and 380 wounded for the Union forces, while the Confederates had 64 killed, 101 wounded and 413 missing or captured.

In case you are relatively new to Civil War casualty statistics, note how many battles there are in which the Union killed and wounded exceeded the Confederate losses, often dramatically. That was what came of exposed Union forces hurling themselves face first into fortified Confederate defensive positions and straight into cannon and musket fire. It is inconceivable today that this kept happening over and over, year after year, with ever-increasing carnage.

These guns were not their grandfather's inaccurate smooth bore weapons of the Revolutionary War. For example, a smooth bore Brown Bess musket used during the Revolutionary War was accurate to about 50 feet, whereas a rifled 1861 Springfield musket of the Civil War could be accurate to *500 yards*! Add to that a well-trained soldier could fire three rounds per minute, and Civil War battles were nothing short of choreographed murder.

Two prime examples of this insanity are Fredericksburg and Gettysburg. At Fredericksburg (which will be discussed in more detail in chapter 11), Confederate forces were behind a stone wall on Marye's Heights, supported by artillery, and wave after wave of Union soldiers walked across an open field into the meat grinder. Total Union casualties were about 12,500 killed, wounded, missing, and captured. Confederate casualties were less than half that, at just over 6,000. That is because stone walls stop bullets, northern wool uniforms do not.

The tables were turned at Gettysburg, specifically during what is popularly known as Pickett's Charge. This time, Union forces were behind a stone wall that was two to three feet high (higher than what remains there today) and Confederate troops had to traverse an open field almost a mile long, unprotected, directly into artillery and musket fire. Once again, stone walls stop bullets, the southern cloth uniforms did not. Union casualties were about 1,500 killed and wounded. Confederate casualties were over 6,500, or about 50%.

It is no wonder the Union soldiers were shouting, "Fredericksburg! Fredericksburg!" to the doomed rebels before them. Apparently, Civil War revenge is best served behind a stone wall.

Of course, I do understand that during war, enemies have to engage at some point, but this!

So now that is off my chest, back to Albion and New Bern.

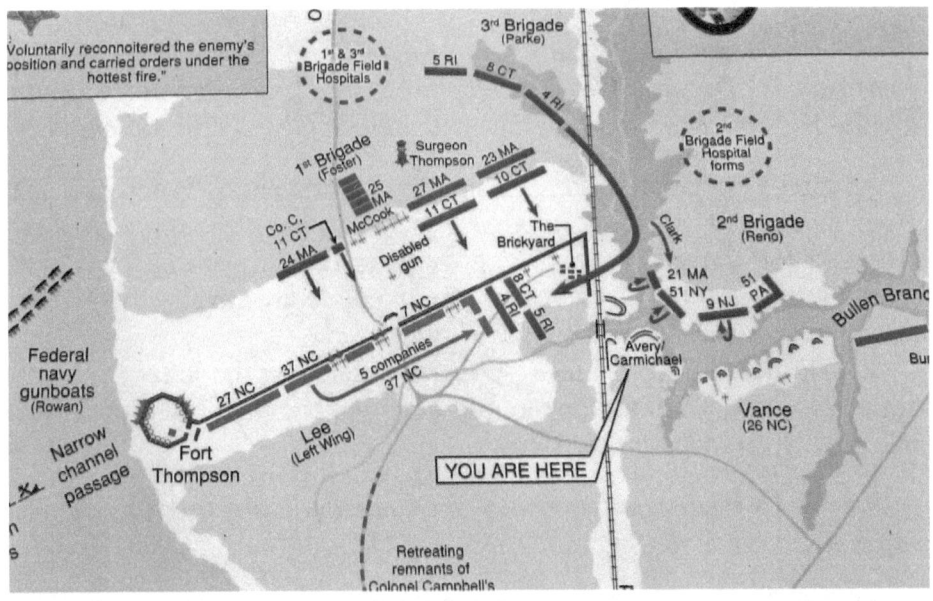

This is one of the very informative interpretative signs along the New Bern Civil War Battlefield Park trails. When Bob and I first arrived at the park, there wasn't a Park Ranger on duty, and we were trying to get our bearings. Apparently, we looked confused, as a local law enforcement officer—who had happened to stop by to use the bathroom—asked if he could help. It turned out, he had a remarkable, Park Ranger-level of knowledge about the battlefield and told us exactly where to go to follow the path of the 8th CT. It was another of those amazing moments when the right person was in the right place at the right time to help us over the years of research and travels for this project.

I think reading the letter in the Trunk Collection 30 years ago mentioning Albion and New Bern was the point when that spark of interest in him began. It was an unsigned letter from a soldier to Reverend Thompson with some good-natured ribbing:

Ask brave Albion if his knees did not shake when the shot came whistling around his head.

To me, this showed that not only were people thinking about Albion, they knew they could joke with him, so I began paying more attention to this one soldier in the vast letter collection.

If Albion's knees did shake, they wouldn't have had too much time to relax, and Burnside's soldiers wouldn't have long to rest on their laurels.

March 17 Monday *Received a letter and papers from Emily. We drew our clothes today. There is a report that we shall have to move forward. Grant us victory, O God.*

March 18 Tuesday *Wrote a letter to Emily. Sent a cavalry sword to Clayton. We expect to go tomorrow to Beaufort. Give us the victory, God.*

A note of explanation here. When the Confederates evacuated, they left behind *a lot* of food, clothes, and weapons. Albion must have scavenged for souvenirs along with everyone else, resulting in Clayton becoming the very happy recipient of a Confederate cavalry sword. One can only wonder where that sword is today…

NOTE: See the Appendix A, Other Soldiers, for the letter from John Smilie, 24th MA, who had apparently acquired the pistol of Confederate General L.O. Branch at New Bern.

March 19 Wednesday evening. *We came on board to go, perhaps to Beaufort. Do not feel very well. Help us, O Lord.*

March 21 Friday. *We were landed today and are to take a forced march. Help us, O god, to give us the victory.*

March 22 Saturday. *We marched forward until around 4 A.M. when we stopped at some barracks. We did not have anything to eat. We had a very hard time. Though it be hard, we will conquer in the strength of Christ.*

The 8th CT had left for their march without drawing any rations. The roads were once again muddy, swampy, and standing in water. Wet, tired, and hungry, this was just a typical day of the week for a Civil War soldier. Finally, they reached their objective:

March 23, Sunday morning Carolina City, North Carolina. We marched yesterday to this place. The rebels had burned a hospital. Even a large building is burning at the fort, supposed to be [illegible] perfect

March 25 Tuesday We have not moved yet from Carolina City. It is very smoky and dirty.

In addition to the fires set by the retreating Confederates, Union soldiers had found barrels of pine resin which burns well on camp fires, but smokes and gets black soot all over everything and everyone—not ideal camping conditions, especially when the soldiers had no tents.

March 26 Wednesday evening. Received a paper from Clayton. Rainy. Our tents have not come.

Another of those roadside signs for which researchers are most thankful...

March 27 Thursday evening. I was on guard today. Grant us Thy spirit, Lord.

March 28 Friday evening. Did not do anything but lay around. We do not know when we are to leave.

With some down time, Albion had the luxury of becoming philosophical and reflective:

March 29 Saturday evening. Another week has past, gone to Eternity. Help me to do as I wished that others should do to me. One of the greatest Evils into which a man in the Army is apt to fall is selfishness. It affects men most curiously, some who left free hearted will return selfish and crabbed.

March 30 Sunday and other Sabbath has passed. Another Sabbath in which I have heard nothing that is as blessedful as of Christ to accept the things that He has given me. And the Son of the Lord shall return with songs and everlasting joy upon their heads that shall obtain joy and gladness forever and defiling shall flee away.

April 1 *Another month has passed. In that time we have had a hard battle. I have been in great danger, but Christ has kept me from all harm. We detached with others to clear away the ground for our camp. The woods caught fire and we worked quite hard to put it out.*

April 4 *We are on the island where the fort is.*

What Albion didn't record was that on April 2, Company A of the 8th CT was rowed across to Bogues Banks, the island which held their next objective, Fort Macon. If the Union could take the fort, then Beaufort Harbor, North Carolina's second-largest port, would be under their control.

The 8th was tasked with supporting the artillery which would be preparing their siege gun emplacements, but apparently there wasn't much to that assignment for at least a week.

April 5 Saturday evening *Another week is gone but have not done anything as yet. "Hold fast that which He hast that no man can take Thy Crown."*

April 7 Monday evening *We do not and have not had much to do. Expect to go out on picket tonight. Rains hard.*

April 8 Tuesday evening *The* [illegible] *is coming over on the Island. Received 3 papers from Clayton.*

Could it have been the mail that was coming to the island?

April 9 Wednesday evening*. It has been a most disagreeable day, rainy and windy. Help me faithfully to do my duty.*

I know I'm biased, but I found this April 10 diary entry amusing:

April 10 Thursday evening *It was quite cold and I lay in bed most of the day. Lazy life, or lazy boy.*

It is good that Albion had the luxury of being lazy, with no fighting to be done—especially as some of his friends and fellow soldiers were currently fighting for their lives.

Chapter 8
"as tough as you could please"
Burnside's North Carolina Campaign: Fort Macon
April-July 1862

April 11 Friday evening *The tents came over today. We heard today of the death of Sam Bosworth and Isaac Tuller. Great God, how great are Thy ways. Past finding out why it was not me.*

This is a sentiment shared by countless soldiers around the world throughout history—the guilt complex of watching your friends die and wondering how you survived. At this time, typhoid was sweeping through the nearby camps due to poor sanitation, decimating the ranks of both soldiers and officers, killing dozens of men.

Typhoid fever is an illness you get from S. Typhi bacterium. It causes a high fever, flu-like symptoms, and diarrhea. You can be contagious with typhoid even if you don't feel sick. Typhoid can be life-threatening and should be treated promptly with antibiotics. If you live in or travel to an area where typhoid is common, you should get vaccinated.[1]

Unfortunately for Bosworth and Tuller, and the estimated more than 100,000 soldiers who died of typhoid during the war, there were no antibiotics yet, and a vaccine wasn't developed until 1896 by English and German scientists.

As these two men were obviously important enough to Albion to mention, I looked into their stories.

Samuel P. Bosworth of Hartford, CT, enlisted on September 18, 1861 and was mustered into Company A of the 8th CT on September 25. Sam died April 8[2], 1862, of "disease," presumably typhoid, and is buried in the New Bern National Cemetery in North Carolina, Section 13, site 2276, if you want to pay your respects. Unfortunately, as of yet, I have been unable to find out more about his short life.

However, on the same day Sam enlisted, a Charles C. Bosworth of Hartford also enlisted, so we might be able to say there were related, possibly brothers, but that will take more research. Charles was discharged from the 8th CT, Company A, on October 3, 1862, due to "disease."

That could have been it for him serving in the war, but he reenlisted from Cornwall, CT on January 28, 1864 in the 2nd Connecticut Volunteer

---

[1] Cleveland Clinic website: https://my.clevelandclinic.org/health/diseases/17730-typhoid-fever

[2] His records at the cemetery say April 8, the roster in *Connecticut Men of the Civil War* lists his death as April 7, 1862.

Heavy Artillery. Ten months later, on October 19, 1864, Charles was wounded in the wrist at the Battle of Cedar Creek in the Shenandoah Valley. He was able to remain in service until his discharge on May 3, 1865. In July, he already applied for a pension, so the illness and injury must have left him with lasting problems.

A somber moment at the grave of Samuel Bosworth, amidst a sea of graves at the New Bern National Cemetery. (I'm wearing my Albion Brooks shirt.)

Isaac H. Tuller was a clerk living in Canton, CT, when he enlisted and was mustered into the 8th CT, Company A, on September 25, 1861. Tuller died of typhoid on April 9[3], 1862. His poignant story was detailed in one of the excellent *John Banks' Civil War Blogs*[4], which described how Tuller and two friends from Canton, Henry D. Sexton and Martin L. Wadhams, wrote a letter in December, 1861, to Sophronia Barber of Canton Center to thank her for "*some mittens and stockings which we are informed you helped knit.*" Nine months later, all three young men were dead; Tuller to typhoid, Sexton to jaundice, and Wadhams was killed at Antietam.

On May 12, 1862, Captain Henry Hoyt wrote to Tuller's sister, Hattie:

Your brother died at 2 o'clock on the morning of April 9th of typhoid fever...You have lost a noble brother. I have lost a man whose loss we all

---

[3] Various records also have the date at April 7 or 8, 1862.
[4] *John Banks' Civil War Blog: Death at New Bern: 'You have lost a noble brother'* (john-banks.blogspot.com), May 17, 2012

deeply feel. He was noble hearted and generous to a fault. He was in the General Hospital at Newbern... He was at that time now sick, but the surgeon informed me that he did not consider him dangerous. I heard from him occasionally and that he was getting better. About the 15th we were startled by the news of his death...He was buried in the Newbern Cemetery with his uniform on.

How many letters like this were written to homes across the North and South, and how many hearts were broken upon reading them? While Captain Hoyt states that Tuller was buried at the Newbern Cemetery, his remains appear to go missing during the transfers several years later to the New Bern National Cemetery (established 1867). There is a monument in Collinsville, CT with Tuller's name, but it is a cenotaph to all the local soldiers whose bodies were never returned home.

On our visit to the New Bern National Cemetery in November, 2024, I took a lot of photos. It wasn't until we came back home and I was organizing those photos that something caught my attention. Close to the grave of Sam Bosworth was this stone, flat on the ground for some reason:

It read "N B CO A 8 REGT CONN INF April 8 1862" 13.2278. Naturally, I wanted to know who N B was, however, no one in Co A of the 8th CT had those initials. Knowing that the wooden headboards used to mark Civil War soldiers' graves can easily deteriorate, I wondered if this could be Isaac Tuller? He and Bosworth died within a day of each other, were likely initially buried near one another, and so could possibly have been disinterred and reinterred at the National Cemetery together. Could "N B" be referring to the original New Bern cemetery for a soldier from the 8th CT whose name had been obliterated from his headboard over the years?

A lot of speculation, and perhaps I am assuming too much. I know there are many other unknowns, including "P---H.M. CO A 8th CT REGT CONN INF April 7 1862" #2325. Again, there are no soldiers listed in the roster of the 8th CT Co A with those initials.

I spent a lot of time on this, researching and corresponding with New Bern historians, but as one recently told me, unless the original burial records are found, this may be an unanswerable question. However, I am not giving up. I very strongly feel that if a soldier gave up his life for this country, the least we can do is give him his name at his grave.

So, Bosworth, Tuller, Sexton, and Wadhams, all young men in Company A, probably all friends, and acquaintances and possibly friends with Albion, all gone too soon. It is no wonder that Albion's thoughts increasingly turned to death, as in the army it could come anytime, anywhere, and most likely would, eventually. Maybe even the following day with yet another close call:

April 12 Saturday evening. We were sent out Saturday morning to drill. Met the rebel pickets. We had quite a skirmish, balls whistling around my head quite close. The shells burst quite close but did no harm.

April 15 I was on picket last night.

April 17 Thursday evening Received a letter from William. My health is very good for which, our Father, I thank Thee. We were paid $26.00 a day or two ago.

April 20 Sunday evening another Sabbath is gone. How different from those that I spent in my own New England home. I pray that there will be many more to spend there. They expect to bombard the fort in two or three days.

April 22 Tuesday evening. We are on guard every other day. How cold I have been in the service of Christ.

April 26 Saturday evening. We commenced to bombard the fort yesterday about 5 A.M. About 5 or 6 P.M. a flag of truce was sent. They surrendered this morning. Only one man was killed and many have life by virtue of God.

A picture is worth a thousand words. The view from Fort Macon shows its obvious importance for coastal defense.

Once again, Albion gives us a maddeningly brief account of a battle in his diary, but then is far more descriptive when he wrote home:

Newbern, North Carolina May 10, 1862
Dear Brother and Sister,
I received your kind letter a few days ago and you do not know how it seems to have news from home. I have read quite a number of papers.
Of course you heard weeks ago of the taking of Fort Macon. Perhaps you have read accounts of the whole scene written better than I could hope to write.
The last time that I wrote you we were in Newbern. We were ordered to march to Carolina City, a place about 5 miles from the Fort. We had to march about 20 miles. Those that could not march fast were left behind to come on and a slower rate. We started late in the afternoon and the way that we had to go was a caution. The roads were quite bad. About 11 or 12:00 PM we came to some barracks which the rebels had built and there we stopped for the night. We started again in the morning and arrived at Carolina City in the afternoon.
But the most sport that we had was the driving in of the rebel pickets. Five companies of the 8th were sent out one morning (Co. A being one). You know that the Fort is on a very narrow island. When one company is deployed as skirmishers it nearly reaches from shore to shore.
The first line of skirmishers who had the Sharps rifles commenced firing but their ammunition gave out and Company A had to take their

place. The rebels were retreating quite slowly when we formed our line and for a while the bullets whistled quite thick, but soon the rebels thought of their children and sweethearts and they turned and put for the Fort while we followed hard on their heels.

The day of the bombardment we (Co. A) were behind the same bank. When the battery of 3 guns was placed, a cannonball came through the bank and dropped on one of my tent-mates but did not hurt him any account. We had only one man killed. He was one of the gunners. He was standing on the bank to watch when they fired from the Fort and the last ball that was fired from the Fort by the rebels struck him in the breast killing him instantly. However, we were rewarded for all our toil and dangers, for the glorious old flag waves over Fort Macon. Our Father has kept me. Thanks be to His name.

I was happy to see this marker near Fort Macon, indicating where the Union artillery—and therefore the 8th CT—was positioned. Again, I urge people to visit these sites as you get a perspective no amount of books or YouTube videos can provide.

The weather is growing quite warm but so far my health has been very good and I am as tough as you could please.

Give my love to all.

We came back to Newbern a short time after the Fort was taken. We are in quite a pleasant camp. What comes next I know not, but, let it come: we are prepared.

Ask Romans Snow if he remembers the time when he dared Orlando and I to enlist, in Mr. Thompson's parlor.

What is the prospect do you think, the war will end soon? I do not want to come home until it is over. I am glad that I enlisted.

Write just as often as you can. Send papers and ask Orlando to write. Tell him that we have a glorious chance to drill, plenty of room, a heavy gun, forty rounds of cartridges and hot enough to roast pig.

Goodbye your affectionate brother Albion D. Brook

Where to begin unpacking this letter? For starters, even here, Albion minimizes the 11-12 hours spent hunched over in a trench next to the artillery under a hail of shot and shell. He also didn't mention that after suffering the brunt of the barrage, once the fort surrendered the next morning, the Confederate flag was given to the 5th Rhode Island, who had relieved the 8th CT once they firing ceased. This was seen by members of the 8th CT as a great slight and injustice, but perhaps Albion didn't mention it because he was just happy for the victory, and to be in one piece. Of course, I can't know for certain whether or not he was bitter and angry about it, but Albion rarely wasted ink on bitterness or anger.

Other points of interest in this letter:
- "A cannonball came through the bank and dropped on one of my tent-mates but did not hurt him any account." Well, there's a story to tell the grandkids!
- The gunner who was killed with the last shot had warned the men of an incoming round, but didn't move in time. Albion wrote that it "struck him in the breast killing him instantly." What he didn't write was that the front of the gunner's chest was completely torn off, exposing his organs.
- Albion states he is "as tough as you could please," that whatever is to come to "let it come," as "we are prepared." What a transition from the school boy six months earlier!
- The transcript reads "Romans Snow," but given Albion's handwriting and the transcription interpretations, I didn't know if this was accurate. Doing some census digging, I didn't find "Romans," but I did find Bridgeport resident Heman S. Snow, also sometimes spelled Herman or Harmon. Snow was a machinist, possibly working at the sewing machine factory? Regardless, this was particularly interesting about Snow daring Albion and Clayton's brother, Orlando, to join the army. I can just picture them all sitting in Rev. Thompson's parlor, a man with whom I became very familiar thirty years ago, with kind Mrs. Thompson no doubt serving tea and goodies.
- Last, but not least, Albion's humor shines through as he responds to Orlando's interest in joining the army: "Tell him that we have a glorious chance to drill, plenty of room, a heavy gun, forty rounds of cartridges and hot enough to roast pig."

One final point about Fort Macon. It was built between 1826-34 as a coastal defense for Beaufort Harbor, and its cannons were placed to fire upon ships—not an enemy approaching on land. So, while the fort was able to drive off the Union's gunboats, they lacked the mortars to lob shells inland. Also, the Union artillery had Parrot rifled cannons, whose 30-pound projectiles were able to penetrate the thick masonry walls of the fort. Between them, and the Union mortars, the fort was struck 600 times! When the walls of the fort's powder magazine began cracking, putting ten thousand pounds of gunpowder at risk of blowing the 400 Confederates to pieces, the flag of truce went up!

It should also be noted that once again, all the Confederates were paroled and released. Given the future horrific state of the prison camps for captured soldiers, such as Andersonville in Georgia (13,000 Union soldiers died, or 28%) and in Elmira, NY (almost 3,000 Confederate soldiers died, or 24%), every parolee should have been thanking their lucky stars they got away before these awful prisons began.

The fort's casemates would provide great protection, until a powder magazine explodes!

The interior of Fort Macon looks very much as it did during the Civil War.

The front page of *Frank Leslie's* newspaper, May 17, 1862, at the lowering of the Confederate flag at Fort Macon after the surrender.

April 27 Sunday evening *On picket today. Do not feel very well. O that I had the spirit of Christ.*

April 30th Wednesday evening *We have been expecting to move for a day or two. Probably we shall go tomorrow. Help us do our duty.*

May 1 Thursday *We moved to Morehead city.*

May 3 Saturday *We landed and came into camp in New Bern. Received a letter from Emily last night.*

Once again, these last few days' entries could use more detail. On their trip back across the Bogues Sound to Morehead City, Company A of the 8th Connecticut had the unfortunate passage on the overloaded baggage barge which kept getting stuck in the shallows. Soldiers were compelled to hop overboard into the water to get them underway again. Their 100-mile steamer ride on the *Highland Light* was not so adventurous, although they did have to sleep on the ship. However, given their three weeks on the *Chasseur* during winter in rough seas, this must have seemed like a luxury cruise by comparison.

Their camp on the west bank of the Neuse River, a mile south of New Bern, was a pleasant spot, the weather was good, and on May 7, they received new, large Sibley tents, although they apparently hardly used them.

May 5 Monday evening On guard..

May 6 Tuesday evening Help me to do my duty. I am almost 19 years old. I, who suffer.

The Prairie Traveler, Marcy, Randolph, Harper & Bros., New York, 1859, page 143.

How sad! First, to realize all that had happened to Albion so far, and he was only 18 throughout the hardships and horrors! He almost never complained, and often practiced an economy of words, so just those three words really struck me, "I, who suffer." This was no place for a bright, sensitive, spiritual young man to spend his 19th birthday, but then, that could have been said for hundreds of thousands of men throughout the war.

May 7 Wednesday evening We are never inside our tents.

May 8 Thursday evening Very pleasant

May 9 Friday evening I am 19 years old. Sweet mother, help me to do as I ought.

One more thought on Albion's birthday—he was also to celebrate, such as it was, his 20th and 21st birthdays in the army, and never again to be with family on that day, as he was killed a few weeks after his 21st birthday.

May 11 Sunday evening and another Sabbath is gone and how different from those that I spent in our New England home, but, while there is need, I am willing to stay here.

May 15 Thursday We have not had a prayer meeting for a long time. We're going to try and stay here. Help us, we pray.

May 17 Saturday evening Another week has gone. Help us to do our duty. We are Pilgrims here on this earth.

May 18 Sunday evening *Today for the first time in four months I've heard the ring of a church bell. I thought of my New England home and the old dear church at home. I almost imagined I was there, but always after, the rattle of drums disturbs the dream and I looked upon myself as a soldier for Uncle Sam,--a soldier who has left his all for the purpose of defending our government alone or as a nation, to do what I have to do,-- my duty and see that the confederates do not win the match, [illegible] or at an hour of trial know not the Son of Man.*

A lonely, homesick boy, who is nonetheless determined and dedicated.

May 20 Tuesday evening *It has been almost six months since I left home. How short the time seems. I have come safely through dangerous times. God, he knows that I have been faithful.*

Newbern, N.C., May 22, 1862
Dear Brother and Sister,
I have just sent by express a box with some clothing which I wish you would keep until I come home. I sent also by express $27.00 a few days ago.
It is quite warm here just now. We have to drill about 3 hours per day. Our food is not extra. We have soft bread once in three or four days and fresh meat about the same. The officers are quite strict as to discipline. We have had some hard times and now that the regiment has a resting spell we are to be improved in drill etc.
But the regiment does not look much as it did at Annapolis when you and Mr. Thompson were there. There have been five discharged from our company since we came back from Fort Macon. Some companies in the regiment have had, I believe, 12 or 13 discharge. Quite a number are sick, so that we cannot muster, I think over 600 men, but my health has been very good and I am about the only one in the tent that has stood the hard times and not been sick, though when we left Annapolis I was not well and had a very bad cough. Quite a number have told me since, that they thought it would about finish me.
We do not know where we move from here. There it is a rumor that we go soon, but I think it is only a camp story. In fact, you can hardly believe anything and the best way is not to fret but wait and see.
Our camp is quite a pretty place. We have just received new tents. We're on the bank of the river, the banks of which are covered by a strip of woods. We can bathe twice a day, in the morning before six, and in the afternoon about five.

We expect to come home, while some think in two months, some in two years, but at least I expect to be gone from home a year from the time I enlisted.

We do not hear much news. There is a faint rumor of the capture of Richmond but we do not know much about anything.

My love to all. Tell them, or those that asked, that I'm for the Union and I am in good spirits.

He obviously didn't mail the letter right away, as there is an addition at the end dated May 31, 1862:

We have just been paid off. I sent $21.00 a few days ago and I send in this letter $35.00 more together with the box by express. If you can, I wish you would take the box in which I send the clothes and send it full of something. Take my pay for this. Please send a couple of pineapple cheeses, a bottle of pickles and, if it is not too much trouble, send me a large pickle bottle full of applesauce and fill the box up with such things as you wish. My health is very good. Captain Hoyt has promoted me to corporal; the office is quite easy, a great deal easier than being a private as I do not have to stand guard for more than once in 20 or 30 days. Give my love to all, kiss the children for me and pray that I may be kept from temptation.

P. S. Send as many cookies as you can, and 6 or 8 pounds of dried beef and two or three cans of concentrated milk.

There is literally a lot to unpack in this letter and the subsequent box. First of all, the announcement of Albion's promotion to corporal takes a back seat to his request for pineapple cheeses (a type of cheddar hung in a net which gave it a pineapple shape and diamond-patterned markings), pickles, and applesauce! Priorities! And the postscript is priceless!

"P. S. Send as many cookies as you can…"

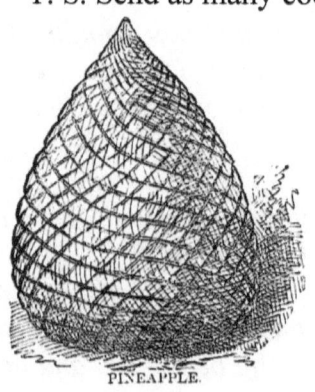
PINEAPPLE.

On a more serious note, it is clear that more than a year into the war, and there was still the pervasive illusion that it wouldn't last long, with some soldiers thinking they would be home in a couple of months. Even Albion only reasonably expected "to be gone from home a year from the time I enlisted," which would be just until November.

Also, typhoid was once again hitting the camps.

There were also "faint rumors of the capture of Richmond." This was during McClellan's Peninsula Campaign, and it was the hope of every Union soldier that Richmond would fall as it meant getting home sooner, but, of course, it was not to be anytime soon. We forget how slowly news traveled, even in the army, and rumors are always faster than truth.

May 23 Friday evening Our new Chaplain spoke in a meeting. He seems to be a good sort of man. I hope for the sake of the Christian men in the regiment that he may be a fine worker for Christ.

The "new Chaplain" was John Moses Morris, a graduate of Yale College and Yale Divinity School. He was ordained on April 23, 1862, and enlisted two days later. He was the ideal chaplain as far as Albion was concerned, as he was highly educated and helped with Albion's studies, including Greek and Latin. Unfortunately, he resigned September 19, 1863, but he went back to Connecticut to be the editor of the very informative *Connecticut War Record* newspaper. Perhaps even more valuable to researchers, Morris and William Croffut wrote *The Military and Civil History of Connecticut During the War of 1861-65*[5].

Morris had a number of important positions in Washington, D.C., and was no doubt destined for even greater things, but he passed away in 1873 at the age of just 36 from tuberculous.

May 24 Saturday evening On guard. Quiet reigns.

May 28 Captain Hoyt gave me a corporal's place. Lieutenant Marsh[6], Captain of Company F; Broatch[7], second lieutenant of Company A. Help me O God in my station, low as it is, to do my duty to God and man.

May 29 We gave Broatch a sword. Captain Hoyt wanted me to present it to him. I did not want to, but Captain Hoyt wanted me too, so I did.

This is curious that Albion did not want to present the sword to Broatch, and actually recorded his feelings. Was Albion shy, or did he not like the man?

May 30 I have paid to [illegible] paid me for the watch. Help me to do my duty O God.

---

[5] *The Military and Civil History of Connecticut During the War of 1861-65*, Croffut, W.A., Morris, John, Ledyard Bill, New York, 1869.

[6] Wolcott P. Marsh of Hartford, CT was discharged December 22, 1862 due to a chronic illness contracted in the army, but lived until 1894.

[7] William J. Broatch of Hartford, CT survived the war and remained in the army, was promoted to Captain, and was discharged in 1870.

June 2 *Sent $33.00 to* [illegible] *in a letter today to Orlando. Lord, help me to do my duty.*

June 6 Friday evening *Rain. Did not drill. Help me to do my duty.*

June 7 Saturday evening*. Another week has gone by. Help me, O god, to do my duty. We are moving on toward the haven of eternity.*

June 8 Sunday evening. *Heard this morning the soft mellow tones of a church bell. It brought to mind the pleasant New England. When shall I hear church bells ringing from the tower of my own dear church.*

June 10 Tuesday *received a letter yesterday from Nellie*

June 11 *My health is good. Praise the Lord. He has given me so many blessings.*

June 13 *Went to a brigade drill. Came back very tired. Have not heard from my box.*

June 14 *Saturday night. Another day has gone, gone to eternity.*

June 19 *Thursday evening. Winds and rains. Help this heart to obey the will of God.*

June 23 *Went down to the battlefield. Many, oh many are the trials which we are called on to endure.*

June 24 *Received a box from Clate together with a letter from Mrs. Higby. Everything in the box had kept well.*

June 28 Saturday evening. *Received a letter from Orlando and William Brooks. We expect to move very soon, God willing. Help us to do our duty. Help me, O God.*

July 1 *It is reported that we're going to Charleston, South Carolina. I hope that we are. Help us to do our duty, Father.*

July 2, 1862 *We left Newbern and came from Morehead city. We most likely shall start tomorrow.*

July 5 *What a day was yesterday. No more like the fourth then a ballroom is to like a graveyard. God grant that I may never see the like again.*

July 6 *On board the steamer* Admiral *off Hatteras. We started about 10 A.M. We are bound most likely for Richmond. What we are to endure, God alone knows. Grant me grace, O Father, to do my duty. Help me in every hour of danger; and if it is to be thy will that I die, help me to die like a Christian and like a brave soldier.*

July 8 Tuesday morning. *It is said that we go to Richmond where most likely we shall see such fighting as we have never seen before. McClellan has been driven back. They have had several days of hard fighting and have fallen back 20 miles.*

Albion is referring to the ill-fated Seven Days Battles, which were part of McClellan's ill-fated Peninsula Campaign, in his ill-fated plan to take Richmond. Word had reached Burnside's troops in North Carolina that McClellan had taken Richmond so their plans were changed. Then word came that Lee had driven back the Union forces (at the staggering cost of 20,000 Confederate casualties and 16,000 Union), so plans were changed again. The bottom line for the 8th CT was that the North Carolina Expedition was at an end, confusion reigned, and they were heading north to an uncertain future.

Fortress Monroe July 8, 1862
Dear brother and sister,
I think that we shall start in a day or two for Richmond. We expect very heavy fighting but do not be alarmed. I am prepared to meet whatever comes.
Give my love to all. This may be the last letter I shall write until Richmond is taken. May God bless you all.
Good bye, your affectionate brother, Albion

July 9 Wednesday. *Companies C, H and F have been put on another boat. We do not know whether we go with the regiment or not.*

July 14 *We and companies H and F came to Newport News to join the regiment where we go into camp. There will be an awful battle before Richmond. What will be my fate, God alone knows. Our fair is very hard. Coffee and hard bread.*

Burnside's coastal invasion, though fraught with trials and tribulations, was ultimately a moderate success, achieving three of its objectives—Roanoke Island, New Bern, and Fort Macon—although not pressing forward to Wilmington or the interior. It also turned raw, naïve soldiers like Albion into fighting men who experienced the worst of weather, miserable marching conditions, hunger, disease, death, and the brutal, bloody realities of battle.

On the other hand, there was still the illusion that the war probably wouldn't last much longer. How much longer it lasted would shock everyone, and how much more brutal and bloody it would become, was beyond any sane man's imaginings.

Water, water everywhere—so many rivers, bays, streams, and creeks to traverse! 1861 map of Hampton Roads area. Geography and Map Division, Library of Congress. LCCN 99439180

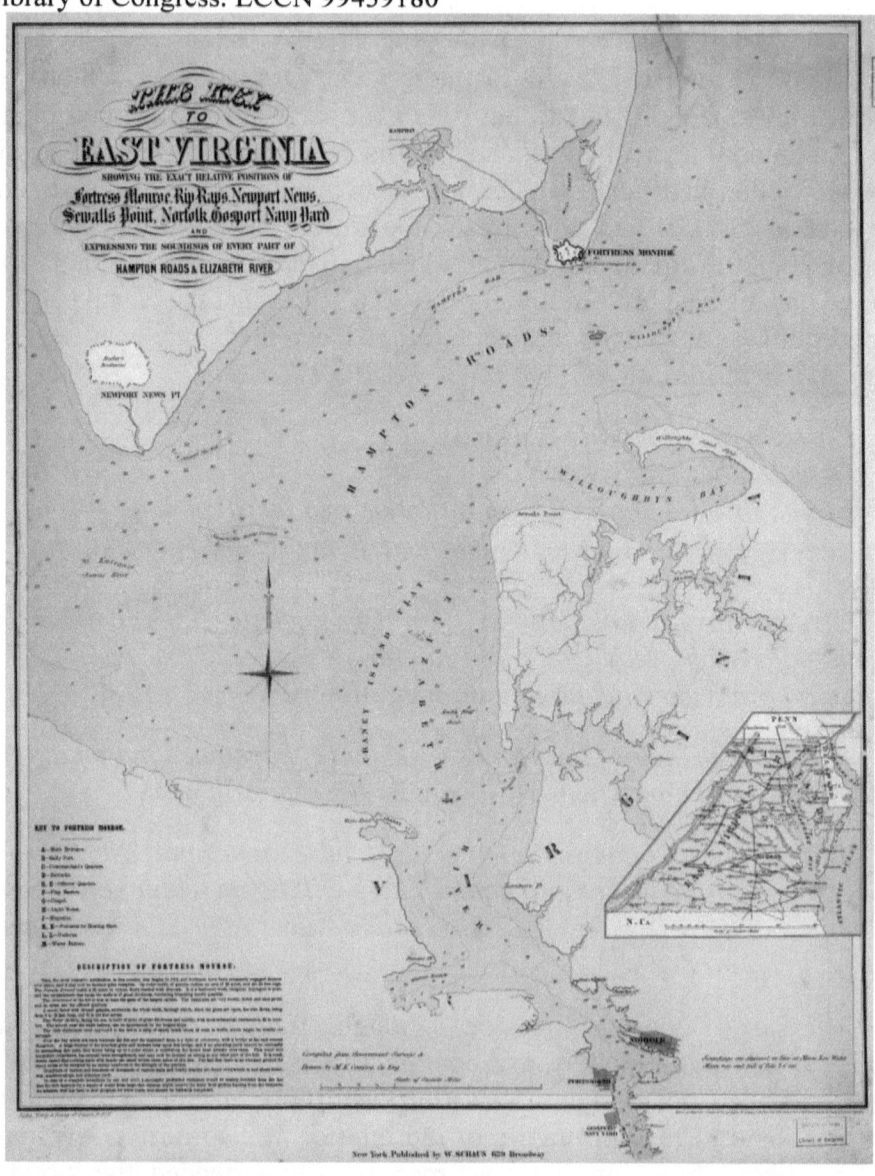

9
The Calm Before Antietam

As generals debated back and forth as to what the next move would be, the 8th Connecticut settled into their new camp at Newport News, Va. Other than it being so abominably hot that daytime activities were limited, the camp had one other distinguishing characteristic—the famous battle between the ironclads *Monitor* and *Merrimac* took place in these waters off Newport News on March 9, 1862.

The day before, the Confederate ironclad *Virginia*—rechristened from the *USS Merrimack*—had attacked the wooden Union ships here, destroying the *Cumberland* and the *Congress*, while the *Minnesota* ran aground. The morning of the 9th, the *Virginia* planned to finish off the *Minnesota*, but the *USS Monitor* steamed in, and the two ironclad ships duked it out. While neither ship succeeded in sinking the other, they figuratively sank all the wooden navies of the world as the age of metal-hulled warships was born.

I wonder if Albion pondered all this as he looked out from his camp at the masts of the *Cumberland*, with her sails still attached, rising from the water like tall tombstones, with the burned wreck of the *Congress* also in sight?

He apparently had plenty of time on his hands to ponder, as there didn't appear to be much else to do.

July 19 Saturday evening. *Another week has gone, gone to eternity. We are doing nothing as yet. Wrote to Clate and E.M. Seelye.*

July 24 Thursday evening. *Received a paper from B. Howe. Have not had a letter. Clate sent me a rubber blanket. They that trust in God shall be as with Zion.*

That short sentence, "Clate sent me a rubber blanket," speaks volumes, as the rubber blanket, popularly called a gum blanket, was a highly sought after commodity amongst soldiers on both sides of the conflict. The Confederacy lacked the raw materials and factories to produce them in the great numbers that they were needed. However, the North had no lack of factories, and they had another ace up their rubberized sleeves; Charles Goodyear's 1844 patent #3633—the process to vulcanize rubber.

With a piece of canvas covered in vulcanized rubber, which made a soft, pliable, waterproof surface, soldiers of the world finally could sleep on the wet ground and wake up warm and dry. In addition to the comfort aspect, which cannot be overstated, how many illnesses did gum blankets prevent, or keep from worsening by shielding the owner from the debilitating cold and dampness? Albion must have literally been a happy camper with Clayton's gift.

July 26 Saturday evening Received a letter from Emily. She wrote a letter which did me good. Thanks be to Him who gave me such a sister.

It is heartwarming to know that Albion truly appreciated and was very grateful for all Emily had done for him—taking him in when his mother died, acting as a sister, mother, and teacher. It must also have been very heartwarming to Emily when she read that diary entry after his death.

Newport News, July 27, 1862
Dear Brother and Sister,
I received your letter yesterday and I can assure you that it did me some good. It is good to know that those that we love at home, are not discouraged, are not cast down by the length of the war and the loss of life.

The people are answering the call right well. Many in Bridgeport whom I did not expect, have enlisted and soon I hope to see them and go shoulder to shoulder into battle with them.

I hope that William will succeed in raising a company. He is doing no more than is his duty. I did not want him to enlist before he finished his studies, but now as he is finished, I say, come and do his duty.

If Clate will enlist, it would be a good thing to enlist as Quartermaster, but then I should not advise him to come.

I should like to have you send me a box, but <u>do not</u> trouble yourself for I know that you have enough to do and if you cannot, as well as not, let it go.

We do not have any fruit here except a few green peaches. Ask Clate to put in a box of Colt's pistol caps.

Burnside has got quite a large division here. We may stay here one month and we may stay here one week, but I think we shall stay here more than a week.

I have written a letter to Ezra Scelzer. I received all that was sent. The cakes were very nice. Many thanks to those that sent the things.

It is Sunday. How different from the Sabbaths in my own New England home, but here we are to defend the right. I am glad that I enlisted at the time that I did.

Give my love to all. May God bless you all for the kindness you have shown to me, and after this war is over, I hope to meet you again in your happy home.

Tell Orlando that he is doing his duty. Give my love to him.

Write soon.

Your affectionate brother Albion D. Brooks

William Brooks was helping to organize the 16th Maine Volunteer Infantry Regiment, now that his studies at Waterville College were complete. William was mustered in as the First Lieutenant of Company E, August 16, 1862.

Orlando Kingman enlisted in August of 1862, with the 2nd Company of Massachusetts Volunteer Sharpshooters

Clayton very much wanted to do his part in the war effort, and was most likely embarrassed that his small size disqualified him at the start of the war. He kept trying to find some position, but preferably starting at the top of the ranks, not the bottom.

Newport News, VA. July 28, 1862
Dear Brother,
Captain Hoyt received your letter yesterday and he asked me to answer your letter because his time is so taken up that he cannot answer letters from his own correspondents.

He does not know of any chance. In the first place the Colonel does not have any aide that ranks higher than a Sergeant. He is called the Colonel's orderly.

He thinks that the best place would be to obtain a place as Quartermaster. You would rank as First Lieutenant and you could take your horse along with you, but you would have to obtain a place in some of the new regiments. I can tell you that a man that will do his duty as Quartermaster is doing as much for the good of the army as any man in the service.

I wish that you would take some of my money and buy an Atlas not over 12 by 16 inches and send it to me by mail, or any other way you see fit.

I received the blanket you sent. It is a very nice one. Many thanks for the trouble you have taken.

Give my love to all.
Your Brother, Albion D. Brooks

Here was a 19-year-old, giving thoughtful advice to his 32-year-old brother-in-law, who was a husband, father, and a very successful businessman!

July 28 *We had a very good meeting. Help us to do our duty.*

August 1 *We were paid today. Shall send home $31.00. We expect to move tomorrow or very soon. Most likely we shall see some hard fighting, but I will try to do my duty, and help me, O Father.*

After about three weeks in camp at Newport News, they were on the move again.

August 2 *We went on board the steamer last night. We started about 3 A.M. We most likely are going to reinforce Pope[1]. Help us do our duty.*

Unfortunately, Albion's diary came to a close with the following entry. It is likely he began new diaries, but if he did, the whereabouts of the rest of 1862 and all of 1863 is not currently known. Only the 1864 diary, his last, resides in the Connecticut Museum of Culture and History archives.

After all young Albion had been through, it is perfectly understandable that his thoughts were on his own possible death. Given his nature and character, it is also understandable that he didn't want his loved ones to grieve for him.

August 3 *We arrived at Aquia Creek this morning. I will close this book. For eight months it has served me faithfully. It has ever been with me in battle and in camp and I never look at it without its calling to mind many pleasant hours. If I fall on the battlefield and some stranger picks up this book and reads, I beg him not to judge harshly. If some of my own dear friends read this when I am gone, I ask them to keep back the sorrow in their hearts and be proud that one did his duty, that he gave up his life trusting in the living faith of Christ. Three cheers for the Red, White and Blue.*

From Aquia Creek, the 8th CT took a short train ride to a station close to Fredericksburg, on the opposite side of the Rappahannock River. Excessive heat made the march to their bivouac location very difficult.

---

[1] Major General John Pope in command of the Union Army of Virginia.

Aquia Creek in 1861 (LOC 4206, no. 4) and the present-day park, which, except for the interpretive signs, gives no hint of its active past.

Burnside's headquarters was in the large Lacy House and the men set up camp around it. McClellan met with Burnside there, and one cannot help but wonder if Albion and his fellow soldiers tried to get a look at him.

Things became tense when it was discovered that Lee's army was headed north and was somewhere in between Burnside's men and Pope's army. Plans were made to evacuate the Fredericksburg area (a decision which would have dire consequences in four months) and whatever wasn't shipped out was burned, including bridges. And both soldiers and officers were ordered to travel light.

A fight was coming.

Burnside's Headquarters and Union camp in Falmouth, VA, in this Alexander Gardner photo from December, 1862 (LOC 4165-G, no. 23) and the elegant present-day building and grounds.

Fortunately, while we have no diaries during this time period, the letters continued, and so did Albion's sense of humor.

Fredericksburg, VA., Aug. 7, 1862
Dear Sister,
Here I am with the great and awful 8th Regiment Company A. We are here probably for the purpose of knocking down a stone wall between us and Richmond. Some of us, I suppose, will get knocked down too, but then the wall must and shall be leveled to the ground. We shall try and do our duty to Our Country and to God and, trusting in the Great Father of all, we are going forward.

We do not expect to stay a great while.

View from the Lacy House across the Rappahannock River to Fredericksburg.

We came from Newport News in a steamer: the scenery along the banks of the river reminded me of New England and I thought that we had not made much headway in Virginia. I did not expect to come back here to fight when I left Annapolis for North Carolina. But then they (the rebels) have changed the war all to one place and we must go to fight them. But we shall whip them in the end although it costs many lives.

I am glad that the President has commenced in earnest. Let him call out the men. I did not like, at first, the idea of drafting, but now I say, "Draft."

Did you send the Atlas that I sent for and the box. Did you send a box? If you have not, let it go, but I should like the Atlas and the only way that I can get it will be through the mail.

Throughout the war, Albion requested books. While other men drank and gambled, he studied Greek, Latin, and algebra. An atlas, while instructive, would also be quite practical for the Civil War soldier who had no idea where he was going.

The letter continued, dated August 9.

I received a letter last night from Ezra Selbye[2]. I shall answer as soon as possible. Have you heard from William? What success is he having forming a company? Good for him. I hope that he will succeed.

The place where we are is quite pleasant, the weather is very warm which will make it very hard marching.

---

[2] This name has been transcribed by Albion's descendants as Ezra Scelzer and Ezra Selbye, neither of whom I have as yet tracked down.

Lieut. Broatch from this from company is at home recruiting. You may see him in Bridgeport.

Give my love to all. Write as soon as you can for I shall not have a great chance to get your letters,--and as often as you can for it does the soldier good to receive your letters.
Your affectionate brother
Bonas Dias
Albion D. Brooks.
I sent by express from Fortress Monroe $31.00
Direct to Burnside Division Near Fredericksburg, VA
Via Washington

Once again, the 8th CT was on the move, and the much-awaited atlas finally arrived!

Aquia Creek, Sept. 3, 1862
Dear Brother and Sister,
We left Fredericksburg two or three days ago which I suppose is now in the hands of the rebels. We expect to leave for Washington today or tomorrow.

I am very well, give my love to all.

I wish that you would take a dollar of my money and send me some stamps. Do write as soon as you can. Direct to Burnside's Division Via Washington.

I would write more if I could but the mail is just going. Kiss all the children for me.
Your affectionate brother
Albion
I received the box and the Atlas. Many, many thanks.

There would be no more letters for 16 days as Albion spent long days of marching and fighting unlike anything he, or the country, had ever seen.

First, however, there was some pomp and circumstance to be had. It's hard to believe that Albion left no record of September 5, 1862, at least none that has yet been found, as the 8th Connecticut marched up Pennsylvania Avenue in Washington, DC, to the compliments of the newspapers. It must have been a proud moment for Albion and all the men of humble and small-town origins to march in their nation's capital as soldiers defending their country!

Now part of the 9th Corps, the greatest trial for the 8th CT was just days away, for as they were marching proudly down the streets of Washington, D.C., Lee's army was crossing the Potomac into Maryland.

10
Antietam: The Bloodiest Day

Albion's new atlas probably came in handy as the 8th CT joined the throngs of troops headed north out of Washington, D.C. on the morning of Sunday, September 7, in what would be 10 days of marching, covering over 100 miles.

Leesborough, Brookville, Laytonville, Damascus, Ridgeville, New Market, Frederick, Middletown, Fox's Gap, Boonsboro, and Keedysville were all points along the way to Sharpsburg. It was often slow going as men competed for space along the dusty roads with horses, supply and baggage wagons, artillery, and everything else a massive army needs. Then heavy rain on September 11 added to their discomfort.

Confederate cavalry and some infantry were not far ahead of the Union forces. New Market had just been occupied by the rebels the night before Union forces arrived, and in Frederick there was a brief, but violent, engagement in the streets, but the Confederate forces soon departed. While the 8th CT heard the sounds of battle as they approached the city, the fight was over by the time they arrived.

Sections of Frederick, MD, still retain their old appearance and charm.

Robert E. Lee had thought that Maryland—being a slave state—might be sympathetic to their cause and welcome the Rebels. He was mistaken.

Dr. Charles E. Goldsborough, a Union surgeon stationed at a hospital in Frederick, witnessed firsthand the occupation of rebel forces he called "Lee's Misérables," lean, hungry, poorly-dressed men who epitomized "squalor and abject wretchedness." The people of Frederick had not been happy by the weeklong Confederate occupation. About 40,000 rebels camped around the city and came into town to buy food, shoes, etc. While they were polite and well-behaved, they "paid" for their purchases in worthless Confederate money, which was just the same as stealing.

No wonder the people of Frederick cheered and waved the stars and stripes once the rebels had fled and the Union troops marched in. It must have been a refreshing change for Albion and the 8th CT who, up until now, had often entered unfriendly "Secesh" towns. To "liberate" an occupied Union town must have been both a great morale boost, as well as being very disconcerting, realizing that Confederates had the ability to take northern towns.

The National Road—the first federally-funded, improved highway, built 1811-1837—and its connecting roads, stretched from Baltimore to St. Louis, and right through Middletown, MD. Both the Confederate and Union troops took the National Road to South Mountain, seen in the distance. The Union used this church steeple as an observation post for the Battle of South Mountain.

The fighting at the Battle of South Mountain was concentrated at Crampton's, Fox's, and Turner's Gaps. On Sunday morning, September 14, the 8th CT was part of the Ninth Corps that attacked at Fox's Gap, although the 8th didn't enter the fray until later in the afternoon. Fighting was fierce, with firing continuing even after dark. The next morning, the 8th prepared for a counterattack, but the rebels had gone to join the gathering forces near Sharpsburg.

The casualties that day were: Union 443 killed, 1,807 wounded, and 75 missing. Confederates 325 killed, 1,560 wounded, 800 missing.

As the fierce fighting on South Mountain waned in the evening, Union Ninth Corps Commander General Jesse Reno rode into a field by Wise's cabin. As fate would have it, Confederate General Hood's Texans had just arrived and fired the final Confederate volley, seriously wounding Reno. He was brought to the headquarters of his friend, General Samuel Sturgis, where Reno said, "Hallo, Sam, I'm dead." Indeed, within minutes, the first Corps Commander to be killed during the Civil War passed away.

The 8th CT continued on, arriving late at night on the 15th in Keedysville. On the 16th, they could hear the artillery of both sides a few miles away, while the infantry began forming their positions for the onslaught of September 17. Antietam would be the single bloodiest day in the country's history.

Casualties:
Union 2,108 killed, 9,549 wounded, 753 missing, total 12,413.
Confederate 1,567 killed, 7,752 wounded, 1,018 missing, total 10,337
Overall total: 22,750
In one day.

Next time you're at a concert or sporting event with about 20,000 people, imagine every one of those people being killed or wounded by the end of the day. Then you must take care of the thousands of wounded men and bury the thousands of dead.

The Cornfield, the West Woods, the Bloody Lane, Dunker Church, Burnside's Bridge—volumes and volumes have been written about every detail of the Battle of Antietam. Here, we are looking at it through the eyes of just one soldier. From a quick note home to let his family know he was alive and safe, as the death notices were beginning to fill local newspapers across the country, to the anxiety about William, his brother, to vivid descriptions of the perilous fight and near-misses, I will let Albion's words speak uninterrupted.

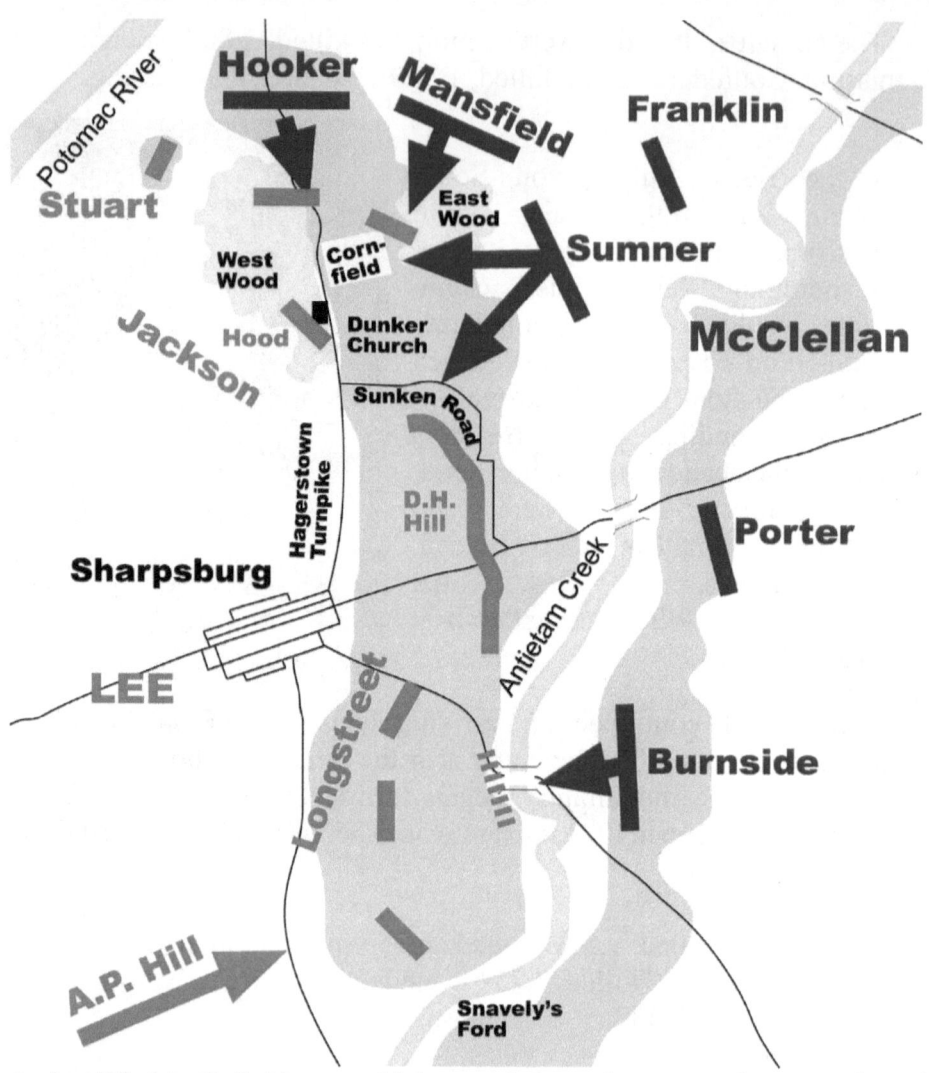

A simplified battlefield map which nonetheless gives a good perspective of what happened and where. (Hlj, Public domain, via Wikimedia Commons.)

Shepherdstown, Maryland, September 19
Dear Brother and Sister

We have had an awful fight but I am safe. About half of our company are killed or wounded. Give my love to all. God bless you. Pray for me.

Brother
Albion

September 20--Near the Potomac

This evening we have retreated across the river.

Company A lost in the fight 8 killed and 8 or 9 wounded, one or two of which will probably die.

We had three Sergeants killed and our 1st Lieutenant.

I saw William two weeks ago but I do not know where his Regiment is now. About ½ of the Regiment is killed or wounded.

Give my love to all.

Your affectionate brother

A. D. Brooks

Antietam, Maryland, October 7, 1862
Dear Brother and Sister

The tumult and smoke of the fight is past and to us Soldiers, even now the sights of misery and blood are beginning to fade from our minds, not but what we pity those of our comrades who fell or who are now suffering from wounds, but because one year of service changes men to such a degree that we take everything as a matter of course.

For myself, I thank God and Him only for my safety. One of my tentmates was killed, three were wounded, and one taken prisoner. The dust and bullets flew around me but not one touched my clothes.

This is the first time that the 8th has had a chance to return the Enemy's fire. The night before the fight the Regiment lay on their arms. All through the night the pickets kept up a firing. In the morning the cannon began to play when the first we knew a cannon ball struck in our ranks killing three men and wounding one. The men killed were about three feet from me. We soon left that place and were not under much of a fire until about 3 o'clock P.M. We crossed a small stream and lay behind a hill for a few moments, the shells bursting over us killing and wounding a few. We were ordered forward and forward we went in line of battle. The bullets spent in the ground around us, but very few, if any, were struck. We had just come to the top of the second or third hill from where we started, when, there in plain sight, stood the Rebels. We stood and fired as fast as we could but from an oversight and blunder of the General, the enemy outflanked us and we fell back, not at all in a panic. After changing our positions we returned the fire of those that flanked us, who very soon left and ran, but many a brave fellow had fallen and our Major withdrew the Regiment, others taking our places.

The blame rests on General Rodman I think, for our being flanked, but he was a brave man and rash. He was shot in the breast.

Our loss you have seen in the papers. The latest list that I have seen was nearly correct.

Mr. Burton of Bridgeport came here a few days ago and is here now. If he stops with the Regiment until we are paid off, I will send home my money by him. The Captain chose to put me in the place of one of the

Sergeants so that my pay is now $7.00 more per month. This time I shall send only $25.00 Bounty and all, but after this I mean to send $50. I have sent home $120 before this. Have you received that amount?

The view from the Union camp on Bolivar Heights above Harper's Ferry. The town is below at the confluence of the Potomac and Shenandoah Rivers.

Near Harpers Ferry - October 8, 1862

We moved our camp yesterday and marched six or seven miles. We're about four miles from Harpers Ferry in one of the most pleasant valleys I ever saw. The valley is not over two or two and one-half miles wide with quite a high a range of mountains on each side. In fact this state is, I think, one of the most pleasant in the Union. The people have some pride and look and act more like the people of my own New England States. It is a state far too pleasant to witness such scenes of horror as have been witnessed within the last month.

I saw William about three weeks ago when we were a day's march from Washington. He was looking very well and seemed to like a soldier's life quite well. God grant, for his own sake, that he may never have to go through the hardships that we have had to.

The 16th Connecticut is in our brigade. We all admire the brave two hundred dollar men. I do not care how much money they gave them, but I think that if those men had <u>done</u> their duty and enlisted a year ago, the war would have been much nearer closed.

I saw a William Hawley a day or so before the fight. He was well and hearty.

Give my love to my new sister. I hope that someday William and I may return and meet you when this war shall have come to an end. I will end this long and dull letter.

Write soon and often as you can. You do not know how much good a letter does to us soldiers. My love to all.

October 10--Sunday morning

Mr. Burton will start for Bridgeport tonight and I send this by him. We have not been paid yet. I shall not send any money in this letter but when we are paid, I shall send $25.00 or $26.00. I shall sell my bounty here.

I notice that the Connecticut papers talk a great deal about the brave 14th and the heroic 16th. Well, so be it. All the fault that I find is that probably not one-half of the 16th fired a gun before they ran and the 14th only had 18 or 20 killed in the whole regiment which is only a little over as many again as Company A had killed. Company A had 8 killed and 12 or 14 wounded out of a Company of 38 or 40 men but not one word have we seen in any paper.

Give my love to all. God bless you!
Albion

Good god, what a nightmare!

Let's unpack this one step at a time. First, there is no exaggeration here, and no sugar-coating anything or false bravado, either. This is an honest, accurate assessment of what unfolded from Albion's perspective.

"…because one year of service changes men to such a degree that we take everything as a matter of course."

How true for Albion! From pious bookworm to hardened soldier, watching men being blown to pieces, their limbs amputated, dying in agony, and gathering the bloated corpses of the dead for burial. Not to mention having to kill other men—when cutting wood on the Sabbath once troubled him.

"The dust and bullets flew around me but not one touched my clothes."

Considering some men were shot three or four times, and the 8th CT had almost 50% casualties, this is remarkable.

"…when the first we knew a cannon ball struck in our ranks killing three men and wounding one. The men killed were about three feet from me."

Three feet from instant death! This incident by Henry Rohrbach's orchard, east of the Antietam Creek, was also written about by other soldiers—and no wonder, as a 12-pound solid shot tearing apart someone next to you is not easily forgotten. Among those killed was Sergeant George H. Marsh of Company A, along with three privates of Company K. Two others were wounded. However, Sgt. Marsh was not actually struck by the cannon ball, but died in a unique way.

Hartford Courant, October 1, 1862:
The body of Sergeant Marsh arrived by the noon train yesterday and the funeral service took place at 3 o'clock from his father's residence, and

was very largely attended. It has been stated that Sergeant Marsh was killed by a piece of railroad iron hitting him, but such was not the case. He was lying on the ground when a ball entered the ground in front of him and came out of the earth a few feet from where he lay. The concussion caused his death, as he was not hit by any thing.

Few people comprehend the incredible force of artillery projectiles, and many a soldier learned a hard lesson. In my book, *Civil War Memories*, there's a tragic incident described by a disabled veteran that happened more times than one would imagine.

"Did you ever see a cannon-ball rolling along the ground, whirling and bouncing and looking as harmless as a toy balloon?...In one great battle there was a terrific cannonading, and our division was in line of battle waiting for the whirlwind to strike us...every few minutes a shell would burst near us or large cannon-balls would come rolling obliquely from the left front. One of these rolled almost along our line. We could see it coming; it bounced 10 or 12 feet when it struck a rock and log, then, whirling along toward us. It was almost as large as a foot-ball, and in motion seemed as smooth and polished as finished steel. It had a queer effect on all the men. I saw a dozen get ready to stop it with their feet. I heard the Captain shout for them to let the thing alone, but it fascinated me. The idea came into my mind that I could stop it easily, and that I must. So in spite of all the shouts and commands I put my foot out to give it a little kick and---I had no foot, or rather I had one foot less."[1]

"...we crossed a small stream..."

The Antietam Creek, and they crossed about 1pm, south of Burnside's Bridge at Snavely's Ford.

"We had just come to the top of the second or third hill from where we started, when, there in plain sight, stood the Rebels. We stood and fired as fast as we could but from an oversight and blunder of the General, the enemy outflanked us and we fell back, not at all in a panic. After changing our positions we returned the fire of those that flanked us, who very soon left and ran, but many a brave fellow had fallen and our Major withdrew the Regiment, others taking our places."

---

[1] Zimmermann, Linda, *Civil War Memories*, Eagle Press, New York, 1998, page 81

Indeed, mistakes were made and the 8th CT ended up going half a mile beyond the rest of the Union line, unsupported, and receiving fire from three different directions. And even though other soldiers ran, the 8th left the field in good order, still fighting, as even Confederate officers of the 37th North Carolina reported, that the 8th CT "held ground quite stubbornly, fought splendidly, and went off very deliberately, firing back at the 37th and waving its flag."[2]

"The blame rests on General Rodman I think, for our being flanked, but he was a brave man and rash. He was shot in the breast."

Albion rarely assigned blame, so when he did, he had good reason, at least from his perspective. At the very least, General Isacc Peace Rodman's orders may not have been clearly communicated, and the sudden appearance of Confederate General A.P. Hill's troops from Haper's Ferry changed everything. Rodman was riding to warn his brigade commanders to shift positions, when he was shot through the left lung, and died thirteen days later in a field hospital.

Rodman was a Quaker who, like Albion, struggled between religious convictions and his sense of duty. Duty won out, and cost him his life.

"The Captain chose to put me in the place of one of the Sergeants so that my pay is now $7.00 more per month."

As so many Sergeants, and officers, were killed in the battle, Albion's sudden promotion would not have been unexpected. And his pay most likely increased from $13 a month to $20 a month, which was a sizable increase.

"The 16th Connecticut is in our brigade. We all admire the brave two hundred dollar men. I do not care how much money they gave them, but I think that if those men had <u>done</u> their duty and enlisted a year ago, the war would have been much nearer closed."

And:

"I notice that the Connecticut papers talk a great deal about the brave 14th and the heroic 16th. Well, so be it. All the fault that I find is that probably not one-half of the 16th fired a gun before they ran and the 14th only had 18 or 20 killed in the whole regiment which is only a little over as many again as Company A had killed. Company A had 8 killed and 12 or 14 wounded out of a Company of 38 or 40 men but not one word have we seen in any paper.

---

[2] Liska and Perlotto, page 83

Bitterness from Albion Brooks! Again, a rare example. I scoured a lot of Connecticut newspapers from the time, and he did seem to have a point about the coverage of other regiments, when the 8th CT suffered so much, and comported themselves so gallantly.

However, there are some extenuating circumstances regarding the 16th Connecticut's questionable conduct, in Albion's eyes, at least.

The 16th Connecticut was formed in Hartford, Connecticut, but not until August 24, 1862, and apparently with a $200 enlistment bonus. Within a few days they were sent to Washington, D.C., and then it was straight on to the Battle of Antietam, with essentially no training. Some men had never even fired a gun! Talk about baptism by fire.

So perhaps Albion did witness some of these 3-week-old, untrained soldiers not firing their guns and running, which considering the unflinching conduct of the 8th CT would absolutely be cause for bitterness. But perhaps we, in retrospect, can cut some slack to the 16th CT, and perhaps, they should have never been thrown into this battle without proper training, where they lost 43 killed and almost 150 wounded.

"Give my love to my new sister."

Albion's brother, William, serving in Company E of the 16th Maine, for whom he was constantly concerned about his whereabouts and health, had married Angie R. Wilson on August 6, 1862. It was a very short honeymoon as just ten days later William was mustered into service and soon headed for the Maryland Campaign. Angie moved to Bridgeport to stay with Clayton and Emily while William was away.

The 16th Maine was at South Mountain and Antietam, although they were detached to guard duty at Antietam seeing no action. Albion probably heard that the 16th Maine was in the area, and was anxious for news of his brother, in lieu of so many casualties.

William was fine, but in just three months, Albion would have reason to fear for his brother's safety at Fredericksburg.

Then there is this letter, written by Clayton to Emily from Albion's camp near Harper's Ferry, West Virginia, just a month after the Battle of Antietam, where he had come for a visit.

Camp Bolivar, Bolivar Heights   October 18, 1862
Dear Emma,
I arrived safe and sound in this place at 2 o'clock this Wednesday afternoon. We had a short trip to New York and a pleasant one. We went on without delay save for one of our trunks, the one we packed at home. The checkman made a mistake and brought the wrong one, and so we came on and he will send it by express to this place.

I was surprised to find so many troops here. There are at least 23,000 here. I am delighted with the place here. I have not seen Albion as yet, nor William, but shall probably tomorrow. The boys were all very glad to see us. I have seen Mr. Batchlor and he is well. Mr. Molan[3], Snow, Corley, Col. Morris and Will Hawley and Rev.

The Colonel who is acting Brigadier General has promised to furnish horses for us to go to the battle ground of Antietam. It is about 12 or 15 miles off. We may or may not, as the weather permits. I may not come on home as soon as I expected if I wish to see all the boys. They were all very glad to see us and send love to the Bridgeport ladies.

I am so glad to be here and see how they live. And then the scenery here is so beautiful. It is the prettiest I ever saw in my whole life and the Hudson is nothing to it.

Yours

Clayton

Okay, does anyone else find this kind of…disturbing? Clayton did help the Christian Commission, and he was very generous, but his attitude does not sit right with me. Perhaps I am way off base, but this seems to be part of Clayton's desire to play soldier, without actually having to fight. He is "delighted" by the camp, and the scenery, like it's a fun sightseeing tour. How about the thousands of dead and wounded soldiers? No mention of them. Handing out religious pamphlets is all well and good, but if Clayton was too small to fight, but still wanted to help, why not volunteer to help in the field hospitals? If women could do it, so could he.

Also, Clayton was an expert, champion marksman who had won many shooting competitions. What regiment *wouldn't* have wanted him? If he was too small to carry his gun and knapsack on long marches, put him on a horse—or put him in the cavalry. Perhaps at the start of the war, when soldiers enlisted for just three months, because no one thought that the war could last longer than that, an undersized man was looked at as a liability. However, after more than a year of bloody fighting, reality had set in and an expert marksman was worth his weight in gold, no matter how light that weight was.

It just seems that if Clayton truly wanted to fight for his country, he would have found a way. Again, this is just my opinion, but I had to go on the record with it.

Back to Albion and Antietam, he wrote a very poignant letter from Fredericksburg, VA, two months later, thinking back to those who were killed:

---

[3] According to the 1860 Bridgeport census, the Molans were neighbors.

November 20, 1862
Dear Brother and Sister,
Here I am in the city of Fredericksburg. Everything looks familiar and it seems good to see something that I have seen before. I have always wanted to come back to this place because, when we left three months ago, the rebels (I mean the women) and children laughed and made considerable sport of the Yankees that were running away from the "Secesh."

We have made a complete circle. We left here about three months ago. Many poor fellows left with us who now are beneath the ground on the battle field of Antietam. I have seen what it is to die a soldier's death and to be laid in a soldier's grave. One only from my tent was killed, the most light-hearted and thoughtless in the Company. We have missed his laugh and jokes but he is gone, the boom of the cannon, the crack of the rifle will never awaken him.

Albion's words say it all. Death did not discriminate between the good and the bad, and friends could be gone in a heartbeat. And no soldier who had been at Antietam could now have any illusions that *he* might not be the next to be put "beneath the ground" in that "soldier's grave."

Antietam continued to haunt Albion, even after a year and a half, as is evidenced by his February 25, 1864 diary entry. His reenlistment furlough was almost over and he was contemplating returning to battle. He knew what awaited him, and he would be carrying the trauma of his past experiences back with him. Of all the horrors he had endured, it was at Antietam where his thoughts dwelled.

...the cannon of Antietam still seems to thunder in my ears...

Gardner photo of the dead on the Sunken Road at Antietam. (LOC 2011649971)

The monument to the 8th CT at Antietam.

The path the 8th CT took at Antietam from Snavely's ford is along the Antietam National Battlefield's "Final Attack Trail." (Due to its unrelenting hills, I called it the "Final Heart Attack Trail.") Walking trails isn't always pleasant in the winter, but there is the great advantage of seeing the terrain free of obscuring vegetation. When Albion describes coming "to the top of the second or third hill," you can envision the scene. Here I am, very cold, but enthusiastic, with more hills to climb until reaching the foremost position of the 8th CT, where their monument stands. Chilling, in more ways than one.

    One final thing, regarding one of Albion's friends. In his October 8, 1862 letter to Clayton and Emily, he let them know that their mutual friend, William Hawley, was doing well, at least right before the Battle of Antietam:

"I saw William Hawley a day or so before the fight. He was well and hearty."

Captain William Henry Hawley, Company K, 14th CT, V.I., was a friend of Albion and Reverend Thompson back in Bridgeport, and I remembered him from my work on *Forging A Nation*. He had written the following letter to Reverend Thompson, dated only "Sunday P.M.," from somewhere in Virginia, and gave no indication of his regiment.

I have just come from <u>church</u> & cannot forbear telling you about our new chapel which is just built by the 108th N.Y. of our brigade, with a canvas roof furnished by the Christian Commission, it is the first house we have had the privilege of occupying for religious worship since entering the service - it is built of pine logs, with oaken benches, & plastered in the inside with Virginia mud. Friday it was dedicated to God with prayer & praise, it was ready last Sabbath, but the battle over the river filled it with wounded, doubly precious will the rude house be to us for it is consecrated with the <u>blood</u> of our brave ones, which staining the floors & benches, some of our heroes were brought in then bleeding & mangled, only to be carried out in a short time dead - In this house we who love Jesus hope to have opportunity of celebrating the Lord's Supper, not since July/62 has that dear privilege been mine –

In the early 1990s when I was working on *Forging A Nation*, I didn't have the luxury of Internet searches for soldier's records and photos. Hawley's was just one of many, many names that I didn't research further at the time. Fast forward 30 years, and his name came up again in Albion's letters, so I thought I would finally see if I could determine his regiment, perhaps find a photo, and learn of his fate. My heart sank when I read the following about the Second Battle of Reams Station, Virginia, August 25, 1864, from a newspaper archive search:

Hartford Courant, Wednesday, August 31, 1864
Among the casualties in the 2d corps in the fight on the Weldon railroad on the 25th inst., as reported in Monday's Tribune, was Capt. William Hawley, staff of Col Smyth, killed.

Litchfield Enquirer, Thursday, September 8, 1864

The 14th Connecticut Regiment bore a very prominent part in this affair, especially in retaking a portion of the works. They charged, alone and unsupported, through a storm of death—dealing missiles upon the enemy, driving them from a strong position and recapturing two or three pieces of artillery. Their loss was cruel, being an aggregate of 50 out of slightly over 200 men. Among them, the brave Capt. William H. Hawley, of Bridgeport, fell dead...

More of William Hawley's story was in an unidentified newspaper clipping on his *Find A Grave* page:

One of the most regretted losses to the regiment was Captain William H. Hawley. He was not only a brave officer, but a man of noble, generous spirit, companionable and with unspotted integrity. He was born in Bridgeport October 5, 1840, and was a bookkeeper when he enlisted, not then being quite twenty-two years of age. Always faithful and efficient when with the regiment, he won distinction as a staff officer and a promising career seemed opening when he was cut down in the severe engagement at Ream's Station. He was shot through the head while directing a skirmish line and fell from his horse, breathing but a few times. His remains were taken to Bridgeport where funeral services under the charge of the city government of Bridgeport were held.

Hawley's grave at Mountain Grove Cemetery in Bridgeport, CT.

Not another bright, kind, young man "cut down" so young! No doubt Hawley was heartbroken by his friend Albion's death, and then he was killed just a little over two months later. Reverend Thompson and all of Albion's and Hawley's friends and family in Bridgeport must have been reeling from loss after heartbreaking loss.

One only needs to read the seemingly endless casualty lists in the newspapers to realize that death touched almost every household in some way. And one also only needs to see the undertaker advertisements for recovering soldiers' remains and bringing them home—like with Captain Hawley—to realize that death became a profitable business during the Civil War.

In yet another example of someone being at the right place at the right time with important information, early one morning on the way to Antietam we stopped in nearby Keedysville so I could photograph a sign for the German Reformed Church, which was McClellan's Headquarters on September 15, 1862, then was a field hospital after the battle.

A gentleman walking a dog stopped and asked if I had an interest in field hospitals, and I showed him my Albion shirt and said I was writing a book about him and wanted to follow the path of the 8th CT at Antietam. To my amazement, he knew *exactly* where the 8th CT had been. We started talking, and his level of knowledge was astonishing. In my head, I'm thinking, who is this guy, Mr. Antietam Encyclopedia? In fact, he is.

I saw he was wearing a Save Historic Antietam Foundation hat, so I asked if he was connected with that group. He said, "Yes. I'm the president." I then think, no way, this can't be Tom Clemens I just happened to run into.

In fact, he was. Mr. Clemens is also a history professor emeritus at Hagerstown Community College, a NPS volunteer interpreter and living history presenter, and editor of Ezra Carman's massive, three-volume *The Maryland Campaign of September, 1862*. Could I have met a more knowledgeable historian walking his dog in a small town early one morning in the few minutes I stopped to take photos?

11
Two Brooks in Fredericksburg

There is maddeningly little correspondence from the period between Antietam and the end of 1862, with not one word about the Battle of Fredericksburg on December 13, 1862. So much happened, and while Albion and the 8th did not face the brunt of the fighting this time, another Brooks did—Albion's brother 1st Lieutenant William E. Brooks, Company E, 16th Maine Infantry. In fact, the situation for the 16th Maine at Fredericksburg was eerily similar to what happened to the 8th CT at Antietam, but unlike Albion who escaped unscathed, William would not be so lucky.

However, before the drama of Fredericksburg unfolded, the soldiers first had to get there. Albion's 9th Corps began to leave their camp at Pleasant Valley, near Berlin, Maryland, the end of October, crossing the Potomac and heading south. The 8th CT crossed on October 28, after being packed and ready to go for days, and their first stop was Lovettsville, Va. Then it was Wheatland and Philomont to Ashby's Gap, where Albion wrote the following:

Alfred Waud's sketch of Ashby's Gap, c.1862-64, LOC 2004660572. This is some steep terrain and would be quite an exhausting march carrying a musket and pack. There are some amazing views at the top.

Near Ashby's Gap, Va., Nov. 4, 1862
Dear Brother and Sister,
I received your letter of the 26th of Oct. just now and it was right. We came.
Here we are after a march of one week or so, the distance traveled varying from 4 to 15 miles per day. Most of the time we have fared quite

well though I think if the men had not become their own quartermasters and drawn their own rations of chickens, pigs, sheep, etc., we should have lived harder.

It is a splendid country here. I do not blame the rebels for trying so hard to hold the state in their power, and so far they have done very well, but Burnside is after them on this side of the mountain, and McClellan, the other. I think we may give them a hard pull. Be that as it may, I hope the next fight will decide something for one side or the other.

I find that there is considerably more care in being the orderly of a Company than being 5th sergeant, but then, one has a good chance in the future to rise higher.

I wrote a letter to you three or four days ago and in case you do not receive it, I will repeat some of it. I received the trunk while I was in Pleasant Valley; the meat was nearly spoiled but the other things were not much hurt, but I had to dispose of everything as I could not hear or find anything of William.

We have not been paid yet and do not know when we shall. When we came here we just had sight of a rebel battery as they limbered up their guns and left double quick. What is ahead I do not know and I do not want to. My faith in God is as strong as ever and, come good or ill, I am prepared.

We have possession of the Gap. I believe we may go through or we may go down the valley this side of the mountain, but what they have to do, must be done quickly. Already the forests are beginning to show bare limbs. Nights, the wind and frost tell the sentence on his part, that winter is coming. Soon the rain will come after which the roads will be a "Slough of Despond" to the Soldiers.

Give my love to all my friends, to Sister Angie and the children. I should be happy to receive a letter from Sister Angie.

Your affectionate brother
Albion D. Brooks

P. S. Will you write as to the whereabouts of William? I saw a South Reading boy on the march the other day.

Some additional information:
- "Here we are after a march of one week or so, the distance traveled varying from 4 to 15 miles per day." Actually, two of the days they marched 17 and 19 miles.
- "Burnside is after them on this side of the mountain, and McClellan, the other." General McClellan was about to be relieved of his command, to be replaced by Burnside.

- "Be that as it may, I hope the next fight will decide something for one side or the other." That's an odd thing to say, "for one side or the other," as if he didn't care if the South won, but then perhaps Albion has had his fill of death and destruction and just wants this war to end. Remember, the war was originally expected to last just a few months. When those few months passed, it was still generally expected to not last one year.

- "I could not hear or find anything of William." And: "Will you write as to the whereabouts of William?" Albion seemed to have a constant anxiety about his brother's whereabouts and well-being, far more than for his own safety.

- "What is ahead I do not know and I do not want to. My faith in God is as strong as ever and, come good or ill, I am prepared." Most people would love to have a crystal ball to see into the future, but the Civil War soldier constantly facing death was probably content to get through the day in one piece, and wake up in the morning.

- "Already the forests are beginning to show bare limbs. Nights, the wind and frost tell the sentence on his part, that winter is coming. Soon the rain will come after which the roads will be a 'Slough of Despond' to the Soldiers." How do you not love Albion and the way he writes!? But seriously, when so many soldiers were illiterate, or would scrawl out something like, "It's gettin' real cold and gonna be real muddy soon," Albion is almost poetic. (And he had me at "Slough of Despond," which has always been one of my favorite phrases.)

- "I saw a South Reading boy on the march the other day." Clayton was born in South Reading, MA, and Albion lived there for two years in the post office working for Clayton's father, Samuel Kingman.

After leaving Ashby's Gap it was on to Manassas Gap, Orlean, Gaskin's Mill, Bealeton, Elk Run, and finally to Fredericksburg, where he penned this letter:

Fredericksburg, Va., November 20, 1862
Dear Brother and Sister,
Here I am in the city of Fredericksburg. Everything looks familiar and it seems good to see something that I have seen before. I have always wanted to come back to this place because, when we left three months ago,

the rebels (I mean the women) and children laughed and made considerable sport of the Yankees that were running away from the "Secesh."

We have made a complete circle. We left here about three months ago. Many poor fellows left with us who now are beneath the ground on the battle field of Antietam. I have seen what it is to die a soldier's death and to be laid in a soldier's grave. One only from my tent was killed, the most light-hearted and thoughtless in the Company. We have missed his laugh and jokes but he is gone, the boom of the cannon, the crack of the rifle will never awaken him.

I wish that you would buy me a gold pen and pen holder and send them by mail. I want a good pen, but the pen holder I want is one that I can carry, pen and all, in my pocket. Charge the cost to me.

Have you had a pair of boots made yet? I wish that I could get a pair as it is beginning to be muddy and wet here. The best way that you could send them, if you have not, would be to do them all separately, mark _very_ plain, and send by mail.

We may stay here one week or one day but I think that I should receive them in less than a week.

The march from Pleasant Valley here was very hard some of the time. We must have traveled about 175 miles. Did not see anything of William though I have always looked out for him. In what Division and Corps is he? I am glad that Burnside is at the head. I think that something will be done. He led us on at Newbern and he can do the same to Richmond.

Give my love to all. May God be with you and bless you all is the prayer of your affectionate brother
Albion D. Brooks

Direct to Albion D. Brooks
Co. A 8th CT, 9 Army Corps 2 Brig 3 Div.. Via Fredericksburg, Va.

- "I wish that you would buy me a gold pen and pen holder." Just after writing about the death of so many of his comrades at Antietam, he completely switched gears and asks for a gold pen! As Albion had stated previously, however, a year in the army changes a man so that he takes everything as a matter of course.

- "The best way that you could send them, if you have not, would be to do them all separately, mark _very_ plain, and send by mail." Unfortunately, packages sent to soldiers had a way of "disappearing," as did money soldiers sent home. A box marked "Brand New Boots" would have been a prime target for thieves.

- "Did not see anything of William though I have always looked out for him. In what Division and Corps is he?" Once again, the concern for his brother is palpable.

- "I am glad that Burnside is at the head. I think that something will be done. He led us on at Newbern and he can do the same to Richmond." Uh, no. Burnside would do something, alright—delay and bungle his way into one of the worst military disasters of the Civil War.

The 8th CT would make camp on the grounds of the Lacy House again—while the officers were snug and warm inside the house, of course—where they had been back in August. The house was on Stafford Heights in Falmouth, across the Rappahannock River, with an excellent view of Fredericksburg and the river below. The house was originally called Chatham Manor, and was built between 1768 and 1771. Its owner during the Civil War was Confederate Major J. Horace Lacy, who must have been none too pleased that his beautiful home was occupied by Yankees.

Lacy survived the war, but had to sell the house to pay debts. However, before you feel too sorry for this former slave owner and staunch secessionist, he owned another home on 5,000 acres called Ellwood, which had been in his wife's family. If you visit Ellwood, which is now also part of the National Park system, along with the Lacy House, you will find something rather unique in the Jones-Lacy cemetery. According to the National Military Park website, "The house served for months as a Confederate hospital after the Battle of Chancellorsville. During the battle, Stonewall Jackson's chaplain—J. Horace Lacy's brother, Beverley—retrieved the general's amputated arm and buried it in the Jones-Lacy family cemetery at Ellwood."

As the impending battle of Fredericksburg approached, Burnside had more of those "mortifying and vexatious delays," this time mostly due to his own inaction. Rather than quickly cross the river and attack the Confederates before they became firmly entrenched, Burnside sat in the Lacy House until the Confederates gathered their forces and became firmly entrenched.

In the dark, early hours of December 11, Burnside ordered the pontoon bridges to be placed directly across from Fredericksburg, where the Confederates were waiting at very close range for enough daylight to start shooting the Union soldiers like targets in a shooting gallery. Union artillery had clearly not driven away these rebel troops, and the murder continued.

Needing more victims to be sacrificed at the pontoon bridge, the 8th CT was asked to assemble 100 volunteers. There is no information as to whether Albion was one of those volunteers, but apparently a considerable number was raised—somewhere between 60-100 according to varying accounts—and the 8th CT lambs marched to the slaughter zone. Remarkably, they were told to *not* bring their weapons! Apparently, they were going to be too busy getting shot to fight back.

Not surprisingly, it was quickly determined that they had no chance in hell, as one soldier was killed and two wounded immediately, and they marched back up to camp. It wasn't until late afternoon that Union soldiers rowed across the river and cleared out the Confederates, so the pontoon bridge could finally be built. Why this wasn't done first is one of the many baffling mysteries of Burnside's thought processes.

Attempting to build the pontoon bridges across the Rappahannock. (Kurz and Allison LC-DIG-pga-01851)

On December 12, the 8th CT crossed the pontoon bridge into Fredericksburg and spent the night sleeping on the streets of the town. On December 13, the real carnage began as wave after wave of Union regiments crossed an open field toward the stone wall at the base of Marye's Heights under withering musket and artillery fire. The 8th CT expected to follow their fallen comrades and had formed a line with their brigade along the railroad tracks, but were fortunately held back. They slept there that night, listening to the cries of the wounded strewn across the battlefield before them, interspersed with over one thousand dead men.

Confederate position at the base of Marye's Heights: *Cobb's and Kershaw's troops behind stone wall,* A.C. Redwood,1886, LC-USZ62-134479.

At sunset, the final large Union assault was led by General Andrew Humphreys and his division of Pennsylvania men. Across an open field into musket and artillery fire, 1,019 men were cut down. (Alfred Waud, LC-DIG-ppmsca-22479)

Total Union casualties were 1,284 killed, 9,600 wounded, 1,769 missing/captured, for a total of 12,653. The Confederates lost 608 killed, 4,116 wounded, and 653 missing/captured, for a total of 5,377. The grand total was 18,030.

Mercifully, the slaughter did not resume the next day—but Burnside had plans for Monday, December 15. Astonishingly, after witnessing thousands of men being shot to pieces, he thought it would be a good idea to personally lead his beloved 9th Corps on another attack! Fortunately, for Albion and the 9th Corps, Burnside changed his mind, or the casualties list would have been much greater.

The *Commercial* newspaper of Cincinnati summed up the battle perfectly, "It can hardly be in human nature for men to show more valor or generals to manifest less judgment, than were perceptible on our side that day." Indeed, the soldiers showed incredible fortitude, but such bravery was ultimately foolishly wasted in what Pennsylvania Governor Andrew Curtin described succinctly as, "It was not a battle, it was a butchery."

The 8th CT was detailed to carry the wounded, and with almost 10,000 of them, it must have been a long, grisly job. The Lacy House became a field hospital, and became soaked in blood and gore. While Albion must have been grateful to be alive and unhurt, at some point he learned that this battle had taken a personal toll—his brother Lt. William Brooks, who was with the 16th Maine.

On November 26, 1862, William wrote to Emily from "Near Brook's Station," which was about 10 miles north of Fredericksburg where there was a Union camp:

I am tough as you please, entirely free of jaundice. I was off duty five weeks and if I could only have visited you, I should have liked it much. Brooks' Station is about 6 miles from Aquia Creek and we see and hear the engine as it goes jumping along, though yesterday they had not got cars, probably will have by tomorrow.

Yesterday morning about sunrise we heard cannonading of Fredericksburg and we thought surely the Rebels were getting it, but as there were but few rounds I guess no one was hurt bad. I wish we would go and take up our winter quarters in Richmond, not as prisoners but as victors.

If we do anything we must do it quickly, for Virginia soil will not be very good to carry on a winter campaign, judging from what a little rain has done.

I do so hope that Burnside will succeed. If he does not, it cannot fail to make for more hopeless the present struggle and McClellan will have to be returned to the command of the army which would be bad for the administration.

We have very little news here, in fact we might as well be out of the world as in it—as for knowledge of what is going on, even a mile from us. It is getting a little cold and uncomfortable and I want to be on the move. I trust we shall soon.

Please give me Albion's address.

Obviously, William didn't know that Albion was already in Fredericksburg, and he would soon be, as well. It was a battle which almost resulted in him being "out of the world"—permanently. Family historian Agnes Thompson wrote the following:

It is interesting to note the protective attitude of the young Albion toward his older brother, William. William, however, had his troubles. In the battle of Fredericksburg, on December 13, 1862, he was wounded. A charge had been ordered and William, at the head of his company, led his men straight toward the confederates. But a retreat had been ordered at almost the same time. William, suddenly realizing that he was alone, was about to retreat when he was struck in the leg by a piece of shell. One of his men, seeing him fall, and believing him to be mortally wounded, rescued his sword to give to the family, telling William that he would tell them how he died.

But Captain Brooks was not destined to die. He lay exposed all during the remainder of the fight, the target of sharpshooters, until he lay back and feigned death. After the tide of battle had receded, he was picked up and taken to a hospital, where he recovered after some months of suffering.

If only we had some word, a letter, a quick note, as to when Albion learned of his brother's serious wounds—as there were two. While a regimental roster of Maine soldiers states that he was wounded in the shoulder, the family account said the leg. However, I found the handwritten "List of Casualties of the Sixteenth Maine Volunteers," and found it was both! William was wounded in the right leg *and* the left arm, and obviously seriously enough that one soldier believed the wounds were fatal.

One can only imagine the distress and anxiety this caused the family, and particularly Albion, who as Agnes Thompson noted, had such a strong "protective attitude" toward his older brother. We can only hope he was able to see William and help comfort and care for him for at least a short time.

A friend and former classmate of William's, Quartermaster Sgt. Henry J. Cushing[1] of the 21st Maine, wrote to him a few weeks later, expressing the fear he had for William at Fredericksburg:

Camp Maine, East New York
January 6th, 1863
My Dear Chum Brooks,
It seems your regiment was in the battle of Fredericksburg and was badly cut up. I was very anxious in regard to you and other friends until I heard. I trembled for a while lest I might hear that you were killed. I was glad to know you were inflicted with nothing worse than flesh wounds. Poor Levitt, I learned, has died from his severe wounds, and Stevens[2] has returned home. You are now acting Captain, of course, if you are able

The 16th Maine was another of those regiments, like the 16th CT, that was mustered in August of 1862 and quickly sent out to the Maryland Campaign. However, they suffered an even greater disadvantage and indignity—they were sent out without their tents or clothing. For all of September, October, and for almost all of November, the barely-trained, ill-equipped men slept out in the cold and rain with nothing more than their blankets, if they were lucky. Many didn't even have a blanket.

Rather than garner sympathy from their fellow soldiers, they were derided. A hospital steward named Eaton wrote[3], "September, October, and then the long march in November to the Rappahannock through storms of sleet and snow; without shelter, without overcoats, shoeless, hatless, and hundreds without so much as a flannel blouse, many without blankets; and through all that long, sad and weary tramp, we were jeered at, insulted, and called the 'Blanket Brigade'!"

So much for the milk of human kindness! The constant exposure to the cold, wet conditions caused over 300 of the 16th Maine to be lost to illness in those first few months before they ever saw battle—and these were Maine boys used to the cold. It wasn't until November 27—Thanksgiving Day—that their tents and baggage arrived. The soldiers

---

[1] Henry J. Cushing, born in Skowhegan, Maine in 1837. After the war he graduated from Harvard Medical school and was a doctor in Merrimack, MA, until his death in 1902 from heart disease.

[2] Captain William A. Stevens, 16th Maine, wounded at Fredericksburg, December 13, 1862. Wounded and taken prisoner at Gettysburg, July 1, 1863. Killed June 17, 1864 near Petersburg by a rebel sharpshooter. When told that the wound was fatal, he told his brother he would die "calm and happy."

[3] *The 16th Maine*, www.mainestory.info/maine-stories/the-16th-maine.html

truly had something to be thankful for that day, as they could finally change their underwear for the first time in almost three months!

Their relief was short-lived, however, as they were soon to be engaged in the Battle of Fredericksburg. Led by Lt. Col. Charles Tilden, a former clerk, the 16th Maine was on the left side of the Union line. They attacked the right side of the Confederate line, where it wasn't as steep as Marye's Heights. They were remarkably successful given the circumstances, reaching and entering the Confederate breastworks, taking prisoners and the rebel's flags.

Unfortunately, Like Albion and the 8th CT at Antietam, the other regiments didn't follow them, and they were left completely unsupported and alone. When the order came to retreat, they were exposed to the full wrath of Confederate muskets and artillery, as they were the only targets there. It is at this point that William Brooks was so seriously wounded. And he was not alone—Captain Waldron of Company I, 16th Maine, wrote, "Out of four hundred and seventeen men who went into the fight, but one hundred and fifty-four answered the rollcall that night."[4] In the following days, some of the missing returned, but that still left just 192 members of the 16th Maine available for duty after only less than four months of service.

With this bravery and terrible sacrifice at least came respect, as Major Abner Ralph Small (a lieutenant with the 16th Maine at the time of the battle) later described in his regimental history:

"The past was redeemed, the voice of insult and reproach was forever silenced. The regiments, which had hitherto ignored our claim to an honorable name, joined heartily with the Second Division in three cheers and a tiger for the Sixteenth, whose casualties were half the loss of the First Brigade."[5]

For William, his brief service was over, and with a "surgeon's certificate" attesting to the severity of his wounds, he resigned with the rank of Captain on February 26, 1863. He got to go home to his wife and family. William and Angie had five children, the first born in 1865, a son he named after Albion. Unfortunately, Albion's namesake died at age five, but the four other children survived, some into the 1940s. Reverend William E. Brooks also enjoyed a long and illustrious career as a minister.

In short, *William lived the life that Albion should have had.*

---

[4] *The Sixteenth Maine Regiment in the War of the Rebellion*, 1861-1865, Abner Small, Portland, Me. : Published for the Regimental Association by B. Thurston & Co. 1886, page 67

[5] Small, page 70

12
Wrestling Mud

Camp 8th C.V. Falmouth, Va., January 21st, 1863
Dear Brother and Sister,
I received the letter with the cap yesterday. Many thanks to Sister Angie for it was just what I wanted.

We expect to have a fight in a day or two; probably before this reaches you, we shall be fighting. Keep up good courage, though I do not expect to get rid of fighting as we did before.

All that I ask of those at home is that they pray for the success of the Army.

Give my love to all. I have sent $40.00 in two letters. Write as soon as you can.

Your affectionate brother
Albion D. Brooks

P. S. I send in this my $10.00 bounty.
If you send a pair of boots out by Captain Hoyt, have a very thick sole on them.

We have orders to be ready at an hour's notice for a day or two but it has rained quite hard and so we have not moved yet.
Albion

- "I do not expect to get rid of fighting as we did before." It took well over a year and some horrific battles, but reality had finally set in with Albion, his fellow soldiers, and the country.

- "If you send a pair of boots out by Captain Hoyt, have a very thick sole on them." Clearly, Albion's friendship with Captain Hoyt was close and comfortable enough that his superior officer would carry a pair of boots from Connecticut to Virginia for him!

- "We expect to have a fight in a day or two; probably before this reaches you, we shall be fighting…We have orders to be ready at an hour's notice for a day or two but it has rained quite hard and so we have not moved yet." Albion is referring to yet another Burnside plan that ended terribly: the infamous Mud March.

General Burnside needed redemption, and the Union needed a win, after the disaster at Fredericksburg. Burnside decided on a plan to swiftly move on Richmond and on January 20, 1863, the day before Albion's letter, the announcement was made to the troops from Burnside's general order that:

> *"...the great and auspicious moment has arrived to strike a great and mortal blow to the rebellion, and to gain that decisive victory which is due to the country."*

Albion had every expectation of seeing fighting in and around the Confederate capital that would rival the carnage of Antietam and Fredericksburg. However, Burnside's plans of a quick, surprise attack were to suffer more of those "most mortifying and vexatious delays," but this time they were not due solely to Union incompetence or Confederate resistance. This time there was another enemy—Mother Nature. That night, it began to rain.

On January 21, troops were supposed to cross the Rappahannock River on pontoon bridges. The plan called for five bridges and a total crossing time of four hours. Once again, like before Fredericksburg, the pontoons were late. Just a single bridge was constructed and the constant rain turned the roads into quagmires of mud—or a "slough of despond" as Albion and I like to say. Yet still, Burnside insisted on pushing on, despite the rain continuing on. And on. And on.

This was no ordinary storm. With Burnside's luck it was nothing less than a full-blown Nor'easter, with heavy rain, winds, and temperatures dipping down into the thirties. The mud swallowed wagon wheels and the legs of men and horses to a depth of two feet. Anyone who has ever tried to trudge through deep mud or snow knows how quickly you become exhausted and demoralized, but still Burnside insisted on forging ahead.

On January 22, Burnside got the brilliant idea to issue whiskey to the struggling soldiers, because obviously alcohol was the perfect solution to tired, angry, frustrated men. Very soon, the army had a lot of tired, angry, frustrated, *and drunk* men who started punching each other. Fighting broke out across entire regiments.

Meanwhile, Confederates across the river were watching the entire debacle with great amusement. They even put up signs taunting the hapless Union soldiers like, "This way to Richmond," and "Burnside's Army Stuck in the Mud." To add injury to these insults, men, horses, and mules died of exposure and exhaustion. And still the rain continued to fall.

Finally, on January 23, with the element of surprise long gone, and the chaos and hopelessness of the situation apparent, Burnside realized that "the great and auspicious moment" had been cancelled due to rain. On

January 25, Lincoln finally relieved Burnside of command of the Army of the Potomac.

The brutal conditions of the Mud March are well portrayed in this Alfred Waud sketch. *Winter Campaigning. The Army of the Potomac on the move. Sketched near Falmouth--Jan. 21st,* LC-DIG-ppmsca-22444.

What of Albion and the 8th CT in this catastrophe of wrestling all that mud? Mercifully, their departure had been delayed, and they remained in camp throughout it all.

The following is a rare letter in the collection *to* Albion, from Emily and Clayton:

Bridgeport, Feb. 16
Dear Albion,
We received your letter of February 10th and were glad to hear from you again. A few lines are always welcome. We wish you would get a furlough, if you can, for it may be a long time before you have another opportunity as good. We mean to send you a box next Thursday by "Hinsdale's" express. We expect him to deliver it to you, but you had better look out for it.
We shall send towels for each man of your company and one for the "Chaplain" of the Regiment. Mince pies so that you can treat once and then have some left. What else I do not know.
You'll have to thank Clayton and Angie for what you receive this time for I am only convalescent, not quite strong enough to cook. Please write soon and let us know when and where you move.

Yours as ever
Emily

We were glad to hear from you. I wrote a line to you via Washington today before I received yours of the 10th. Work here is brisk and I am in good spirits now and hope to remain so, if all war business goes on prospering.

Remember me to the Chaplain of the Bully Eighth. We send him a towel and you can present them to the company.
Our regards to all
Yours ever,
Clayton

- "We received your letter of February 10th" Unfortunately, this letter is not in the collection, so we do not know its contents, but it was most likely to inform Emily and Clayton that the 8th CT had suddenly left camp the morning of February 6. After taking a train to Aquia Creek, they then went back on board a steamer which brought them to Newport News the following day.

- "We wish you would get a furlough." Well, yes, so did Albion and every other soldier. If only it was that simple.

- "I am only convalescent, not quite strong enough to cook." There's no indication as to what was wrong with Emily. The year 1863 was one of the few years she *wasn't* giving birth to a daughter! They had five daughters, much to Clayton's dismay, as he wanted a son.

- "Work here is brisk and I am in good spirits now and hope to remain so, if all war business goes on prospering." The war was financially very good to Clayton. There is always a lot of money to be made in wars, which is one reason they keep happening.

Newport News, Va., Camp 8th CT, March 1st, 1863
Dear Brother and Sister,
Many, many thanks for the barrel that you sent (received 26th Feb). I did not expect near as much and the Company returned many thanks for the towels sent by you. I gave the towel to the Chaplain. He told me to return his warmest thanks to the donor, which thing, Mrs. Kingman, I now do.

I have been to church today. We had quite a good sermon and it called to mind the Old Church in Bridgeport. It rained quite hard last night but it cleared away this morning and now it is quite pleasant.

All is quiet. We have drill parades etc. It is the best place our regiment has been since it left Annapolis. Our First Lieut. came here on a visit yesterday. He had been in Conn. recruiting ever since last August.

Encampment Of U.S. Troops At Newport News, Va. 1861 & 1862, E. Sachse & Co., 1862

I suppose that you have not heard of the letter with $20.00 yet. There has been nearly $100.00 lost by men in the company. Someone stole it, very likely between Fredericksburg and Aquia Creek.

It cannot be a great while before the 9th Corps again takes the field. We look forward to that time with a kind of dread which any soldier will feel who has been in service long enough to learn the tune of every wind instrument, from a 32 Pound Shell, to a charge of grape and minie balls, but we are ready. Give us the man that led us at Roanoke and Newbern and we will do our part, do as much as a Corps of our size can do (and a little more).

The Army has had a little rest during the muddy season here in Virginia, but the wind will soon dry up the mud; hard roads will take the place of the sloughs and holes which block wagons and everything else now. Then will come the shock of war. It must be settled the next summer.

Oh, that every soldier in this great Army would put his trust in the living God, not trusting in his arms and numbers, but in Him who will give the victory to the right. Oh, that men at home, shame on them, should allow men like Tom Seymour to utter such sentiments as they do. Free country, I suppose they say. Well, so it is, but not while this rebellion holds up should men be allowed to disparage the soldiers and government.

My love to Sister Angie. She must have had a hand in that barrel. If she did, she must take her share of the thanks (rather dry pay, I think). My love to all. Kiss Ella, Mary, and Carrie for me. Write as soon and as often as you can.

Your affectionate brother
Albion D. Brooks
P/S. You did not tell me the price of that pencil. Please buy Andrews and Stoddard's Latin Grammar, *charge it to me and send it by mail.*
Albion

- "It is the best place our regiment has been since it left Annapolis." Indeed, the soldiers were in proper barracks, sleeping on bunks. What a luxury!

- "It cannot be a great while before the 9th Corps again takes the field. We look forward to that time with a kind of dread which any soldier will feel who has been in service long enough to learn the tune of every wind instrument, from a 32 Pound Shell, to a charge of grape and Minie balls, but we are ready." This is pure Albion Brooks, and one of my favorite quotes from his letters. Within the same line in which he expresses the understandable dread of facing battle and the specter of death again, he refers to his familiarity with artillery projectiles and bullets as having learned "the tune of every wind instrument, from a 32 Pound Shell, to a charge of grape and Minie balls." At Antietam, he was only three feet from men torn apart by a solid artillery ball, yet he can make light of it all as if these lethal projectiles are a type of music. I'm sure he was always cognizant of trying not to alarm his sister, but it goes beyond that. Albion just saw the world differently than the average person, and he was never at a lack for a clever or poetic description.

- "Give us the man that led us at Roanoke and Newbern and we will do our part, do as much as a Corps of our size can do (and a little more)." Albion never lost his admiration for General Burnside, even after Fredericksburg, but understandably so. The North Carolina campaign of 1862 was a success, and turned an 18-year-old raw recruit into a proud and capable soldier.

- "Then will come the shock of war. It must be settled the next summer." If only it had been settled in the summer of 1863, perhaps Albion would have lived.

- "Oh, that men at home, shame on them, should allow men like Tom Seymour to utter such sentiments as they do. Free country, I suppose they say. Well, so it is, but not while this rebellion holds up should men be allowed to disparage the soldiers and government." Thomas Seymour was one of the Peace Democrats who were opposed to the war. They believed that it could be resolved by negotiations. Realistically, the Confederates exhibited their opinions on a negotiated settlement of differences when they fired upon Fort Sumter on April 12, 1861. Seymour, who had been Governor of Connecticut from 1850-53, ran unsuccessfully in 1860 and was trying again in 1863. On March 3, 1863, the *Hartford Courant* quoted him: "I abhor the whole scheme of southern invasion with all its horrible consequences of rapine and plunder…depend on it, Heaven will frown on such a cause as this." In short, Seymour did not want a Union military victory, he wanted peace through a negotiated settlement. To the soldier in the field who had sacrificed so much and watched his friends die, the idea that politicians were essentially eager to cave in and make concessions was a bitter pill to swallow, and Albion would have none of it. The state of Connecticut wouldn't have it either, as Seymour was again defeated in 1863.

- "Please buy Andrews and Stoddard's Latin Grammar, charge it to me and send it by mail." Once again, pure Albion. You can take the scholar out of the classroom, but you can't take the classroom out of the scholar. In the midst of war, and as other soldiers are drinking, gambling, and doing all manner of disreputable things, Albion wants a book on Latin grammar so he could continue his studies!

There would be little time for studying, however, as the 8th CT was on the move again on March 13, this time going to Suffolk, Virginia, where they would once again be hit by the unrelenting "shock of war."

13
A Siege and Surprise Attack

Suffolk, Virginia was an important transportation center with its railroads to Portsmouth and Norfolk, as well as to Petersburg, and westward, and access to the Nansemond River, which led to the James River and Newport News, Fortress Monroe, the Chesapeake Bay, and then the open ocean. In the spring of 1863, the Union still occupied Suffolk, and General Lee wanted General Longstreet to drive them out. In addition to the transportation, the Confederate army needed to collect food and supplies in the region, and they didn't need the Union army harassing or preventing them from doing so. The ensuing campaign is called the Siege of Suffolk, which is not technically correct, as the Union army was not cut off, but to the soldiers in the trenches who had to stay on constant alert, sleeping for weeks without tents, it certainly felt like a long, grueling siege.

As for those trenches, Union General John Peck's orders to dig in and build fortifications resulted in 10 miles of earthworks with batteries and rifle pits, which created a formidable ring around the city. The Great Dismal Swamp on the east and the Nansemond River on the west provided additional natural barriers. Confederate troops would counter by constructing 12 miles of their own fortifications.

A clever little poem written by the "Suffolk Correspondent," which appeared on page 3 on the *New York Herald* on April 21, 1863 summed up the considerably altered landscape:

There's earthworks on the little hill,
Earthworks all around;
You cannot wander anywhere
Where earthworks are not found.

The correspondent further added the following regarding the conditions for the Union soldiers:

In these intrenchments sleeping and eating there, ever vigilant, ever ready for a skirmish or general engagement, are our boys—our soldiers, once our friends and neighbors, now fatigued, but not despondent. They are loyal, and will save the Union, provided powder and shot can do it, and practical plans are laid out for them to execute.

Perhaps that last part about "practical plans" was a not-so-subtle jab at all the previous Union blunders?

Map of the Siege of Suffolk by Orrin Sweet Allen, Co. H, 112th NY, 1863. Allen was a jack of all trades, from inventor to dulcimer maker. He survived the war and settled in Oregon, where Allen Blvd. in Beaverton, OR, is named for him. (http://hdl.loc.gov/loc.ndlpcoop/gvhs01.vhs00399)

Late on March 12, 1863, the 8th Connecticut and other regiments were ordered to prepare rations and be ready to move quickly. After hurriedly packing, re-packing, and re-re-packing, and then waiting around for hours, in true, inimitable army fashion, the 8th and 16th Connecticut finally stepped aboard the *Georgia* about 3pm on March 13th and steamed towards Portsmouth. Then the railroad carried them to Suffolk. However, whatever energy the soldiers were spared traveling by steamship and rail, rather than marching, would soon be expended by digging and cutting down trees.

Longstreet had about 20,000 men. The numbers of Union troops engaged changed dramatically over the course of the siege: the initial 13-15,000 men, swelled to 29,000. The Union's Naval forces on the Nansemond gave them a further advantage. However, neither the Union's superior numbers, nor their extensive fortifications, would deter the Confederates from trying to take Suffolk. And trying. And trying.

The first attack commenced on Saturday, April 11. The 8th CT defended Fort McClellan, one of five forts along the ring of defenses. The Confederates were repulsed, with the 8th CT's losses being just one man wounded—a nice change of pace from them usually being the ones out in the open, assaulting fortifications.

Threat of another attack continued Sunday, and into Monday, before the Confederates fell back to their line of defenses. On Tuesday, the 8th CT was repositioned to the north of Suffolk, where an artillery battle occurred back and forth across the Nansemond River. On Wednesday they had picket duty. The men were kept in constant readiness, and there was little time to rest, as is evidenced in Albion's following letter:

8th C. V. Suffolk, VA., April 20th, 1863
Dear Brother and Sister,
I received your letter quite a number of days ago. You had not, at that time, received the letter with $60.00. It was expressed from Unionville, Connecticut by one of the company who went home on a furlough. I also sent by mail about the same time, my ambrotype.

Well, all is excitement here. The rebels have attacked the place. As yet, there has been nothing but some light skirmishing with the enemy, but I think that unless their forces are drawn off by Hooker, we shall have quite a fight here. Let them come. We will give them all they want. You must have no fears for me for I shall be kept from harm.

We have had quite a time of it. I took my boots off today for the first time in seven days and have slept every night for the same time with overcoat and accouterments on. Most likely we will have the same length of time more to do the same.

We are doing picket on the most exposed part of our lines. When we first commenced we kept shooting away at each other but I do not think a man was hurt on either side. The men on both sides were very poor shots. In the morning I went over a hill, or rather along the banks of the river to one of the posts when they fired at me making a very poor shot. I fired at something blue, which might have been an overcoat but which I think was a bush, as it was not seen to move after the gun was fired. My conscience does not trouble me in the least with having shed blood.

But we may have hard fighting yet and then may God protect the New England boys whether we are behind breastworks or not. We shall do our duty.

Old Connecticut has done her duty right bravely. We are glad that Buckingham is governor.

But I must close. My love to all friends. Kiss the children for me. May God bless you all is my prayer. Pray for me that I may be kept from all harm and, above all, from growing cold in the love of Christ.

Write soon.
Your affectionate brother
Albion D Brooks

- "I also sent by mail about the same time, my ambrotype."

This may be the ambrotype Albion sent home.

- Nothing illustrates the constant stress and strain of the siege like this statement: "I took my boots off today for the first time in seven days and have slept every night for the same time with overcoat and accouterments on. Most likely we will have the same length of time more to do the same."

- "I fired at something blue, which might have been an overcoat but which I think was a bush, as it was not seen to move after the gun was fired. My conscience does not trouble me in the least with having shed blood." We know Albion initially had a moral dilemma about cutting firewood on the Sabbath, let alone breaking the sacred commandment, "Thou shall not kill." Claiming to have shot "a bush" appears to be his awkward attempt to make a joke and assuage guilt. When Albion says his "conscience doesn't trouble me in the least," I have no doubt his conscience was troubling him for all he had done since joining the army.

- "We are glad that Buckingham is governor." At a time when soldiers in the field were unable to vote in their state elections, the contest between incumbent Republican Governor William Buckingham and Democrat Thomas Seymour was of great concern to Connecticut soldiers. Seymour was a "Peace Democrat," commonly called "Copperheads," who were against the war and wanted a negotiated settlement with the Confederacy. Needless to say, after so much sacrifice, Union soldiers wanted total victory, not bending to the rebels in a negotiated settlement.

What Albion completely fails to mention in this letter, for reasons known only to him, was the battle of the previous day, April 19. Perhaps he did not want to cause Emily any anxiety, but he robbed us of his account of what was one of the most remarkable engagements of the war. We so often concentrate on the major battles, and rightfully so, but often to the detriment of the smaller—dare I say—gems that occurred throughout the war. One such gem was the Union victory at Hill's Point Battery (also called Fort Huger) on the Nansemond River.

The river is narrow by Hill's Point, and the Confederates recognized that a battery placed at this location would deny Union ships use of this vital lane of transportation. Noticing fresh dirt being piled up along the riverbank, it quickly became obvious that the Confederates indeed had a new battery there, and the Union had a problem. The initial Union plan was to assault Hill's Point on the night of April 18. Soldiers prepared, only to be later told the plan was on hold as it became clear it couldn't be carried off quickly enough before sunrise. The plan then shifted to the evening of April 19, ostensibly giving the troops enough light to attack, but preventing a Confederate counterattack as darkness fell.

The view of the narrow Nansemond River at the modern-day site of the Hill's Point Battery. Clearly, Union ships would have been reduced to matchsticks at this pointblank range. Much to my delight, I found remnants of the original earthworks, which are still are still visible on the bottom right.

The following is Union Brigadier General George Getty's official report[1], interspersed with additional details to make a smoother narrative:

At 5:30 PM on April 19, detachments of 113 men from the Eighth Connecticut and 140 men from the Eighty-ninth New York were embarked on the Stepping Stones *at Dr. Council's landing. A canvas screen, which effectually concealed the men, was drawn up all around the deck,* [and the men were told to remain silent] *and the boat pushed off and steamed rapidly down the stream.*

The ship used in the attack, the *Stepping Stones*.

---

[1] *The War of Rebellion*, Series 1, Vol. 18, pages 304-305, Washington, Government Printing Office, 1887

As she approached the battery, not a shot was fired or a sound heard to indicate the presence of the enemy. He was waiting, with all his guns double shotted with canister, until the vessel should come abreast and within 50 yards of his battery. At 300 yards above the battery Lieutenant Lamson headed his boat inshore, but striking on a spile she glanced off, and, borne on the ebb-tide, was on the eve of shooting in front of the battery, when Lieutenant Lamson, with admirable presence of mind, reversed the paddle-wheels and backed her aground. [The gangplanks were put down to disembark the men, but they "floated away."[2] *Stuck fast in the mud about 10 feet out from shore, "a yellow streak of water of unknown depth"[3] lying between the stern and the riverbank, it seemed as though bad luck had struck again. "Reacting quickly, Captain [Hazard] Stevens pushed his way through the crowd of soldiers, leapt into the river and shouted for the men to follow, the mud and water reaching only up to the waist.[4]" The men jumped off from both ends of the boat up to their waists in mud and water, scrambled hastily ashore, and with a cheer dashed for the battery. In an instant Lieutenant Lamson had landed his howitzers and followed. The enemy, apprised of our approach by the cheers, opened a hot fire of musketry, and was enabled even to reverse and fire one of his guns; but seeing himself cut off, and receiving one or two discharges of canister from Lamson's howitzers, he surrendered.* [Sgt. Seth Plumb of the 8th CT elaborated: *Our bayonets were at the breasts of the nearest men in the Fort, and were all shouting surrender when up came a white handkerchief on a short pole, but just an instant after, one of the guns at the other end of the Fort let fly a charge of grape at us, and then the boys hollered "shoot them" "kill them" and charged their bayonets into their very throats, but the rebels begged for life, and strange to say not one of them was pricked with a bayonet.[5]*]

The capture of 5 guns [all of which had originally been Union artillery that the Confederates had captured at Harpers Ferry], *7 officers, and 130 men, the liberation of five gunboats above, and the occupation of a point of vital importance to the enemy and an admirable point of operations for us were the results of one of the most brilliant achievements of the war. Our loss was 4 killed and 10 wounded.*

The battery retaken, our whole attention was turned to fortifying the position and preparing for attack.

---

[2] Liska and Perlotto, pg. 114

[3] Cormier, Steven A. *The Siege of Suffolk: The Forgotten Campaign*. Howard, Inc., Lynchburg, VA, 1989.

[4] Cormier

[5] Liska and Perlotto, pg. 114

Historians don't often say, "Wow!" but I think it applies in this case to "one of the most brilliant achievements of the war." Had Lt. Lamson not been able to run the *Stepping Stones* aground before floating into the crosshairs of the deadly artillery fire, had Captain Hazard Stevens not hesitated to leap into water of unknown depth and rallied the men, and had Lamson not somehow managed to quickly get the howitzers ashore in support, the Battle of Hill's Point Battery may have been another embarrassing Union failure in the footnotes of history.

However, the labors of the 8th CT and 89th NY were not over, as General Getty pointed out, "The battery retaken, our whole attention was turned to fortifying the position and preparing for attack." The command of that task was given to Col. Arthur H. Dutton, Twenty-first Connecticut Infantry, commanding the Third Brigade. The following is from his report[6]:

I was now directed by Brigadier-General Getty to assume command of the post and put it in a state of defense during the night. The force at my disposal for the purpose consisted of detachments of the Eighth Connecticut, Eighty-ninth New York, Tenth New Hampshire, and Ninth Vermont, in all about 700 men. The soldiers, although fatigued and fasting, worked with the most commendable zeal to intrench themselves, as we fully expected an attack in the morning.

To the two detachments first named [8th CT and 89th NY] *especial credit is due. They had been under arms nearly all day; had most gallantly captured the battery in the evening; had been a considerable time without food, and were drenched with the water through which they were forced to wade in landing, yet not a murmur was heard from them throughout...*

At early daylight a line of the enemy's skirmishers was discovered advancing about 1,000 yards distant. They covered themselves behind trees and fences and a few were observed entering a house a few hundred yards in front of our left...

It now became apparent that the enemy did not meditate and attack, but contented itself with annoying our pickets by occasional scattering shots. I accordingly gave directions that the house above alluded to should be fired and the woods shelled. This being accomplished we were troubled no more...

In this connection I cannot forbear paying a tribute to the valor and energy of the naval forces under Lieutenant Lamson. This gallant officer has at all times shown himself most willing to render invaluable assistance

---

[6] *Official Records*, pages 317-318

to the land forces with men and material, fearlessly imperiling the safety of himself, his men, and his vessels.

Roswell Hawkes Lamson

At this point, I must take a detour to discuss Lamson and Stevens.

Roswell Hawkes Lamson's family had been pioneers to Oregon from Iowa in 1847 when he was nine-years-old. In 1858, he was the first man from Oregon to be appointed to the United States Naval Academy, finishing second in his class in 1862. He had to take his final exams at sea as he had already been assigned to duty. Following his exploits during the Siege of Suffolk, in 1864, he became commander of the *USS Gettysburg*, and in January 1865, led a group of sailors and Marines in the successful assault on Fort Fisher—but not before spending an unpleasant, and dangerous, night in a ditch, pinned down by enemy fire.

Surviving the war, he toured Europe, married his cousin, had seven children—sadly, only two of whom reached adulthood—and had a long career as a U.S. District Court clerk. In recognition of his heroism throughout the war, in the twentieth century, three U.S. Navy destroyers were named in his honor.

Hazard Stevens

Captain Hazard Stevens was born in Newport, Rhode Island in 1842, but like Lamson, he headed to the west coast with his family in 1854, where his father, Isaac Ingalls Stevens—who had graduated first in his class at the West Point Military Academy—became the controversial and polarizing first governor of the Washington Territory. At the outbreak of the war, both Isaac and his son, Hazard, joined the 79th New York Volunteer Infantry, known as the Cameron Highlanders.

During the Battle of Chantilly on September 1, 1862, now General Isaac Stevens, in command of the entire division, grabbed the fallen colors of the 79th NY, despite the wounded color bearer (the sixth color bearer to be wounded at that point) yelling, "For God's sake, General, don't take the colors!"[7] General Stevens nonetheless rallied the men with a shout of

---

[7] Welker, David A. *Tempest at Ox Hill: The Battle of Chantilly*, Hachette Book Group, p. 223-234, 2007.

"Highlanders! My Highlanders, follow your general!" During the charge, Stevens was shot in the head and died on the spot. His son, Hazard, was severely wounded during the battle, twice, in the hip and arm, but obviously survived.

The death of General Isaac Stevens at Chantilly by Alonzo Chappel.

General Isaac Ingalls Stevens by Timothy O'Sullivan. A powerful portrait, perhaps my favorite Civil War photo.

In recognition for his bravery at Hill's Point, Captain Hazard Stevens was awarded the Medal of Honor, with the citation reading: "Gallantly led a party that assaulted and captured the fort."

Obviously not one to rest on his laurels, Hazard Stevens, along with P. B. Van Trump, became the first men to make a documented ascent of Mt. Ranier on August 17, 1870. He became a lawyer, wrote a biography of his father, and once again ascended Mt. Ranier at the age of 63. He died in 1918 at the age of 76, and is buried in Newport, Rhode Island, next to his equally famous father.

I have taken this slight detour in the narrative of the Siege of Suffolk to highlight some fascinating men involved, because, well, they are fascinating, and had noteworthy lives. I also did it to provide a contrast to Albion Brooks—whose life was taken at just 21, who never had the chance to go to Europe, get married, become a father, climb a mountain, write a book, grow old, or make his mark on the world like Lamson and Stevens. Had he not been killed at Cold Harbor, it is likely Albion would have soon been promoted to Lieutenant, and had the opportunity to be a leader of men, where—both objectively and subjectively—I believe he would have excelled.

Of course, we will never know where life would have taken Albion, but for now, there's still a siege going on.

Once again trading rifles for shovels, the 8th CT continued strengthening their fortifications, doing picket duty, and remaining on alert. Other regiments engaged in skirmishes which dragged into early May. Longstreet realized he couldn't spare the men and ammunition needed to dislodge the Union forces from Suffolk, and on May 4 he retreated across the Blackwater River, thereby finally ending the siege.

The casualties for the three weeks of fighting were 260 killed, wounded, or missing for the Union, and about 500 killed and wounded for the Confederates, with another 400 captured. Ultimately, while the Union retained Suffolk, they were so busy digging, they didn't prevent Longstreet from resupplying his army, and they didn't make a move toward Richmond. By the end of June, Union forces had been removed from Suffolk, as it no longer seemed important enough to tie up troops. Historians may argue whether or not the entire campaign was worth it, but I think everyone can agree it was an historically riveting few weeks.

Suffolk, Virginia, May 19, 1863
Dear Brother and Sister,
I have neglected to answer your kind letter which I received quite a while ago. You must lay the fault to the climate which makes one feel too lazy to quarrel or to do anything else.

All is quiet here now. The rebs left to give Hooker a boost across the river and I think they did it very well. What do the people think of Burnside's crossing now? There was no delay in pontoons this time. Well, I am sorry, sorry that he (Hooker) failed. I did have great hopes that Hooker would be successful and now I hope he will try again. May God give one victory to the poor Army of the Potomac before they are all killed or discharged.

I have heard some rumors that we are or should be consolidated. Well, I hope that it may never be so. It is hard for men to be so low in service and see new Regiments come and we grow smaller and smaller and nothing done to fill it up.

The government was very foolish when it stopped enlistments, last summer, I think it was, and government will make a blunder even greater than that if they raise drafted Regiments by themselves. They will not amount to anything if they are not put where they are obliged to do their duty. I should like to have a few from Bridgeport that I know drafted and put in this company. They would be treated kindly enough, at the same time, they would not shirk and I think when they got home they would not laugh at others for not going and still stay at home themselves.

I received a letter from William a few days ago. He was well and so was Angie.

There have been rumors that we shall stay around here this summer. I hope we shall, not but what I am willing to do my duty but in hopes the Regiment could be filled up, but I think that when we are not wanted here we shall have to join the corps in Kentucky.

You asked me in your letter if I wanted anything. I should like to have you buy Waverly Magazine (a weekly paper) every week and send it to me and charge the same to me. You did not say whether you have sent the coat or not.

Give my love to all who may inquire. Kiss the children for me. Write as often as you can. Pray that I may be kept, that my love of Christ will ever be warm.

Your affectionate brother,
Albion D. Brooks

Will you have half a dozen photographs (card size) taken from my likeness and send them to me?
Albion

Albion was, of course, referring to Hooker's disaster at Chancellorsville, which has been written about ad infinitum, so it needs no description here. What I did find almost humorous—if it wasn't so true—was his opinion of the mighty Army of the Potomac, one of the largest and best-equipped fighting forces created to date.

May God give one victory to the poor Army of the Potomac before they are all killed or discharged.

Albion wrote one final letter from Suffolk that summer:

Suffolk, Virginia June 7, 1863
Dear Brother and Sister,
It is Sunday and I feel just like writing a letter to you.

It has been warm for the last week but last night we had a heavy thundershower and now it is as clear and cool as one could wish. I hope that you in New England are having as fine a Sabbath as we are here. I wish that I could be home today and go inside of a Church. I think that I have not been inside a Church since I was in Annapolis, eighteen months ago. Of course, there have been prayer meetings and preaching by the Chaplain.

My health is very good. If we should come home this summer we should have to make considerable of an effort to shake off the sloth that has grown upon us in the Army. Warm weather makes one feel dull and for myself, I do not have anything much to do only look out for the Company.

We have sent James Burton (Clate remembers him) to the Insane Hospital, Washington, D. C. His insanity was brought on or hastened by the excitement and by falling into the river, but that was not the cause. I am very sorry but perhaps he is the only one to blame. The men have considerable picket duty to do now but we live very well. We received two months pay a week or so ago. I sent $30.00 by Adams express to you. When you write let me know whether you have received it or not.

You need not send the coat back now, but I should like to have you keep it for me. I should want it next fall.

I was sorry, very sorry that Hooker was whipped. Not that I care for him, for I think he defeated Burnside's plan, but for that poor Army of the Potomac. I should not wonder if we had to go to Hooker's Army yet for the two year regiments going home must weaken him a great deal and I understand that all of the forces in Virginia are subject to his call. I hope not, if we leave here I hope it will be to join our old corps in Kentucky.

Burnside sent on a congratulatory order to the 3rd Div. He said that we were not forgotten.

If the people of the North allow a General that has captured more for the Union cause, or at least as much as any General, to be hissed at by Copperheads and at peace meetings, they do not deserve a government, and for doing what no other Generals could, ordered to do so.

But then, if we can only put down this rebellion is all I care for by any way, any means that can be used. The soil of the South is drenched with the blood of thousands, and I fear it will be by many more before this war is over. I do not want to give up and know that thousands of New England men have been slain in defending the Old Flag and it all amounts to nothing.

But I must close. I wrote to Ezra Scelze a long while ago. I do not know whether he received it or not. Give my love to all who may inquire.

Kiss the children for me. Pray for me that my heart may be kept free. Write soon and as often as you can.

Your affectionate brother, Albion D. Brooks

Clearly, Albion's loyalty and affection for Burnside had not waned, and he had no love for the Copperheads. Perhaps the most curious item in the letter, however, was the rather cryptic reference to James Burton, who had to be sent to the Insane Hospital in Washington, D.C. What I discovered about Burton was startling and quite disturbing, and his story will be explored in the following chapter.

Until recently, the site of the Hill's Point Battery was pristine and would have made an excellent battlefield park. Sadly, that all changed as developers have destroyed yet another historic site. I guess we should at least be grateful they kept a tiny section on the point where the fort stood. (Google maps)

On my visit in November, 2024, the sounds of construction filled the air as houses were now being packed together right on the edge of the fort.

14
The Disturbing Case of James Burton

Suffolk, Virginia June 7, 1863:

We have sent James Burton (Clate remembers him), to the Insane Hospital, Washington D.C. His insanity was brought on or hastened by the excitement and by falling into the river but that was not the cause. I am very sorry but perhaps he is the only one to blame.

    This is a rather cryptic statement: "but that was not the cause." Albion rarely underlined words, so what was this mysterious cause for which James Burton himself was supposedly responsible for his own insanity, and why didn't Albion spell it out?

    The "excitement" to which Albion refers was the recent Siege of Suffolk, during which the 8th CT was in a constant state of readiness, night and day, for at least a week, during which time Albion "took my boots off today for the first time in seven days and have slept every night for the same time with overcoat and accouterments on. Most likely we will have the same length of time more to do the same."

    The reference to "falling into the river" most likely occurred during the attack on the Hill's Point Battery, when the soldiers were forced to jump into the chest-deep muddy water, scramble onto the riverbank, then successfully charge the Confederate battery under intense musket and artillery fire.

    Clearly, these events must have been extremely stressful, yet Albion thinks the real reason for Burton's mental breakdown was something unrelated. What could Burton have done to himself? Excessive drinking seemed to be a possibility, as it was rampant in the army, and something Albion despised. In 1860, 17-year-old Albion complained about the sailors landing in Bridgeport and going straight to the "grog shops" on Water Street for "that liquid which is worse than fire." Then on February 24, 1864 in his diary, he wrote, "There is a great deal of drunkenness in the Regiment and I have seen so much that I can almost vomit at the sight of a drunken man."

    Did the trauma of war drive James Burton to drink himself into a type of Alcohol-Induced Psychotic Disorder? If so, why didn't Albion just say that Burton drank too much?

    Then, there's the fact that Burton's gravestone in Mountain Grove Cemetery in Bridgeport only has the following inscription about his military service:

JAMES BURTON
1843-1906
CO. E 1ST REGT.
CONN. VOLS.
ASLEEP IN JESUS

Why does it reference his three months with the 1st CT, yet there is no mention of his almost two years with the 8th CT? Did this insanity and its mysterious cause lead his family to sweep his service under the carpet and hope that it would be forgotten?

It all didn't add up, and it was a puzzle I needed to solve. So, in May of 2024, I requested the service records of James Burton from the National Archives, which unfortunately would take many months to receive. In the meantime, I searched for more information about Burton and his family.

The Burtons came from England in the 1600s and for generations lived in Fairfield County, Connecticut, in the town of Stratford and nearby areas. In the 1850 census of Bridgeport, CT, (which is just a few miles from Stratford) Alden Burton (1800-1879) is listed as the "City Watchman" with property valued at $6,000. Considering farm land cost about $20 per acre, the average wage was less than $2,000 per year, and a very large, new house with six bedrooms could be built for $1,800, Alden was doing okay for himself.

By 1860, his occupation had changed to a "merchant" and his real estate and personal assets had grown to $13,000. By 1870, he was a "retired grocer" and his wealth had increased to what must have been a very comfortable nest egg of $20,000.

Alden had married Abigail Avis Shelton, 1811-1852, who was from an even more prestigious family, which included the governor of Connecticut in the mid-1600s, Thomas Welles. The Sheltons were also earls, barons, countesses, and duchesses back in England with very high positions and connections. For example, Abigail was a direct descendant of the aunt of Anne Boleyn, whose marriage to Henry VIII didn't end well. The family lineage could be traced way back to the French aristocracy before the Norman Conquest of 1066.

Unfortunately, Abigail was to know great tragedy. She had previously been married to Noah Monroe, and they had a daughter, Mary. When their daughter was just 9 months old, Noah passed away at the age of just 32 in December of 1836. Just 5 months later, the new widow also lost her 1-year-old daughter, Mary. Abigail then married Alden Burton in 1840, but she passed away at age 41 in 1852. It is all a stark reminder of the high mortality rates among all age groups in the 19th Century.

Hopefully, both Abigail and Alden found some happiness when their twin boys, John and James, were born on January 10, 1843. This was the same year Albion was born, and like Albion, their mother, Abigail (coincidentally also the same name as Albion's mother), passed away when they were just 9-years-old. Sometime before the 1860 census, the boys got a stepmother named Charity, but I was unable to find any additional information about her, other than her name appearing as a widow in the 1880 Bridgeport census. By age 17, the twins are listed as being clerks in the 1860 census. The following year, everyone's lives would change.

When the war began, 18-year-old James was among the many eager young men who didn't hesitate to join Company E of the 1st Connecticut Volunteers. According to the *History of the First Connecticut Volunteers* written by its colonel, George S. Burnham, who had initially enlisted as Captain of Rifle Company A, "The First Regiment of the three months' men was recruited under the proclamation of President Lincoln, issued Monday, April 15, 1861, and the call of Governor Buckingham issued the day following. Anticipating the call of the Governor, recruiting had begun so promptly that by the 16th many companies were ready to report with more than the minimum required."

Confusion and chaos reigned in the early days of the war, but according to Burnham, the Connecticut men had everything under control.

"These were days of intense excitement in Washington, and false alarms were frequent, but cool heads were in control of the Connecticut Brigade."

Then came their first taste of a real battle, and a very real defeat:

At midnight of Saturday, July 20th, the brigade was advanced via Warrentown road toward Bull Run, and was detached to guard the Warrentown road during the detour of the flanking column via Sudley Ford. It remained in this position until about 10 A.M., when it was beyond Youngs Branch, farther west.

Colonel Keyes in his official report said:

"The order to advance was given at about ten o'clock A.M., and from that hour to four P.M. my brigade was in constant activity on the field of battle. The First Regiment Connecticut Volunteers was met by a body of cavalry and infantry, which it repelled, and at several other encounters at different parts of the line the enemy constantly retired before us.

"Before recrossing Bull Run, and until my brigade mingled with the retreating mass, it maintained perfect freedom from panic, and at the moment I received the order for retreat, and for some time afterward, it

was in as good order as in the morning on the road. Half an hour earlier I supposed the victory to be ours."

Before night-fall the entire brigade reached its former campground at Centerville in good order, and under orders, bivouacked as was supposed for the night; the men suffering much from fatigue, at once going to sleep on their arms. About 10 o'clock P.M. peremptory orders came to continue the retreat to Falls Church. The road was now comparatively clear, as the disorganized part of the army was already far advanced on its way to Washington. About 9 A.M. the next day the regiment arrived at Falls Church, and, in a drenching rain, struck its tents and dispatched its entire camp and garrison equipage, together with that of the Second Maine, which had left the brigade, to Alexandria.

If Burnham and Keyes are to be taken at their word, while other Union soldiers ran in fear, the 1st Connecticut performed honorably and did their duty during the heat of battle. However, just the next day, their official duty was done as their brief 3-month enlistment was already over.

The First remained in Washington until July 27th, when (their term of service having expired on the 22d) it started for New Haven, where, after tedious delays, it arrived and was mustered out on July 31st.

Their term of service saw no one killed, 6 wounded, 6 captured, and 25 discharged due to disability.

Apparently, James Burton's short, frenetic service with the 1st CT with his baptism of fire and a crushing defeat, did not dissuade him from reenlisting less than two months later, on September 25, 1861, this time in Company A of the 8th CT. New recruits, such as Albion, may have looked upon Burton as an experienced veteran.

Everyone in the 8th CT was to gain far more experience with battles and the hardships of army life, staring with Burnside's North Carolina campaign and reaching an awful peak at Antietam. They were still reeling from their losses at Antietam when they were called into line of battle for Fredericksburg, but were fortunately spared marching into the Confederate meat grinder. Winter brought some rest, but as the weather warmed, fighting season began, and the Siege of Suffolk was an unrelenting period of fighting and expecting to fight.

In addition to all this stress and anxiety, Burton no doubt was concerned about his twin brother, John, who had joined the 48th New York Vol. Inf. The following is John's record of service:

BURTON, JOHN.—Age, 19 years, Enlisted, August 9, 1861, at Bridgeport, Conn., to serve three years; mustered in as private, Co. E, August 26, 1861; wounded and captured in action and paroled July 18, 1863, at Fort Wagner, S.C.; promoted corporal, no date; wounded in action, May 16, 1864, at Drewry's Bluff, Va,; discharged on expiration, of term of service.[1]

John Burton was to be wounded twice, and captured. While his first wound was received after James was committed to the Insane Hospital, we can't dismiss the possibility that a deep concern for his twin brother's safety may also strained the nerves of an already battle-weary James.

Yet with all this, Albion still blamed James Burton for his own mental breakdown.

It was six long months before I finally received the email that Burton's records were available for download. Immediately stopping what I was doing, I rushed upstairs to my office to retrieve the files and, once and for all, end the speculation and discover the secret of James Burton's insanity. I was not prepared for what I found, and I admit my jaw dropped with a startled gasp.

From Sabin Stocking[2], Assistant Surgeon of the 8th CT, dated May 20, 1863, Suffolk, VA:

I hereby certify that I have carefully examined James Burton a private of CO. A. 8th Regt. Conn. Vols. and find that he is rendered unfit for duty by reason of insanity apparently the result of masturbation.

This insanity has existed for forty days. Said soldier was never insane before entering the service.

Wait, what!? "Apparently the result of masturbation," really? Not the result of years of watching men dying horrible deaths? Not the heat, cold, disease, hunger, exhaustion, fear of battles, stress of camp life, and long,

---

[1] https://dmna.ny.gov/historic/reghist/civil/rosters/Infantry/48th_Infantry_CW_Roster.pdf

[2] According to Stocking's *Find A Grave* page: Civil War Assistant Surgeon, 8th Regiment, Connecticut Volunteer Infantry. Promoted from Assistant Surgeon, 8th Regiment CVI to Surgeon, 17th Regiment, CVI on May 31, 1864. Mustered out July 19, 1865.

From *The Stocking Ancestry*: "Dr. Sabin Stocking and Matilda Buck had no children. He was a physician of celebrity, res. in Glastonbury, where he built up a large and lucrative practice extending far beyond his native town. He served as regimental surgeon in the Civil War, from August 29, 1862, to July 19, 1865."

Born 1807, died 1891, age 83.

grueling marches? Not the constant specter of death that could strike any soldier, in any way, at any time?

No, according to the 'wisdom' of the time, it was the insidious self-abuse of masturbation that had so far caused 40 days of insanity, going back to around April 10, 1863.

I immediately searched for other such cases during the Civil War, and found an 1864 letter[3] which recently sold at a private auction, from former Confederate Lt. William Dandridge Pitts of the 40th Virginia Infantry. Pitts was writing to the superintendent of the Western Lunatic Asylum in Staunton, VA, regarding the condition of his brother, Private Charles Pitts, who had also been with the 40th VA until he was discharged for "illness." In the letter, Pitts reveals the cause of this illness to the superintendent:

I have had some conversation with the physician who attended my brother previous to his going to the asylum, and he advises me to inform you of the fact, that he had learned from some of my brother's associates, who were in (military) camp with him, that he was addicted to masturbation, while in camp. He (the physician) is also persuaded of this fact from the conversations he has had with my brother.

The prevailing thought in the 19th century was as absurd as one can imagine:

American doctors, using the most modern "scientific" methods at their disposal, convinced themselves that masturbation was the underlying cause of nearly all social problems and diseases, ranging from rape, divorce, "pederasty," poverty, and criminal activity, to paralysis, epilepsy, venereal disease, nervousness, heart disease, fever, tuberculosis, apoplexy, insanity, idiocy, and even death.[4]

Rather than hypersexuality in all its forms being the *result* of mental illness brought on by stress and trauma, it was viewed as the *cause* of mental illness. Fortunately, modern science has a more enlightened view on the role which trauma plays. From an article published by the National Institute of Health:

---

[3]https://www.liveauctioneers.com/price-result/civil-war-soldier-addicted-to-masturbation/

[4] *History of Sexual Medicine: The Antimasturbation Crusade in Antebellum American Medicine,* Dr. Frederick Hodges, *The Journal of Sexual Medicine,* Volume 2, Issue 5, September 2005, Pages 722-731

There was a statistically significant direct effect of post-traumatic symptoms on hypersexual behavior... We found the relationship between hypersexuality and trauma describing a possible etiological pathway...Hypersexuality can be considered as a reactive form of a major affective psychopathology representing a tip of the iceberg hiding the real issues of a suffering personality.[5]

So, this was the terrible secret about which religious, God-fearing, sin-fearing Albion Brooks dared not write. It was the awful shame which made Burton's family hide his years of service with the 8th CT.

There was something more in Burton's file—on January 20, 1865, in Bridgeport, CT, James Burton, who was 5' 6 ½" tall, with blue eyes, brown hair, and a "florid complexion" tried to reenlist! Soldiers who had been discharged for reasons such as Burton's were not allowed to serve again, but remarkably, in the enlistment document, the line which asks if he had ever been discharged "on account of disability" was crossed out!

Was Burton really able to reenlist by crossing out the line about a previous disability? There was a James Burton in the 1st CT Heavy Artillery, as well as one in the 2nd CT Heavy Artillery, but as it was a common name and the National Archive file ended with this document, there is not enough information, yet, to say how far this ill-conceived reenlistment proceeded.

Not until 1870 is there a clear record of his whereabouts—back home in Bridgeport living with his father and stepmother, and working as a clerk in a lumber yard. Apparently, his mental health had improved enough that he actually got married sometime soon after the census, as the birth of his first child, Abbie (no doubt named after James' mother) was recorded in 1871, with his wife being Mary Quinn. There was another daughter, also listed as Abbie, born in 1874, and a third daughter, Florence, in 1880.

Meanwhile, in the 1870 census, his twin brother, John, was living in Brooklyn, NY, as a salesman with $5,500 in property. He was married to a woman named Ellen, and they had three children. Unfortunately, his young wife must have died soon after the census, as by 1872 he was married to Isabella Quinn, the sister of Mary Quinn. The twin brothers married sisters!

Despite the fact that their father, Alden, passed away in 1879, it would be nice to think that these were relatively happy post-war years for the brothers, but that happiness was not to last. John Burton died in 1884 at

---

[5] National Institute of Health, Fontanesi, Marchetti, Et al, *Hypersexuality and Trauma*, https://pubmed.ncbi.nlm.nih.gov/33229025/, 2020

the age of just 41. In 1889, James had applied for a pension due to disability, and in the 1890 census he is divorced and living as a boarder.

Had James' mental illness returned? Due to the fact that he sustained no recorded physical wounds during his time of service, it would seem likely that was the case as the basis of his claim of disability. I was tempted to request James' pension records, but the Burton case was a rabbit hole in which I had already gone far deeper than I had intended, and I still had a mountain of Albion material to absorb and write.

In 1906, James Burton died, and there was enough money from someone to give him a substantial headstone—which mentions his service with the 1st CT, but makes no mention of his service with the 8th CT.

Hopefully, we, as a society, have come far enough to understand more about the effects of trauma on mental illness. Albion's 19th-century belief that James Burton was to blame for his insanity was just wrong. The shame his family felt about his insanity and its alleged cause was also wrong. Hiding James Burton's years of service with the 8th CT, which included the bravery everyone in the 8th CT exhibited during the hell of Antietam, was wrong.

I would like to acknowledge and thank James Burton for his service during the Civil War—*all of it*. War leaves a lot of scars that can't be seen, scars that often lingered for the rest of a soldier's life, and James no doubt carried those scars to the grave four decades later. For what it's worth, I would like to apologize to James Burton on behalf of an ignorant society, that, rather than treating his mental illness, mistreated him and his legacy.

An early 20th Century photo one of the oldest buildings of the facility called the Government Hospital for the Insane. As physically wounded soldiers began to be brought here, too, they would sign their letters from "St. Elizabth's Hospital," lest their family and friends think they had gone insane. (LOC cph.3c04691)

15
After the Siege: The Raid

The Siege of Suffolk was over, the 8th CT was back in Portsmouth, VA, and Albion and the other soldiers could take off their boots at night and sleep unmolested. Which isn't to say they still weren't kept busy strengthening fortifications, but at least they had some time to decompress—but not for too long.

Portsmouth, Virginia, June 16, 1863
Dear Brother and Sister,
It has been quite a long while since I wrote to you. I began a letter to you when Captain Hoyt started for home, but did not send it by him.

We received four months' pay today. I send in this letter $20.00 and shall send the same amount in my next letter.

I have not seen anything of my Express bundle. I think that it is lost, but I wish that you would ask Captain Hoyt, when he returns, to call at the Office in Washington and see if it is there. I am very sorry to lose the books as they are just the thing needed here. I wish that you had put the pen in a letter and sent it on, as it is, both are, most likely lost.

The weather today makes me think of old New England. There was a warm south wind as much unlike winter as we could wish, but the rain will come one of these days and then, alas for any shoes and poor sick soldiers.

The affairs of the country are, I think, rather mixed,--judging from what I have seen I should think there was a war. The soldiers were beginning to be impatient for their pay and I don't blame them a bit. As it was, they were disappointed at only receiving four months' pay.

Perhaps you would like to know whether I am sick of war. Perhaps you think at times that all thoughts of those at home have gone from my mind, but it is not so. I wish that I could be home, but not until the Old Flag that I have followed for nearly a year and a half is given up and the regiment of the 8th is mustered out of the service of Uncle Sam.

I remailed a letter to Captain Hoyt, that, judging from the writing, was from you at Bridgeport.

Give my love to sister Angie. Tell her to have patience and forgive, and I will answer her letter as soon as possible, for we soldiers cannot do things in a hurry.

My love to all friends. I do not pretend to write to only those at home. Kiss the children for me. Pray God that I may keep my heart warm with the love of Christ and that I may do my duty as one that will answer before the Bar of God.

Your affectionate brother,
Albion D. Brooks
P. S. Have you heard from George? In what company is William?

- While it is nice that Albion has the luxury of time to worry about his lost books, I am sorry they were lost. I am also continually delighted that in the midst of the horrors of war and the countless bad habits in which soldiers indulged, he wants to study Greek, Latin, and algebra! It should also be noted that he feels comfortable enough to ask his sister to ask Captain Hoyt, a family friend, but nonetheless his superior officer, to run an errand for him in Washington and pick up the box of books if they were there.
- I am even more unabashedly delighted by Albion's wonderful sense of humor. Bravo, young Albion: "The affairs of the country are, I think, rather mixed,--judging from what I have seen I should think there was a war."
- Then there is the poignant assertion that as much as he would love to go home, he will continue to follow the "Old Flag" until the job is done.

The 8th CT battle flags to which Albion Brooks was devoted, are on display at the Connecticut State Capitol in the Hall of Flags. Many additional Connecticut battle flags are on display.

- Sadly, the letter ends once again with questions regarding his brothers, George and William. In addition to concerns for their safety, it would have been a morale boost for Albion to hear from his big brothers.

One of the intense goosebump moments over the years of research was when I walked into the Connecticut Hall of Flags with its many battle flags, understanding what the men who followed them endured. And a chill went up my spine when I saw the distinctive open, pointed finial of one of the 8th CT flags and realized these were the actual flags Albion saw during battle.

Camp routine was to change several days after this letter during a grueling raid up the peninsula, the efforts of which debatably resulted in very little return on the Union Army's investment of precious manpower. In the following letter, Albion had just returned from what would mockingly be referred to as the Blackberry Raid.

2 Brig. 2 Div. 7th Army Corps
Near Portsmouth, Va., July 15th, 1863
Dear Brother and Sister,
We have just returned from our long and hard tramp. We welcomed our old tents as we would home after an absence of three weeks and after having traveled a good 150 miles.

It was about as hard a march as I have ever had. Most of the time the heat was very great, and on one day there were about 20 cases of sunstroke, but not more than two or three died.

What did we do, I suppose you ask. Well, we up and marched back again and tore up railroads--two or three rails in the road between Richmond and Fredericksburg. The bridge was too strongly guarded and the General commanding concluded he would not burn it and so let it alone after one or two men had been blown into Eternity.

I hope there is no one that thinks of starving the rebels. If they do, I wish that they could have been with us on the march. I never saw so many acres of wheat, oats, corn, etc. as I did between the railroad and the Whitehouse and if one third or one sixth of the rest of the South raises as much grain you might better give up the war then delay in the least hoping that hunger would make the least difference with the men in the South. They probably have obeyed through the wish of Davis that they should plant rice instead of cotton, tobacco, etc.

There was one thing rather singular. We went up there to destroy the bridge, we failed and returned, but we camped for two or three days on a farm of a rich planter who had hundreds if not thousands of acres of wheat, and who was not afraid in the least to say that he would help the rebels all he could, but as far as I can learn, not a stalk of his wheat was burned.

We have been changed into the 7th Corps. The men do not like it at all. They groaned for Dix and cheered for Burnside. I hope that it is only for the present, though as long as we are under Dix we shall have an easy time.

We are hearing glorious news. I hope there will be coming nothing but such for a time to come.

I received Clate's letter with the $5.00 just after I came back. It could not have come at a better time. Kiss the children for me. Give my love to all who may enquire.
Your brother
Albion D. Brooks

Before describing the Blackberry Raid, let's unpack some of the other news, in fact, "glorious news." Of course, Albion is referring to the major Union victories at Gettysburg, July 1-3, and Vicksburg, which finally surrendered on July 4. If you need to brush up on your Civil War history, an Internet enquiry as to the number of books on each subject states that there are 78 books on Gettysburg and 39 on Vicksburg, so I won't devote too much time and space here. Suffice to say that the fall of Vicksburg and resulting control of the Mississippi River is often described by historians as splitting the Confederacy in half, while Gettysburg put the nail in the coffin of the South's ambitions to invade the North, not to mention their hopes of gaining foreign recognition and assistance. The dream of the Confederacy became a Dead Man Walking, and all that was left to determine was how much suffering and destruction they could tolerate, and just how many dead men would be the result.

Some Confederate soldiers were in denial about these major defeats, as is evidenced by a letter written from Albion's brother, William Brooks, to their sister Emily and Clayton, while William was working for the Christian Commission in Nashville, TN, on July 22, 1863.

I went over to the prison hospital this A.M...There is a rebel Chaplain among them, taken prisoner, Hamilton (?) by name, belonging to the 26 Alabama, who is a very good man in religious matters but who is a most consummate fool in Politics. It was but last Saturday, I think, that he would not believe that Vicksburg had fallen, thought it all a hoax and will perhaps continue to think that Lee is in New York, perhaps Boston. If he is so foolish, what must the really ignorant be? This is not only a war for Freedom, but to show whether it is better for a man to be foolish or wise.

Albion and the 8th CT were clearly not happy with joining the 7th Corps as they "groaned for Dix." John Adams Dix was born in New Hampshire in 1798 and had one of those wildly diverse 19th century lives which included joining the Army during the War of 1812 at age 14, and becoming a U.S. Senator, Secretary of the Treasury, postmaster of New York City, governor of New York, and president of the Union and Pacific railroad. Dix was also a Major General during the war, but apparently did not instill confidence in the troops, and many thought he was too old for field command.

Dix is perhaps most famous for his 1861 order as Secretary of the Treasury to anyone in New Orleans daring to show disrespect to the United States of America: "If any one attempts to haul down the American flag, shoot him on the spot," a phrase which found its ways in various forms on popular tokens.

In September of 1862, Lee's first attempt at a grand invasion of the North, which he envisioned would bring a swift end to the war, was relatively brief and essentially failed to meet any of his grand goals. However, nine months later, the need for supplies, and to shift hostilities into Northern territory, was just as pressing, and Lee prepared for a second invasion, this time into Pennsylvania, renowned for rich farmlands that would bring tears to the eyes of a hungry rebel.

Towards the end of June, over 70,000 men in Lee's army had crossed western Maryland and entered Pennsylvania. Over 90,000 Union forces were also headed north toward Pennsylvania. However, both massive armies were uncertain of the other's location. They would ultimately collide in the little town of Gettysburg, but they were not the only chess pieces on the board.

With the bulk of the Confederate army going north, General Dix decided that he would take 20,000 Union troops from Portsmouth and once again head up the peninsula toward Richmond. At the very least, Dix hoped to disrupt Confederate supply lines and distract their forces enough that they could keep reinforcements away from Lee, in fear for Richmond's safety.

From Portsmouth, the 8th Connecticut took a steamer to Yorktown on June 22. Four days later, they were at White House Landing, so named because of the historic mansion where George Washington and Martha

Custis were married in 1759. In 1857, the mansion was inherited by Robert E. Lee's son, William "Rooney" Lee, and at the beginning of the war the property became an important supply depot on the Pamunkey River. At the end of McClellan's botched Peninsula Campaign, he ordered the depot burned, and sadly this historic home also became a casualty of war.

White House, May 17th, 1862_LCCN2014646904 James Gibson

The White House, before and after.

Mathew Brady's *Illustrated History of the Civil War*, pg.292

White House Landing, Va., 1862. LC-DIG-cwpb-01807

Current railroad bridge at White house Landing.

I am compelled to mention that there was no direct access to take the previous picture of the railroad bridge, as there are homes along the river bank. Undeterred—well, slightly deterred—there was this very steep embankment up to the railroad tracks which I had to crawl on all fours to climb up, and then unceremoniously slide down on my butt. Historical research is not for wimps.

On July 1—as the battle of Gettysburg commenced—Dix's troops crossed the Pamunkey River to Lanesville, and thus began the "long and hard tramp" to the north and west in brutally hot weather. On their way to Hanover Junction, just 25 miles north of Richmond, the weary soldiers marched between 8 and 16 miles per day. Overcome by the extreme heat, many men collapsed, with some dying.

Confederate General D. H. Hill quickly realized that this was not a serious assault on Richmond, but rather merely a lame attempt to look like one. With his unique sense of humor, Hill wrote that this bogus Union campaign "was not a feint, but a faint."

Albion mentions coming upon the farm of a "rich planter," who happened to be George Taylor, remarkably known to Sargent Seth Plumb of Co. E of the 8th Connecticut. Taylor— "an old tyrant" who abused his slaves—spent summers in Litchfield, Connecticut, and attended the same church as Plumb.[1] Albion marveled at the vast quantities of crops and Taylor's open support of the Confederacy, and couldn't understand why then, weren't those crops burned?

Even if what the hungry Union troops didn't eat from Taylor's farm wasn't burned, he lost something of enormous monetary value to him—his slaves. According to Sargent Jay Nettleton, Co. I, 8th Connecticut:

---

[1] Liska and Perlotto, page 125

This Taylor's farm is a paradise...He is a King and his estate a kingdom...He counts his plantations not many less than ten and his acres by the thousands, and slaves in all some 900.[2]

Those enslaved men, women, and children didn't hesitate to escape to freedom with the Union army as they headed back down the peninsula. Given an average slave auction price of roughly $1,500, which equals to over $57,000 in today's money, that means that over $50 million in George Taylor's net worth simply walked away. And, without the forced labor to grow and harvest his crops and manage the farms, his future financial prospects were bleak. (Pardon me if I don't shed a tear for Taylor.)

Ad for George Taylor's produce May 25, 1863, *Richmond Times Dispatch.*

One of the major objectives of this mission had been to destroy the bridge across the South Anna River, but it had been too strongly defended, so the Union troops gave up and headed back down the peninsula. Albion sums up the results in his own inimitable style:

What did we do, I suppose you ask. Well, we up and marched back again and tore up railroads--two or three rails in the road between Richmond and Fredericksburg. The bridge was too strongly guarded and the General commanding concluded he would not burn it and so let it alone after one or two men had been blown into Eternity.

By this point, the reader may be wondering how the Blackberry Raid got its name. The simple answer is—blackberries. New Englanders had never seen such vast quantities of the berries which grew thick along the path of their march through the Virginia countryside. Everyone, of all ranks, indulged by the handful, hatful, and bucketful of the blackberries, some to the point of overindulging, but the little black fruits were a bright spot in an otherwise cruel, exhausting, and for some, fatal, march of futility.

---

[2] Liska and Perlotto, page 125

16
Camp and Home

The following letter contains nothing very newsworthy, written in the calmness and stability of camp. Once again, Albion voices some frustration in the lack of correspondence from his brother, William, and also asks for news of his other brother, George, who was with the 1st Regiment California Vol. Infantry. Around this time, the 1st CA was somewhere in the New Mexico Territory fighting the Apache and Navajo—a side of the Civil War years unknown to many people.

Camp 8th Connecticut, Portsmouth, Va.
August 4th, 1863
Dear Brother and Sister,
It is past Roll Call and not feeling like retiring just at the present time, I will answer your letter received some days ago.
The weather has been very warm for a week or so. Showers which came nearly every day do not come hardly oftener than once a week, now. The health of the men is very good. The warm weather has made me feel a little dumpish, but I'm coming out in good style.
We were paid today. I shall send home $30.00 in a few days, probably by Adams Express.
We have a very good place here, about a quarter of a mile from salt water and just far enough from town so that the men will not be running away all the time. The camp is finished off in good style and their rations are very good.
We rather expected that we might have to go to South Carolina, but did not. The 1st and 5th Brigades have gone so that there are only two Brigades of the old division left.
I have received all the papers except this week's. Mail comes through in three or four days and Express in about the same.
I was sorry, very sorry to hear any such thing as that you wrote about Mr. H. Alas, that he should forget God, that he should fail in the last. But I have faith that he will return to Him whom he has forgotten. He had his faults, but oh, you should have seen how that man worked and prayed for my conversion. You would be astonished. Do help him as much you can and, if possible, set his feet again in the path from which he has almost slipped.
Captain Hoyt was home on a furlough of eight days but did not stay in Bridgeport but a day or two. As he did not see you, very likely you did not see him. Isn't that logic?

I have not heard from William for a long time. Sometimes I am almost angry at his long silence, but then it is not, I know, but what he thinks of me often, but a habit of his, his letters go week after week.

We are expecting the drafted men here in a few days as they do not seem to stay put in New Haven, but I think they will grow tired of such fun after they join their Regiments. I did hope that we should go home without having drafted men with us but we must have them. In our company there are only 12 or 14 privates. Give my love to all my friends. Kiss the children for me. May you all be kept from harm is the prayer of your brother

Albion

P.S. Have you heard anything from George?

The 8th CT, comfortable in their Portsmouth camp, would soon move once again.

Camp 8th Connecticut, South Mills, NC
August 23, 1863
Dear Brother and Sister,

Here we are in the South East corner of the Dismal Swamp, thirty miles from humanity doing picket duty.

We struck camp in Portsmouth on the 19th I think, and after a march of two days we arrived in this desolate place safe and sound. Yet it is not so bad as it might be. The great trouble is that we have not had a chance to get any papers and only one mail which came today and which, by the way, brought me four or five papers which are right welcome I can assure you. I hope that in a few days things will be put to rights and we will receive mail and papers every day.

We are close to the Dismal Swamp Canal. Fish, flesh, and fowls abound and are quite reasonable rates too. We buy potatoes from 50 to 75 cents per bushel, milk 10 cent per quart, which I can tell you is a great luxury.

The Dismal Swamp canal.

Our camp is in a pine grove, quite a nice place.

You spoke about coming here with Emily. If we were in Portsmouth you could do it very well and it would be just what I should like, but, as it is now, I do not advise Emily to come, not but what I want to see her, but for her own comfort as the accommodations in this region are very limited. Of course, Clate could come a great deal better and I should like to see him very much.

We have been doing picket duty up and down the Canal towards Portsmouth and Elizabeth City. The greatest trouble is in the North Carolina fly which bites outrageously, and which, when once they have commenced to pay attention to you, are very hard to get rid of.

"The fly which bites outrageously," a.k.a., Diachloris ferrugatus, the Yellow Fly of the Dismal Swamp. It is a highly aggressive species of horse fly, causing painful bites. Females draw blood for their eggs.

I just sent by mail from Portsmouth a record of the Company. If you have received it I wish that you would put it somewhere safe, so that if I live to come home, I can have it framed. I received also your letter acknowledging receipt of my money, and I hope that you will keep an account of all that you have spent for me so that you will not come out the loser at the end of three years.

Nearly two years have passed since I left Bridgeport. It does not seem possible. It has brought many changes to you, no doubt as well as to me. Out of the Company of 101 men there are 21 here with us now. We have on our roles 38 men; the rest have been killed, have died or been discharged.

I want to go to school after this War is over and if my health is good I may try again to go through college, though I shall be rather old to commence.

I have not received a letter from William for a long time. It seems to me as though he could be a little more brotherly, especially as he has been in the Army and knows how welcome all letters are.

But I must close. Is Emily sick? She has not written for so long a time that I think that must be the reason.

When you write if you have any spare fish hooks and line, send them along in your letter, as the fish are a plenty but the line to catch them is wanting. Give my love to all inquiring friends. Kiss the children for me and,--only thirteen months longer if God spare us, may we see one another again.   Your affectionate brother, Albion D. Brooks

The unfortunate 8th CT, back in the "Dismal Swamp, thirty miles from humanity," with "the North Carolina fly which bites outrageously, and which, when once they have commenced to pay attention to you, are very hard to get rid of."

"Nearly two years have passed since I left Bridgeport. It does not seem possible. It has brought many changes to you, no doubt as well as to me. Out of the Company of 101 men there are 21 here with us now."

What absolutely stark numbers! Eighty percent of the men gone after just two years—*only 21 men on duty from the original 101!* And the changes about which Albion speaks cannot be understated. He left home an innocent, naïve, optimistic, religious, 18-year-old boy, and faced countless horrors and endless tests of his endurance, courage, and faith. Death and suffering became so common that the average soldier often viewed with detachment things which at home before the war would have been emotionally devastating.

Despite all the awful things that happened, and there were so many of those, Albion also matured, found a strength that he probably never knew he possessed, and rather than lose his faith, it seemed to strengthen. Perhaps most importantly, he took the first steps to becoming a leader, not only in army rank, but starting to find his voice to preach, or at least speak up in front of a crowd, which can be very intimidating to the average person.

These were years about which he could be proud of his actions and conduct, and obviously something he wanted to remember always…*if* he lived: "I just sent by mail from Portsmouth a record of the Company. If you have received it, I wish that you would put it somewhere safe, so that if I live to come home, I can have it framed."

And once again, poor, neglected Albion complains in a very rare near-rebuke of that lazy-letter-writing brother of his.

"I have not received a letter from William for a long time. It seems to me as though he could be a little more brotherly, especially as he has been in the Army and knows how welcome all letters are."

Then there is the astonishing part about, "You spoke about coming here with Emily." Traveling into a war zone on a camping trip, in the middle of the Dismal Swamp? Oh, and by the way, Emily had become pregnant about this time (which might explain her suspected sickness?), which would have made the strenuous and hazardous trip all the more strenuous and hazardous to her health. There is no record of this trip taking place, so perhaps Albion was able to talk some sense into Clate.

Of course, once the 8th CT got settled into their Dismal Swamp camp, on September 7 they were on the move back to Portsmouth.

Camp near Portsmouth, VA.
September 12, 1863

Dear Brother and Sister,

I received your kind letter a number of days ago but owing to our moving camp, etc., I have not answered before.

We left South Mills about a week ago. I should rather have stayed where we were. The only advantage here is that we received the mail and papers daily.

We received 160 conscripts 3 or 4 days ago. They seem to be a good set of men. Of course there are quite a number of hard cases but we expect that, and altogether I am not disappointed in the men. I expected a worse set than have come. As they have not been assigned to their companies yet, I do not know what sort of men I shall have, but, rough or smooth, I think that we can get along, if not by words, by something stronger.

The nights are beginning to be cool and are very damp and foggy. My health is very good considering the amount of duty we have had to do.

I wish if it is not too much trouble you would buy me two over shirts and two undershirts. I should like to have the over shirts blue or red and thick flannel. I think the size that Clate wears will be large enough. Have them fine and good.

I will send on the measurements for a pair of boots. Have them like the pair you sent last winter, but do not make them any longer than the measure, and do not have them any larger around the ankle than possible. You may send a pound of tea if you like, half a pound of green and black, - also two pair of socks.

Send the things in a box and charge the same to me. We probably shall be paid in a week or so. You see that I have sent an account of money that I sent home. It is right I believe, though you perhaps can tell best.

Give my love to all of my friends. Kiss the children for me and yourself if you wish. It is Saturday evening here. I should like to look in just now, but, no, one year from the 25th of this month and if God spares me and you, we will see each other again, but it is growing dark.

Your affectionate brother,   Albion D. Brooks.

Amount sent home up to January 22nd, 1863	$162.00
Lost by mail	20.00
	142.00
Sent home March, 1863	60
	202.00

Paid you by William brooks for me	20.00
Sent home June 3, 1863	30.00
July 7, received from you	252.00
	5.00
	247.00
	33.0
Total due me	$280.00

This is taken from the copy of the account that I have kept. I think it is correct but if you do not, of course, say so. Of course there are several other accounts, such as papers you have sent, and some things that have been sent in boxes for which we must settle, or rather for which I must pay you. You alone have kept that account.

P.S. Have a heavy sole put on the boots, as when they are worn out there is no chance of having them mended. I want double uppers, calfskin.

Please send one or two handkerchiefs. I received the hooks and line. They are just the thing and will come in handy anywhere.

I wish you would buy me a Day's Algebra and send it along too.

Well, look at young Albion Brooks being all manly and authoritative about the new conscripts: "As they have not been assigned to their companies yet, I do not know what sort of men I shall have, but, rough or smooth, I think that we can get along, if not by words, by something stronger." You go, Albion!

However, he wasn't fully consumed by testosterone as he requested a copy of "Day's Algebra."

The most pressing items in the letter are the clothing and boots. In writing about what he wants for the shirts, he adds, "I think the size that Clate wears will be large enough." I found this to be a bit surprising, as Clate was so small he was rejected by the army. Albion was recorded as growing from 5-foot, 5 inches, to 5-foot, 7 inches over the course of his enlistment. We can surmise by this that while Albion was substantially taller, he was not very muscular, or at least not much wider in the shoulders and chest than Clate.

As for the boots to which he gives explicit directions as to their construction, when I received his records from the National Archives it dawned on me in a decidedly disconcerting moment, that these would be the boots listed in his final personal effects, the boots in which Albion would be buried.

The following letter was undated, but appears to fall between the September 12th and October 9th letters.

Camp, 8th Conn. Vol. Portsmouth, Va.
Dear Brother and Sister,
I received your kind letter today. Many thanks for your cheerful words. I do not know what I should do if the letters from home were not more cheery than some that are received in this company, but I think that my letters would be short and far between.

We are having quite cold weather, especially the nights which make us think of Old New England.

Our recruits appear to be quite a good class of men. Our lot was 29. Five have deserted. The rest, I think, will stay, at least until they see harder times than they will in this department.

There were two men killed in a New Hampshire regiment. One was a conscript and the other was one of the old men. They got into some dispute and the conscript shot the other man and he, in turn, was choked so that he died.

I did not send home from New Bern any such overshirt as I want. If I sent undershirts they probably will do well enough. I want good overshirts, those that I can wear with a vest if I wish. I do not care whether they are blue, red, or checked. I wish that you would put in a pair of suspenders or two or three pairs of socks. As to the drawers, I can draw a very good article from U.S.

Handkerchiefs will come in very handy, of course. You can send whatever else in clothing you think best, only don't forget the tea.

We were paid today. I shall send by express tomorrow $30. Have you heard from George yet? And likewise from William? I do not know whether he is alive or not, only as you write, which of course is to be relied on. I will write him in a few days.

My study in Greek goes along very well. Chaplain Morris is a very good teacher and I recite to him every day. You remember that I sent for a Day's Algebra (small book). Come to think I have just the book in my trunk with my other books.

Kiss the children for me. Give my love to Angie and to all others who may have interest enough to enquire.

When you send the box, write a letter so that I may know when to expect it. But I must close. Pray for me that I may be true to those at home and to myself. Only a few months longer when, if He wills, we shall meet again.

*Good night
your affectionate brother
Albion D. Brooks*

Now this was some interesting news: "There were two men killed in a New Hampshire regiment. One was a conscript and the other was one of the old men. They got into some dispute and the conscript shot the other man and he, in turn, was choked so that he died." As of yet, I have been unable to find out which New Hampshire regiment and the names of these men.

And no need for *Day's Algebra* after all, as he already has an algebra book with him in his trunk of books—and what Civil War soldier *didn't* carry an algebra book? Also, good to know he is getting along with his Greek studies. Just a typical soldier, nothing to see here…

***Camp 8th Conn. Near Portsmouth, Va.
October 9th, 1863***
My Dear Brother and Sister,
I will take a single sheet of paper this beautiful morning and write a line to those at home.

It is a splendid morning, such a one which makes me homesick. It is nothing but the fall weather at home, and, at times, makes me think that I am there. but Brooks very soon comes back to the reality of the thing, especially about dinner time.

I received the box the morning of the 6th. Everything was as good as when packed except the grapes which were spoiled. Many thanks for the edibles which you sent. I can assure you, they were right welcome. The shirts are just the thing and, as for the boots, I could not ask for a better fit.

There is no news here. All of the men have to work building breastworks. Our conscripts behave very well. We have not received the guns for them yet, and all they have to do is to use the spade, which is not a very agreeable employment to some.

How is the draft in Bridgeport? I have seen no notice in the Standard of its having taken place. That Standard, by the way, is a remarkably dry paper. Either the City of Bridgeport is very quiet or the Editor is not on the alert.

I am glad that Orlando has got home. A very poor place this army is, for any whose health is not good, and I would advise all such to get out if they can. Tell him to write me a letter.

I suppose you have not heard from George as yet.

There has been some sickness around here, most of it sore throat. We have had two men die in the Regiment with it, since we have been here. I had an attack of the same about the 1st of the month, and for a few days, was anything but comfortable, the doctor cured it in a few days.

There is one thing for which I am very sorry. Our chaplain, Mr. Morris, has resigned and gone home. I was hoping with his assistance to make considerable advance in my studies, but now, any such idea is completely knocked in the head. He resigned, I believe, to take charge of the Conn. War Journal, *a paper published in New Haven, I believe.*

How does the South church prosper? Have you a good minister? And how does the Thursday evening meeting progress? Such a thing as a prayer meeting I have not seen these many months, and, unless there is some man in the state of Conn. who will be our Chaplain, we shall be minus all religious teachings for the time to come.

But I have written enough. My love to Angie. Kiss the children for me. My regards to all friends who may enquire.

Your affectionate brother
Albion D. Brooks.

- Orlando was Clate's brother, who had become sick soon after enlisting. (See Appendix for more on Orlando Kingman.)
- No word from his brother George, what a surprise.
- Chaplain Morris did indeed go to the *Connecticut War Journal*, where he most likely was the one responsible for Albion's obituary. The new chaplain, Moses Smith, would be the one whose eloquent letter describing Albion's death brought tears to my eyes and cemented my quest to learn more about him.

There are no letters until October 25, 1863, simply because Albion apparently received a sudden and unexpected furlough home! After almost two years and life-altering changes, how strange and wonderful it must have been to be home. The only record of this time is Albion's subsequent return to camp, already "decidedly homesick."

Camp 8th Conn. Portsmouth, Va.
October 25, 1863
Dear Brother and Sister,
Here I am safe and sound in Portsmouth. I did not stop in New York Friday because why? Because that after I left Bridgeport, I felt decidedly

homesick, and the quicker one could get out of humanity, the better, as long as you were sure you would have to in a very few hours.

I arrived at Fort Monroe Saturday morning and at Portsmouth about 11:00 AM. It commenced to rain early in the morning and if any of my friends in the good old state of Connecticut, have the power to look through to hill and mountain within about four miles of the place where I am now, they would have seen a solitary figure with a valise slung over his shoulder, plodding his way towards camp, bearing, no doubt, a striking resemblance to a wet and cold chicken after a shower, for it did rain most tremendously. By the time I reached camp, my overcoat was soaked. I proceeded to unpack the valise and to replace the miniature.

I found everything all quiet. The execution of Dr. Wright, I think it was, took place the day before I arrived. They had the whole brigade there so that there would be no disturbance. I think they wanted to be on the sure side. You probably will see an account of the affair in the papers. Those that saw him said that he was very calm and that he died like a man.

It is Sunday. You at home, no doubt, are enjoying yourselves. It is rainy and chilly here. In truth, I am sure that I am in the swamp again, but then "only" for eleven months.

Give my respects to all who may inquire. Pray for me always. Kiss Ella, Mary, and Carrie for me.

Your affectionate brother,
Albion D. Brooks

As if having to return to camp after a furlough wasn't bad enough, Albion paints a vivid and pathetic picture of himself bearing "a striking resemblance to a wet and cold chicken" after he had to trudge back to camp through pouring rain.

On a much more serious note, there was an execution which occurred the day before Albion arrived back in camp, which deserves further explanation in the following chapter.

17
Wright and Wrong

The execution to which Albion is referring—a spectacle which he fortunately missed while on furlough—was that of Dr. David Minton Wright, hung for the murder of a Union officer. Initially, the story of Dr. Wright was going to get a footnote, or just a brief explanation in this book, but as I read contemporary newspaper accounts about this case, I realized it required more extensive coverage.

Wright was a prominent local doctor/surgeon known for his great efforts during a yellow fever epidemic in 1855, despite taking ill himself. Wright actually opposed secession and believed in the Union. However, when Virginia seceded, he remained in Norfolk.

On July 11, 1863, after a celebration of his wedding anniversary, Wright—a slave owner—saw something he simply could not tolerate. It was bad enough that the Confederacy just suffered two major losses at Gettysburg and Vicksburg. It was also bad enough that Union troops occupied Norfolk, but at least until this point, they had been *white* troops.

That fateful day, right on Main Street, 29-year-old Lieutenant Alanson L. Sanborn—a white officer—was leading the 1st U.S. Colored Volunteers to the customs house to be reviewed by Norfolk's military governor, General Egbert Ludovicus Viele. This would be no spontaneous crime of passion, as Wright had previously boasted to his friends that he would shoot the first white officer who was leading black soldiers. That day, about 4pm, his opportunity arose.

The following appeared in the *Richmond Times-Dispatch*, page one, Monday, July 20, 1863, Richmond, Virginia:

Yesterday afternoon, at 4 o'clock, Lieut. Sanborn, who was drilling a colored military company, and while in front of Andrew Foster's dry goods store, on Main Street, Norfolk, was shot [with a Colt revolver], *one ball passing in at the mouth and out behind the ear, and another ball passed through the body, entering the left shoulder and out at the right, from which he died in fifteen minutes. Dr. Wright, of Norfolk, is charged with the murder and had a preliminary examination last evening before the Provost Marshal, Major Booly.*

The first witness called was Lieut. Col. Guyon, 148th New York Regiment, who testifies that Lieut. Sanborn had drawn up his company on Main Street, in front of Andrew Foster's store, and was in front of his men dressing them, when Dr. Wright, who was in the store, addressed some remarks to Lieut. Sanborn, who replied if he was further interfered with in that way he would arrest him.

The Doctor thereupon advanced and shot Lieut. S. in the head. The Lieut. then turned upon the Doctor with sword uplifted when the Doctor fired a second time, hitting the Lieutenant first in the hand and passing through from his left to right shoulder. The Lieutenant seized the Doctor and endeavored to wrench the pistol from his hand, and whilst thus struggling they entered the store, a great crowd following them. They continued struggling for several minutes, when the witness took the pistol from Dr. Wright, and arrested him. Lieut. S. died in about fifteen minutes.

The Doctor was committed to jail.

Lieutenant Sanborn was a native of Vermont.

The tragic and senseless murder of Lt. Sanborn was in newspapers across the country for months, shocking even a public used to horrific battlefield reports and casualty lists. The following is from a newspaper in his home state of Vermont.

Orleans Independent Standard, Friday, August 7, 1863, page 2, Irasburgh, VT

The Murder of a Vermonter—Lt. A. L. Sanborn of this state was murdered at Norfolk on the 11th inst. As he was marching a company of colored troops through one of the streets, a prominent citizen and violent secessionist named Mr. Dr. M. Wright (sic), rushed from a store and insulted and abused the lieutenant, applying to him the most opprobrious epithets. The Lieutenant halted his company, and walking towards the doctor said, "I am a United States officer, consider yourself under arrest." The doctor presented a revolver and fired two shots in rapid succession; the first ball passed through the lieutenant's hand, and the second entered the left shoulder, passed through the base of the neck, and came out near the right shoulder blade. The lieutenant rushed upon the doctor after the second shot and bore him back into the store, where he sank to the floor, the blood pouring from his mouth and nose, and immediately expired. The colored soldiers with fixed bayonets followed them into the store, but were prevented from wreaking summary vengeance upon Dr. Wright by a Lt. Col., who seized the Dr. as the Lieutenant fell. He was handed over to the Provost Marshall, and a trial held. The whole testimony showed it to be the most wanton and deliberate murder, and the prisoner was placed in confinement, heavily ironed and under guard, to await the orders of the general commanding.

There are several accounts in which Dr. Wright supposedly said nothing more to Lt. Sanborn than, "Oh! You coward!" That seems a rather sanitized version of Wright's "opprobrious epithets," aka, what is commonly referred to as "cursing a blue streak." And many accounts also have Sanborn giving Wright a warning to cease and desist, before actually announcing he was under arrest. Also, this article says Wright was a "violent secessionist." Violent, obviously, but unless two years of war changed his position on secession, that part was untrue.

A more detailed account of the incident was actually copied from a Philadelphia paper for the *Richmond Dispatch*, including the execution on October 23, 1863, and a daring escape attempt which almost worked.

Richmond Dispatch, page 1, Monday, November 2, 1863, Richmond, Virginia

The execution of Dr. Wright at Norfolk—further particulars.

A correspondent of the Philadelphia Inquirer furnishes that paper with a detailed account of the execution of Dr. D. M. Wright, of Norfolk, VA., on the 23rd ult. It appears that at one time Dr. W. had nearly affected his escape from prison.

The letter says:

On Wednesday [October 21] *Dr. Wright made a request that a light should be furnished with him in his cell that evening. Strange as the request was, no one garded [sic] it with any suspicion. Late that evening he was visited, as usual, by a portion of his family, which on this occasion consisted of his wife, two daughters, and a small son. They all entered their father's cell, and after remaining a short time, the whole party, apparently, retired. To gain the street they have to pass through a little anteroom in the prison, which is occupied by its officers for the transaction of business. Here, one of the party, entering through a door, slightly stumbled. This was noticed by one of the turnkeys, who, after they had just cleverly reached the street, exclaimed, "By---, I believe that was Dr. Wright in disguise." Lieut. Cook, who was sitting among those present in the room, rushed out, and intercepted the party before they had gotten many steps. Walking up to one of them he exclaimed, "That's played out; I know you, Dr. Wright," at the same time lifting up two heavy veils that concealed the face.*

It proved to be as the Lieutenant had asserted. It was Dr. Wright, and he appeared to be but little surprised or embarrassed at the detection, and on being conducted inside the jail remarked that "desperate means were pardonable under desperate circumstances," and then walked back to his cell as unconcernedly as if nothing had occurred. The sequel of how he was disguised can now be most readily shown. When he left the place of his confinement he was clad in the garments of one of his daughters, who remained behind. As her father was re-entering his cell, she was found reclining upon the bed, fully equipped in her father's clothes, the boots peering beneath the covering. She was much chagrined at being found in this position, but was more deeply surprised and pained to find that her scheme for her father's escape had been frustrated. For her imprudent act no restraint was placed upon her, but she was escorted home by one of the officers of the prison. It is asserted, but we know not with what truth, that the doctor had everything in readiness to facilitate this escape, and that his friends were not slow to aid him in it. [Offers of $20,000 in gold had been made by his friends to secure Wright with safe passage to England.] *It was through a mere accident that he was recognized. Being taller than the women, he stooped as much as he dare to make himself appear small, and in doing this he stumbled while passing through a door. This caused his detection, as it more clearly revealed the shape and size of his body, which the keen eye of the turnkey was quick to detect.*

It having been rumored pretty freely throughout the city for several days past that an attempt would be made to rescue the prisoner, the Eighth and Fifteenth Connecticut and Fourth Rhode Island regiments were brought across the river to prevent any such demonstration. One regiment was stationed around the prison, while the other two were in good supporting distance. No surprise or rescue was attempted, and the night passed quietly by.

The Doctor throughout yesterday appeared as cheerful as usual. In the afternoon the Lord's sacrament was administered to him by the Rev Mr Rodman, of Christ's Church. His family remained with him all night and up to four o'clock this morning. A portion of the time was spent in conversation, and the rest was devoted to religious services. Upon their departure they took their last farewell. They all appeared to be deeply moved, and it was truly a solemn and touching scene. Almost up to the hour of execution there lingered a ray of hope. Yesterday, and even this morning, telegrams were sent to the President asking for a further reprieve. All that friends could do for him was done. His counsel even used personal influence in his behalf, but all this was of no avail.

Early this morning the exterior of the prison was surrounded by glistening bayonets, and the interior filled by officials who were preparing everything for the execution. At 9 o'clock, Dr. Wright was taken from his cell and conducted through the prison to the street. To those who were present he bowed, and several he addressed with a few words. He was supported on either side by a clergyman. After viewing the procession, which was drawn up into line, he advanced towards the hearse and requested that the lid of his coffin [which Wright made himself out of cypress] *might be removed, so that he could take a last view of his family, whose portraits* [daguerreotypes] *were arranged all along the sides just above the head.*

... The 118th New York, and 21st Connecticut regiments brought up the rear.

There were few to be seen on the thoroughfares through which the procession passed, except negroes. But the solemn line was viewed from the houses by many. In a number of instances women were observed crying.

*The spot selected for the site of execution was the old Fair Grounds. In the centre (*sic*) of them the gallows was erected.*

At a few minutes before ten o'clock the procession reached here. Already the Eighth and Fifteenth Connecticut regiments, the Fourth Rhode Island regiment and Regan's battery, were drawn up in a hollow square around the gallows. The procession passing inside of it, Dr. Wright's carriage was halted before the scaffold, which he mounted without any apparent nervousness, assisted by Dr. Rodman and another clergyman.— From the scaffold Captain Sheppard now read the charges, finding and sentence of the court by which the condemned was tried. The order for execution was also read. The Doctor listened to them calmly, and without evincing any emotion.

Dr. Rodman now offered up a prayer, at the conclusion of which Dr. Wright advanced a few steps forward, and in a tremulous voice said, "Gentlemen, the act which I committed was done without the slightest malice." His hands were now tied. Bending on his knees, he prayed most fervently for a few minutes. Upon arising, the cap was adjusted over his face, and the executioner, Mr. John Armstrong, of Co. B, 21st Connecticut regiment, stepped from the platform and pulled the rope attached to the bar which supported the drop.

All this time a breathless stillness prevailed, and as the doctor descended through the trap a shudder appeared to run through everyone present.—He fell without a struggle. His death must have been instantaneous, as not a motion was perceived. It was a few minutes after 10 when the signal to lower the trap was given. The body, after hanging a half hour, was examined by Dr. Conover, the Medical Director, Dr. J. H. Lee, of the 21st Connecticut, and several other surgeons, who pronounced life extinct. The body was then cut down and placed in the coffin, to be delivered to his family.

Thus has Dr. David M. Wright paid the forfeit of his life for shooting, in cold blood, Lieut. Sanborn, of the United States colored troops, in the early part of July last. Since the commission of the deed he has endeavored to justify himself in it. He was a man of strong Southern feelings, and this, in a measure, may have prompted him to commit the act.

Now there is a lot to be said about this excellent account, not the least of which was that five regiments of infantry and a company of artillery, the 7th Independent Battery from the 56th NY Volunteers commanded by Captain Peter C. Regan, were deployed to maintain order. Also, the daring escape plan was the work of his daughter, Penelope, who in addition to swapping clothes with her father, had smuggled in a master key to remove his shackles. Also, one of the photographs in the coffin was of Wright's eldest son, who had been killed in Gettysburg, but his family hadn't learned of his death until after Wright was arrested for murder, and they didn't have the heart to tell him

However, there is one line which practically caused me to blow a gasket. In addition to many other things, for several years I have been a true crime podcaster for my show, *Murder in the Hudson Valley*. I have heard all kinds of ridiculous statements made by murderers—often blaming the victim—but never, *ever*, have I read a more ridiculous comment as Dr. Wright's on the gallows:

"Gentlemen, the act which I committed was done without the slightest malice."

Seriously? That would be laughable if it wasn't so outrageous. I can't imagine a much greater expression of malice than shooting a man in the head at a distance of four feet, then shooting him again—and all because Sanborn had committed the unforgivable sin of being a white officer leading black soldiers. There was so much seething hatred in this vile act of murder that it is inconceivable—or at least I hope it is—to modern sensibilities.

It is worth noting another of Wright's statements, which appears in the court records of his trial. Wright staunchly maintained that he was completely justified in murdering Sanborn. In fact, it was self-defense in his warped way of thinking, because he was a slave owner, and how could he be expected to submit to an arrest at the hands of people who may have been his former slaves? In an exchange with the prosecutor, who pressed him on this question of possibly being taken into custody at the hands of black men, Wright responded, "No sir, I could not submit to that."

It should also be noted that President Lincoln personally looked into this case, despite all of the pressing affairs of state. Lincoln asked that Dr. John P. Gray, superintendent of the Utica (NY) Lunatic Asylum, examine Wright to be sure he hadn't been insane at the time of the murder. When the doctor certified that Wright had been sane, Lincoln decided to listen to his advisors that the trial and sentence had been fair and justified. Still, Lincoln showed one slight mercy in delaying the initial execution date of October 16 by one week in order that Wright would have more time to get his affairs in order—a courtesy Wright did not extend to Lt. Sanborn.

Which brings me to an important point, and one I continually stress in my podcasts—what about the victim, what was his story? As we just saw in all the articles, the murderer gets all the coverage, while the victim got no more ink than to mention that he was from Vermont. Even many modern sources mention only that Lt. Sanborn was Wright's victim, but offer no details of who he was. Just what life did Wright cut short in his vicious rage?

Alanson L. Sanborn, born in 1834, was a school teacher, who loved his home in Thetford, Vermont. His parents, Thomas and Mary, were both from a long line of early English settlers to the New Hampshire coast. Alanson had six brothers and sisters, all of whom got married and had children—something he never had the chance to do. He could have stayed comfortably at home, but in a letter home to his mother in May of 1863, he wrote:

"It is my duty and I would rather die in the field fighting for my country than be spared at home in finest ease while my brothers die on the altar of their country."

He saw the recruitment of black soldiers as being "a work of justice. It is a work of humanity… to elevate downtrodden humanity."

This is the man that the supposedly fine, religious, educated, Southern gentleman, Dr. Wright, a physician who devoted his life to relieving the suffering of the sick and injured, considered by many to be a martyr to the cause, shot in the head and body, bleeding out in minutes on the floor of a drug store—all because he dared to be a white man giving dignity and purpose to black men.

There had been some delays in returning Sanborn's body to his family, so it wasn't until early December that he was finally laid to rest in Vermont soil, at the Evergreen Rest Cemetery in Thetford Center. The presiding clergyman at his funeral, Rev. D. S. Frost, said that the war had revealed people like Wright in their true light, and were exposed "in all their moral deformity before the nations of the earth as moral lepers of the human race, fit to be remembered, only to be loathed, abhorred and detested for all coming time."

Rev. Frost also added in contrast, that Alanson Sanborn was one of "freedom's martyrs" who had lived the type of life that revealed "the real heart they possess."

In a way, this case is a microcosm of the passions and motivations that drove many on each side during the Civil War; an example where there are no gray areas, just literally black and white. A prominent doctor glorified by the South for a brutal, senseless act of murder, and a humble New England school teacher wanting to "elevate downtrodden humanity." The symbolism would not have been lost on soldiers like Albion, and undoubtedly added fuel to their fire to crush an unjust rebellion once and for all.

Lt. Alanson L. Sanborn (Courtesy of P.J. Horn)

For those who still adhere to the idea that this war was only about states' rights, remember this face. William Brooks said the war was also about whether a man would be wise or be a fool. Going a step further, it was also about whether a person would choose to be kind and compassionate, or a hate-filled, prejudiced murderer.

18
The "R" Word

Reenlistment. That awful "R" word which sounds so wonderful on paper with its enticements of bonuses and furloughs to homesick and war-weary soldiers.

Just sign here…The war can't last much longer…You don't want to turn your back on your country just when victory is so close…Think of the regiment…It's the patriotic thing to do…There's a big bonus…

However, after returning from his furlough at the end of October 1863, Albion didn't have any thoughts of reenlisting. On the contrary, as the following letter indicates, he was counting the months—and most likely the days, until his enlistment was up and he could go home for good.

Camp 8th Conn. Vol. Portsmouth, Va.
Nov. 13, 1863
Dear Brother and Sister,
As everything is quiet along the street, and no one to molest or make afraid in my tent, I will write a few words to you, brother and sister in the good old state of Connecticut.

It is evening about 7:00. The work of the day is done, at least to me, but not to the soldier who is pacing his feet. He will give you a far different answer. The new moon is shining down on the camp of tents as beautifully as it does on your pleasant home in New England. All is quiet except the occasional bark of a dog. But enough of this.

I think that I wrote all the news in my letter to Angie. Since that epistle was mailed there's been no change in my health. There seems to be a little stir here today. I should judge that they had seen some indications of rebels in the country, if they (the Rebs) want to give us a try, I'm willing, but I think they will find us a hard nut to crack.

There seems to be a small movement in Meade's army. Hope that Meade will not turn around and put for Washington again. It has, up to this time, seemed to be a very curious sort of movement, first one would charge, then the other. Perhaps it is, - was, - strategy.

Give my love to all who may inquire. I am very sorry that I did not see Mr. Strong[1]. Give him my best respects and tell him it is only for 10 months.

---

[1] After combing Bridgeport census records, I suspect this is Emory Foote Strong, who was a schoolteacher in 1860. During the war, Strong was named Lt. Colonel of the Connecticut militia, and after the war he was active in government and was appointed to

Kiss the children for me and any pretty lady who cannot get along without it. But I must close. Excuse the shortness of the letter as it is the third that I have written this week, a feat that I have not done before for two years.

God bless and protect you all.
Your affectionate brother
Albion D. Brooks.

P.S. Clate, will you send me a sheet of the finest Emery cloth that you have in a paper? I wish it to use on my gun and I cannot get any good here. Albion

- A sarcastic, yet insightful, soldier's-eye view of the Civil War to this point: "Hope that Meade will not turn around and put for Washington again. It has, up to this time, seemed to be a very curious sort of movement, first one would charge, then the other. Perhaps it is, - was, - strategy." In October and November of 1863, Meade and Lee met in a series of minor engagements—the Bristoe Station and Mine Run Campaigns. Both Meade and Lee had hoped to deal each other a decisive blow, but by December, Lee had backed off and it was time for the Army of the Potomac to "turn around and put for" winter quarters.
- Albion Brooks mentions women—rarer than a blue moon! "Kiss the children for me and any pretty lady who cannot get along without it."
- Last, and certainly not least, Albion does not sound like someone who wants to stay in the army a minute longer than he has to: "I am very sorry that I did not see Mr. Strong. Give him my best respects and tell him it is only for 10 months."

Before discussing reenlistment, there were two entries at the beginning of Albion's new diary book which he would use for 1864. The first demonstrates his deep gratitude for being taken in by his sister and her husband.

---

be U.S. Marshall. A patriotic schoolteacher—exactly the kind of people to whom Albion, Emily, and Clate, would have gravitated.

May the blessing of God be upon Clayton and Emily for what they have done for one who had no claim upon them. You shall receive your reward. God has blessed you in this world.
Signed
Albion D. Brooks

The other entry—essentially his Last Will and Testament—speaks for itself.

Camp 8th Conn. Vols. Portsmouth, Va.
November 1st, 1863
In case that by any means I should die, it is my wish that my body should be carried North and laid by the side of My Mother in Kingfield, Maine. What money there is left after expenses are paid, I give to my brother, William E. Brooks.

Albion D. Brooks
1st Sergeant Co. A.
8th Reg. Conn. Vols.

So, in November of 1863, Albion saw two possible paths for his future—going home in 10 months if he was lucky, and if not, death. How then, did he come to reenlist?

Recruiting-officers were sent to the regiments in the field; and the soldiers having less than one year to serve were offered the veteran bounty of $702 to re-enlist, with a furlough of thirty days before the expiration of their original term of enlistment. The effort was attended with abundant success.[2]

Regiment.	Commanding Officer.	Location.	No. Re-enlisted.
1st Artillery,	Col. Henry L. Abbot,	Defenses of Washington,	435
1st Cavalry,	" Wm. S. Fish,	Baltimore, Md.,	92
1st Squadron Cavalry,		Army of the Potomac,	43
1st Battery,	Capt. Alfred P. Rockwell,	Department of the South,	46
5th Infantry,	Col. Warren W. Packer,	Army of the Cumberland,	280
6th "	" Redfield Duryee,	Department of the South,	205
7th "	" Joseph R. Hawley,	" "	333
8th "	" John E. Ward,	" of Virginia,	310
9th "	" Thomas W. Cahill,	" of the Gulf,	321
10th "	" John L. Otis,	" of the South,	280
11th "	" Griffin A. Stedman, Jr.	" of Virginia,	268
12th "	" Ledyard Colburn,	" of the Gulf,	436
13th "	" Charles D. Blinn,	" "	298
			3,347

---

[2] Croffut and Morris, pg. 462

That was a lot of money, but in addition to the enticements, the recruiting officers used a carrot and stick approach. The carrot: If you enlisted, you received the bounty, got to go home for a wonderful 30 days, and you had the honor of being called "Veteran." The stick: If you declined to reenlist, all regular furloughs were suspended, and chances were you would be sent to the Army of the Potomac, and no rational soldier wanted to go there!

Of course, there was the consideration of finishing the job with the regiment to which had been devoted so much blood, sweat, suffering, and sacrifice. Albion was a man of honor and duty, and as he said in his letter from Portsmouth, VA to his sister in Bridgeport, CT on June 16, 1863:

I wish that I could be home, but not until the Old Flag that I have followed for nearly a year and a half is given up and the regiment of the 8th is mustered out of the service of Uncle Sam.

Loyalty to his country and regiment—and the nice, big, fat carrot—prevailed, and on December 24, 1863 it became official. Albion Brooks was now committed to three more years, or the duration of the war.

Sadly, it wouldn't matter, as he wouldn't live to see either.

19
The Absence of all that Makes Many Happy and Comfortable

Furlough was over. The bliss of family, homecooked food, warm, soft beds, women, and no one shooting at you, was done and it was time to go back to the drudgery of camp life and the horrors of war. Albion's diary entries detail the process of returning back to the army, and the "level of despair" which accompanied it. While he continues to have faith that God will protect him, he had only 107 days to live.

Bridgeport Connecticut February 16, 1864
Very pleasant day, start tonight for New Haven—our time of misery—and then, how are you.

"So I am with you even unto the end. I will keep you from the arrow that flies by day and the pestilence by night.[1]" Amen B

Wallingford, Connecticut February 18, 1864
The place of rendezvous was changed from Hartford to this place. We are quartered in a very good building have straw, stoves and would like to be in Bridgeport tonight—they think of me—I know here many pleasures because I spent them during the 30 days and God knows they are gone—and another term of service is before us—but He that kept me in days gone by, will keep us in days to come.

February 20/64 Saturday
Quite warm received the Regiment 35 recruits last night but Company A received nary a one.

Expect to leave next week for Ft Monroe—but I think we shall not I hope that we may be with Burnside B

February 23, 1864
Sister, o ye disconsolate[2] to the level of despair that comes from the old coach factory in the town of Wallingford.

We, just within sight of home, cooped up in this prison. We think of the beds, friends, girls, and others that we left behind, and the shade of all the colors of the rainbow, over our faces, we sit down to our rations of "salt horse" and bread—and how we do think of the table only ten or

---

[1] Psalm 91:5-6

[2] The hymn *Come, Ye Disconsolate* was written by Thomas Moore, published in 1816.

twelve miles from home—why did we enlist is the cry of that goes forth—why did we go with the Army for three years longer—oh may the sun shine on our heads—may the everlasting rocks howl and split. May the hills jump up and yelp—may I be older—at least a day or so—before I enlist again to be shut up in an old factory in the old Nutmeg State.

Written by Brooks when said Brooks was in a very dejected state of mind from the absence of all that makes many happy and comfortable.

Albion was clearly very, very depressed, and may have had an extra special reason for being so. He makes a rare mention of girls in the previous diary entry, and then the next entry introduces the mysterious "Mary B." Up until this point, there had never been the slightest mention of Albion having a girlfriend, or even any interest in a girl. Now, he was smitten at the very least, and quite possibly genuinely in love—just as he had to return to the army.

February 24
Sent a letter to Mary B--do not know but what I was in a great hurry. There is a great deal of drunkenness in the Regiment and I have seen so much that I can almost vomit at the sight of a drunken man. Many of the men are worse than when they came home, God forgive the poor fellows who in the knowledge of what they may expect do go without any hope in Christ back to the field.

There is a rumor that we leave this week--I do not care when we do for it is far worse than being in the middle of the Dismal Swamp.

Received the Atlantic Monthly from William, it seems like an old friend. Have spoken to several in regards to their soul, God help the words spoken.   B

The Dismal Swamp—the standard by which all miserable places are measured! The conditions at "the old coach factory" must have been abysmal, and the pain of separation from loved ones is often most acute when you are still in relatively close proximity.

February 25
We expect to leave here tomorrow. There is something that pulls at my heart much harder now than it did two years ago--at the thought of leaving "old Conn." There are some ties which will make me think of Bridgeport very often—and yet there is nothing which gives me any such grounds perhaps just imagination. What is in the future I do not wish to know. I go knowing what I may expect, the cannon of Antietam still seems to thunder

in my ears—O can so many of my comrades go back and not be prepared in the least to meet with God.

How beautiful are the works of our Father.

As I sit here in the third loft of the old building my mind goes back to the days of old—days gone forever. I can call to mind the weeks and months in the army—of the hours of ease and also the hours of horrible Lucifer when nothing but the strong arm of God kept evil away, away back of all those days. I remember the days of my boyhood of that cold bleak day in February when they buried my mother beneath the frozen clods among the hills of Maine and I a boy of just of 10 just stood looking on, O could I have looked forward into the future how my heart would ache and my eyes shed bitter, bitter tears at losing my dear Mother, but it is past. May God teach me from the past--to prepare for the future. He is coming—whither this century or not I do not care to know, enough be it that we shall all rise that day. Enough be it to this poor mind of mine, that God who knows all shall judge me some day not too far distant. Oh poor souls who are going down to Hell why will you die—O why will they be so careless when they know what they have good reasons to expect. B

Here is more indication that Albion's heart was with Mary B. in Bridgeport. He is clearly also in the that tenuous first stage of a relationship where he wonders if she likes him the way he likes her: "There is something that pulls at my heart much harder now than it did two years ago--at the thought of leaving "old Conn." There are some ties which will make me think of Bridgeport very often—and yet there is nothing which gives me any such grounds perhaps just imagination."

He also writes about "knowing what I may expect," heading back into the deadly theater of war, and then writes what I consider to be one of his most haunting lines:

"…the cannon of Antietam still seems to thunder in my ears—"

Almost a year and a half after the living hell of Antietam, and Albion confesses to his personal diary that the trauma is still very much with him. I cannot help but think that in three months when he mentions that he "can hear Grant's cannons" on May 31 on his way to Cold Harbor, that the sound brought thoughts of Antietam flooding back.

It was also heartbreaking to read how his mind had carried him back to the time when he shed "bitter, bitter tears" as a child at the loss of his mother, standing on the frozen ground of that windswept, hillside cemetery during a harsh Maine winter. Perhaps the most chilling line of this diary entry, however, was his prediction:

"God who knows all shall judge me some day not too far distant."

Portsmouth, VA March 2, 1864
We left Wallingford Saturday, came on board the boat with the 11CV there was not near enough room. The left wing of each Regt was given the deck for their quarters—three below--way below freezing. Everything looked great in camp. It seemed like home.

Sad, but true—the army, for all its instability and chaos, was highly structured, nonetheless, and it was really the first place Albion could call a home of his own. It was also a place where he had a position of authority, and was not living on the charity of others.

March 3
Every thing is quiet—hope to have prayer meetings and such like this will keep a man's faith alive. Oh for a Christian conversion here in the Camp.

March 6
I should like to be home to day. Mailed a letter to Ezra S. Rained very hard yesterday. Cold and windy today. Only three years more. But Him who lives keep me—is able to keep me in days to come.
We have church service this afternoon—I have not begun my--or rather any studies yet—have a book of the Chaplain's The History of the Reformation, rather dry subject perhaps but a very well written book and if read as it should be—will do one good.

It bears repeating—with rampant illiteracy and the endless temptations of army life, Albion Brooks spends his free time studying Latin, Greek, algebra, and the "dry" *The History of the Reformation*!

March 6 Sunday Eve
I must record the best prayer meeting that I ever have had while in the Army—there was a large Hospital Tent full. The Chaplain spoke and Jay Nettleton[3] made a prayer—and God gave me strength to speak and pray. Help me do my duty O Father.

March 8
Wrote to John Ople. Raining and cold.

---

[3] Sergeant Samuel Jay Nettleton, Company I, 8th CT, 1832-1912. Nettleton was a farmer in Litchfield, CT, and the father of nine children.

March 10 Thurs PM

We had a very good prayer meeting last evening. Hickman[4] spoke, said that he would try and live a life as he should. It gave me new strength, O that we may have many such come forward and speak.

It is a cold and chilly day—it is raining quite hard and considerable wind.

March 11 Friday AM

To day is a continuation or rather a second edition of yesterday. True the windows of Heaven have not opened yet—but every thing promises that they will soon.

Rain, rain, and more rain—one can only imagine the conditions of the roads. Any attempts at a campaign would be the Mud March on a grander scale. Despite the conditions, however, the 8th CT would soon be on the move again from Portsmouth to Deep Creek.

March 14 Sunday PM
"Sweet Sabbath Eve"

Yet to day has not been much like a Sabbath. We struck camp about 7 o'clock AM—and started at 11 o'clock.

Here we are in or near Deep Creek in a densely(?) Cornfield. Tired, cross, crabby and hungry, but not so hungry as we might be. Rec'd yesterday a letter from Mary B. full of encouragement. She is as fine a woman. Her mind appears to be as good if not better advantage in her letter as she did in her conversation. Received a letter today from Fannie D.

Sabbath eve. How many recollections pleasurable and profitable to my mind. How many scenes come and go before my memory, of pleasant hours spent in Good Old Connecticut, of the Sabbath schools—all of the Old Church and the familiar folks that I—in days gone by—I was accustomed to every Sabbath after Sabbath.

But those things are gone and past, perhaps forever. The Church bell ringing from the tower of my own Church in Bridgeport, my most sweet on those mental ears of mine again, but there is a brighter city, there is a Church on high whose harps never cease to sound. There is a city the Maker and Builder which is God. This world is not but for a time. The soldier in active service knows what it is to want an earthly Friend, many

---

[4] This could be Robert Hickman, who had just enlisted with Company A of the 8th CT on February 25, 1864. On July 17, 1864, he was wounded at Petersburg and discharged on June 5, 1865.

of us will die when there is no Mother or Sister to soothe the pillow, there is one consolation to the Christian soldier but there is a Friend with him that stickith closer than a brother.[5] *Let Antietam or Gettysburg or other battle fields sound a warning in our ears. Prepare to meet your God is the command which our Captain has given us.*

"*So I come quickly.*"

Clearly it wasn't a pleasant stroll, the dozen or so miles to their new camp, as they arrived, "Tired, cross, crabby and hungry."

Albion makes reference to church bells several times in his writings. "The Church bell ringing from the tower of my own Church in Bridgeport, my most sweet on those mental ears of mine." It would be a wonderful tribute after his death, that Emily and Clayton dedicated a church bell to his memory at the Park Congregational Church, a bell which still exists.

The South Church once stood at the corner of Broad and Gilbert Street in Bridgeport, CT. Reverend Thompson was Albion's minister there.

Once again, there is an eerie foreshadowing of his death, when "many of us will die when there is no Mother or Sister to soothe the pillow." But then again, what soldier could realistically expect to survive such wholesale slaughter?

Now for the 800-pound gorilla in this diary entry—Albion is in love! "Rec'd yesterday a letter from Mary B. full of encouragement." Who needs church bells when the woman you love gives you "encouragement?"

"She is as fine a woman. Her mind appears to be as good if not better advantage in her letter as she did in her conversation." Well, be still my beating heart! I hope Albion will forgive my poking fun at him, but is *this* the passionate confession that a 20-year-old man makes to his personal diary, of a "fine woman" with a good "mind"!? No poetry with hair of gold, eyes like deep pools, and lips as red as cherries?

While on the one hand I laughed when I first read this diary entry, I nonetheless felt a pang of heartache for both Albion and Mary B., as they would never meet again, and their young love would be tragically cut

---

[5] Proverbs Chapter 18 Verse 24, King James version

short. I wonder who Mary B. was, if she ever married, and if she lived a long life, did she sometimes think back over the decades to the soldier she once loved?

March 15, "Maternity Eve"

We have worked hard to day in pitching our tent with other like things here these days of weariness to the body bring to mind the day that is coming where we shall never tire.

Death seemed to be on his mind quite often, and understandably so.

The reference to "Maternity Eve" refers to his sister Emily expecting another child, but if her due date was March 16, she would be three weeks late! (See below)

March 19, Saturday AM

Mailed a letter to Mary B. and Emily yesterday, there is a rumor that we shall go to Annapolis soon. Well I hope so but yet I should rather stay here I think, but if Burnside will lead us it will make it somewhat better.

What I wouldn't give to see Albion's letter to Mary B.! I'm sure it was filled with stimulating quotes from Latin and Greek literature, with a significant dose of Biblical references.

And Albion still remains ever-faithful to Burnside, which is more loyalty than I think Burnside deserved.

March 23

Snowed very hard last night. Cold and windy. I have prayed with the Chaplain every night.

March 26, Saturday

Rec'd a letter and study(?) from Wm all well. Warm and windy. The Chaplain's wife has come so that our evening prayer has given up.

March 28, Monday

Wrote a letter yesterday to Will. It was a beautiful Sabbath. We had a sermon from the Chaplain in the morn and a prayer meeting in the evening here. Those Sabbath hours bring to one's mind the memory of those past. They cluster around one's mind and every praying breath of holy things brings down a shiver which makes me think I'm home again. There are many things in the Army which instruct and amuse (?) and if a man will be a man, if he will act well his part he will come forth purified and strengthened for his duty in this world. God knows who will go home safe and those who never again will cast their eyes upon the hills of New

England who never look again into the eyes of those whom they love but come life or death, hardships and evil, oh my our hearts, may my heart be firm upon that Rock which will never be moved.

"Lo, I am with you even unto the end of the world"

Yet another of Albion's poignant and eloquent statements: "...every praying breath of holy things brings down a shiver which makes me think I'm home again."

March 31
Received a letter from Fred Crosby with Photograph.

Went to prayer meeting yesterday eve. Captain Coit[6] spoke, said that he had in days past been a Christian wanted us to pray for him, Lord I thank Him that we have such evidence working of the Holy Spirit.

"Just as I am without one plea."[7]

Shakespeare wrote that "The course of true love never did run smooth." Well, the same applies to trying to decipher someone's handwriting—especially in regard to phrases which are obscure to the decipherer.

I spent a considerable amount of time on the last line of Albion's March 31 diary entry, until I finally determined it read, "Just as I am without one flea." I reasoned it must be an ancient Biblical reference and referred to someone who was fortunate enough not to have any parasites on his body. Oh yes, I had it all figured out—until I did a search and found that I didn't. The word was "plea" not "flea," and was from an 1835 hymn. Great moments in research history...

April 8
Rec'd a letter from OPK[8] and Nellie K. We have started a debating club rather young as yet. I spoke the other eve, all went as "merry as a marriage bell" until my streak of knowledge gave out, and I stopped so sudden that I nearly shook my bones apart.

Another example of Albion making light of his situation. How many of us have been pontificating over a family dinner or around the water cooler at work when our "streak of knowledge" gives out?

---

[6] Captain Charles Morgan Coit, Co B, 8th CT, 1838-1878. Wounded at Fair Oaks, VA, Oct. 27, 1864. Died in 1878 while saving his son from drowning.

[7] *Just as I Am* is a hymn written by Charlotte Elliott in 1835.

[8] Orlando Kingman

April 16/64 Sat Morn

We started the evening of the 14th on a "wild" around Suffolk. We marched to Bowers Hill the water in the road was from two to twenty inches deep and so by the time we arrived at BH our feet were wet, we were tired, cross and hungry. We went on the Cars to Suffolk and started again from there about 3 o'clock in the evening, we marched a few miles out from Suffolk and then made a circle and came back to the river some 4 or 5 miles below town we then marched back again, and arrived as a company about 6 o'clock PM. It was the hardest march I ever had, at least for my feet—we marched through so much water that it made them tender and so that they blistered very easy, we started from Suffolk about 2 o'clock in the evening for camp and arrived here about 8 o'clock AM.

Received a letter yesterday from home from Will. E has given birth to a—girl. Well, I think I could do better than that. It is raining quite cool (?) Brooks

Albion writes that his sister, E—Emily—"has given birth to a—girl." This would be her fourth daughter, Katie Brooks Kingman, born on April 5, 1864. Emily would have one more daughter in 1873—five girls with no boys! Clayton wanted so much to have a son, but then, he could have been a father to Albion for those years he chose to send him away to live with others.

Then came Albion's laugh-out-loud swipe at his brother-in-law fathering nothing but daughters:

"Well, I think I could do better than that."

This was the first time Albion mentioned Bower's Hill, and according to local historian Gerald Kinney:

...Bower's Hill where is located the evidence of the Norfolk & Petersburg and Seaboard & Roanoke Rail Roads. During the Civil War, these railways transported both Confederate and Union troops and supplies from Portsmouth and Norfolk to Weldon, North Carolina, Suffolk, Petersburg, and Roanoke. At the beginning of the Civil War the Seaboard and Roanoke railroad transported new recruits traveling through Portsmouth from Maryland to points west and south.[9]

---

[9] *Mystery Fort, The Civil War Era Fort Located on Jolliff Road, Chesapeake, Virginia*, Gerald Kinney, 2012.
www.cityofchesapeake.net/DocumentCenter/View/4679/Earthwork-Fort-at-Jolliff-Road-PDF

A more colorful and contemporary description of the area was printed in the New York newspaper, *The Troy Daily Whig* in August, 1863:

> *Bowers' Hill is one of the characteristic misnomers etched from the fertile brains of Southern imagery upon local geographical charts, but the topography of this country, from Norfolk to the Blackwater, refutes unequivocally the assumption of a hill, and nowhere, perhaps, is this refutation more palpably illustrated than in this immediate vicinity. This country is decidedly level, and were it not for the dense forests and swamps that flourish on its surface, would present a view as unbroken, almost, as the sea in a perfect calm.*
>
> *Bowers' Hill is located eight miles from Portsmouth, eleven from Suffolk, and is flanked on the south east by the Dismal Swamp, and on the west and north-west by Goose Creek. Thus, Bowers' Hill is very easily fortified, and hence, in a strategic point of view, of great importance, commanding as it does, the main avenue of approach to Portsmouth.*
>
> *It always has been, and still remains, a great object of mystification to your correspondent, why Suffolk, of itself a place of no importance, commercially or otherwise, and a point of no military account to the Rebels, should have been so strongly fortified, – while long chains of forts, earthworks and stockades, upon which our (Clark) soldiers labored so many months, thru' Summer's heat and Winter's rain, should have been erected, incurring as it did, immense expense, when the line of Deep Creek and Bowers' Hill could have been so readily fortified, at little cost, and more effectually held with one-fifth of the imposing force required to hold the dirty, dilapidated borough of Suffolk.*[10]

Other than Bower's Hill not being a hill, as well as being in a region where time and effort was wasted on over-fortifying everything, this correspondent makes no attempt to conceal his contempt for the "dirty, dilapidated borough of Suffolk."

Today, Bower's Hill is still a crossroads, or more accurately a tangle of interstate interchanges, as is evidenced by the Virginia Department of Transportation's 2023 "Bowers Hill Interchange Improvements Study":

> *This study evaluates options to improve the Bowers Hill I-664 Interchange in the cities of Chesapeake, Suffolk and Portsmouth. The Bowers Hill Interchange Improvements Study covers the junction of I-664,*

---

[10] *The Troy Daily Whig*, August 1, 1863, *From 169th Regiment Bower's Hill, 8 miles from Portsmouth, VA July 28, 1863.*

I-64, I-264, U.S. Route 13, U.S. Route 58, U.S. Route 460 and VA Route 191 (Jolliff Road), as well as seven miles of I-664 to College Drive (exit 8A).

As for the exhausting "wild" the 8th CT took around Suffolk, Virginia, it appears to have been a wild goose chase through roads flooded up to "twenty inches deep" with no discernable purpose or results for the common foot soldier. Speaking of feet, for all the hundreds of miles Albion had marched in every conceivable condition, to declare this to be the "hardest march I ever had," speaks volumes to his poor, raw, blistered feet.

Unfortunately, there would be little time for soldiers to rest or their feet to heal as the hell of the Bermuda Hundred campaign was about to commence the following day.

Albion Brooks in this undated, pre-war photo. Youthful and optimistic, he had no idea what the future held.

20
Bermuda Hundred

As winter faded and the Spring fighting season approached, General Grant met with General Benjamin Butler on April 1, 1864 at Fortress Monroe, to hear what plans Butler had in mind. Both generals had similar ideas—Butler should establish a base of operations near City Point and Bermuda Hundred, VA, and move toward Richmond from the south, while Grant would doggedly be engaging Lee to the north in a series of battles which would come to be called the Overland Campaign.

In a letter to Butler dated April 2, 1864, Grant made his wishes abundantly clear:

Lee's army and Richmond being the greater objects toward which our attention must be directed in the next campaign, it is desirable to unite all the force against them. You will collect all the forces from your command that can be spared from garrison duty—I should say not less than 20,000 effective men and—to operate on the south side of the James River, Richmond being your objective point...

The fact that has already been stated, that is, that Richmond is to be your objective point, and that there is to be co-operation between your force and the Army of the Potomac, must be your guide...

What I ask is, that with them, and all you can concentrate from your own command, you seize upon City Point and act from there, looking upon Richmond as your objective point.

If you can send cavalry to Hick's ford and cut the railroad connections at that point it is a good thing to do so. I do not pretend to say how your work is to be done, but simply lay down what, and trust to you and those under you for doing it well...

Grant's orders to Butler seems clear and unambiguous, "Richmond is to be your objective point."

In Grant's report, he then continues:

On the 16th, these instructions were substantially reiterated...Should he, however, fall back into Richmond, I would follow up and make a junction with his (General Butler's) army on the James river; that, could I be certain he would be able to invest Richmond on the south side so as to have his left resting on the James, above the city, I would form the junction there; that circumstances might make this course advisable anyhow; that he should use every exertion to secure footing as far up the south side of the river as he could, and as soon as possible after the receipt of orders to move; that if he could not carry the city, he should at least detain as large a force as possible.

Even to non-military minds, Grant's wishes leave no doubt that Butler's objective was to take Richmond. If not, he should at least get as close to Richmond as possible to establish a rendezvous point with Grant, and it should all be done as quickly as possible.

As Confederate General Beauregard had scant forces to defend Petersburg and Richmond, the Union plan looked good on paper, and Butler's newly formed Army of the James would include over 30,000 men ready and willing to go "On to Richmond." The Union commanding generals, however, well, not so much.

Suffice to say, Butler's commanders, including General William "Baldy" Smith, General Alfred Terry, and General Quincy Gilmore, didn't all get along, were often slow to respond to orders, and were borderline insubordinate. In one instance, Butler met with Corps commanders Smith and Gilmore to discuss his plans to attack Petersburg and asked for input. Smith and Gilmore had nothing to say—until they left the meeting and then promptly began devising their own plan, which understandably infuriated Butler when he found out.

To the soldiers doing the fighting and dying, the squabbles of the general staff were beyond their control. All they knew was that they had orders to follow, and prayed they would come out victorious, and alive.

Let us follow the Bermuda Hundred[1] Campaign through Albion's eyes.

Albion's Diary Entry, April 20, 1864 Enroute to Yorktown
(44 Days until Albion's Death)

We struck camp the 17th we are to go to Yorktown—there I think we shall be under Burnside, for myself I expect to see hard marching and hot fighting—But God who has kept me so far will do best to me and time to come. But many, oh many in the Company do not realize the scenes which I fear we are to go through err long.

Albion was certainly right about the hard fighting to come, but it would be Butler, not Burnside in command. After leaving their camp at Deep Creek, the 8th CT—now part of the 18th Corps—marched to

---

[1] Bermuda Hundred was established by the English in 1613, and refers to a section of land that could sustain one hundred homesteads. The English had also recently established a settlement in Bermuda—as the result of a shipwreck in 1609—and some survivors eventually made their way to Virginia and lived in Bermuda Hundred.

Portsmouth, steamed to Newport News, and finally marched to camp in Yorktown. Troops throughout the region were on the move, so it was no secret that big plans were in motion, and he shared more details with Emily and Clayton in the following letter:

Camp, Conn. Vol. Yorktown, Va.
April 28
My Dear Brother and Sister,
I have just finished my Regimental Rolls for the month of March, and my pen having been started, I cannot stop. Therefore, lifting it from the Rolls, I place it on the sheet of paper and let it go,--whether you will thank me or not, I cannot tell, for giving it its liberty.

Everything is quiet here,--a quiet that precedes the storm.

We have sent everything in the shape of coats, blankets, and camp equipment to Norfolk to be stored, at least the Regiment's things that we can by any way get along without. We expect our shelter tents soon, and I suppose then we will send the tents we have now.

I have not received a letter from home, and by home I mean you, all this long while. I am almost sure that I shall receive a letter by the return mail. I will tell you if I do.

I sent to William a few days ago a letter with $10.00 for you, but will not pay all into a dollar or more, but this will be some other time, will it not?

I think that the coming campaign will be short but heavy. If the forces here march direct to Richmond, three days march will bring us to the point where the Rebels think forbearance ceases to be of virtue, and likely, we, being of different mind, will try to convince them of their folly,--how are you folly.

I have been hoping Burnside would come here and take command but the latest news we have would seem to say that he is going into the Army of the Potomac. Well, I wish him well, and the old 9th, if they go there, but they have a hard, very hard road to travel this summer, I am afraid.

The 7th and 11th Connecticut regiments are on the opposite sides of the river, on Gloucester Point, but I have not been there yet, and in fact, do not know of many in either Regiment with whom I am acquainted.

You at the North are expecting that something will be done this summer, are you not? Well, by the help of God, I hope there will be, and I hope that you at the North, will remember better then you have done in days gone by, that not the arm of flesh gives us the victory, and that "not unto us" belong the praise of conquering but to God. I think that by the people forgetting that one thing, we have had in that fact, disaster when we might have had victory.

I have been over the works, rebel and Union in and around Yorktown and can tell you that McClellan was right when he laid siege to the place. It could not have been taken without the loss of more men and not even then I believe.

There are yet lying around the field shots of all kinds from the grape to the ten-inch, which things, by the way, remind us that we may see some miles farther on, and instead of being loose on the ground, they will be very loose in the air, but then we let those things trouble us least of all,-- we hope by the blessing of God to whip the Rebels.

We have prayer on Sunday and Wednesday evenings. They are very well attended and considerable interest is shown. The Chaplain is an earnest Christian man. But I must close. Give my love to Nellie and Orlando. Tell him to write and not wait for me. I think that I am entitled to that. Do you not? I suppose that William and Angie are in Maine. Kiss the children for me. Write often and may God bless you and yours is the prayer of

Your brother
Albion D. Brooks
Direct 2nd Brigade, 1st Division, 18th AC

In the midst of all the preparations, Albion had the opportunity to go sightseeing at the battlefield of Yorktown, where McClellan had conducted siege operations from April 5 to May 4, 1862. McClellan had planned a major bombardment on May 4, but then discovered the Confederate forces had snuck out the night before. The fact that there were "yet lying around the field shots of all kind" is a modern relic hunter's dream come true! Albion also takes time to joke about soon encountering such things that were "loose on the ground," being "loose in the air."

April 22, 1864
(While dated April 22, the entry covers through May 5)

We were paid to day. There is quite a number of troops, on to Richmond is the cry. Well so be it, in God we may trust.

Yorktown—On board U.S. transport G. Washington. Came on board about 4PM. We are going to City Point—we may have some hard times but give us the victory O Lord.

Friday morn—three miles beyond City Point 10am. We arrived here last night at 7PM landed about 12 night.

City Point depot, July 1864. LC-B817- 7044 LOT 4175

We have not seen any Rebs yet and very likely shall not for the present—but if we march to day we most likely shall come across some Southern Brothers.

But give us the victory is my prayer. Even though it may be my lot to be one of them who shall fall.

May 6, 7pm

The ball opened about half an hour ago—Peter[2] and myself were going to the River when lo, a volley of musketry greeted our ears and a few moments after the cannon began to strike up the bass of the music—some have gone most likely to the other world—God knows how many more will the next few days.

The First Battle of Port Walthall Junction occurred on May 6, and resulted in the Union retreating to the line of entrenchments which were diligently being constructed. Apparently, although the 8th CT was not engaged, Albion was close enough to hear what he sarcastically called "the ball" with the cannon providing "the bass of the music."

May 7 Sat Morn

The firing ceased at dark. There was occasionally a spat in the night—there has not been any firing that I can hear.

---

[2] Checking the 8Th CT roster, there are six soldiers named Peter who possibly could have been with Albion that day. At present, I have no further information to narrow it down.

Army of the James entrenchments on the Bermuda Hundred lines.
LC-DIG-ppmsca-35182

How many for the last time have answered to Roll Call this morning, the only Roll they will ever answer again will be for the Bier of God.—<u>It is a terrible struggle, at least to me</u> that there are so many men with immortal souls, who will be called to stand before their God, within the next three days, and yet not prepared. <u>I wish not to know what</u> is coming. "Sufficient on to the day is the evil thereof."[3] "So I am with you always even unto the end."

½ past 5 Saturday Morn Brooks

Just hours after writing this, the 8th CT would form a skirmish line along the west side of Old Stage Road, followed by the 10th and 13th New Hampshire and 118th New York to their right, in the Second Battle of Port Walthall Junction. Albion explained the battle in his next diary entry.

May 8 Sunday Morn

We started from camp yesterday morn about 6 o'clock AM with nothing in the shape of baggage except Haversacks and canteens. We marched about 3 or 4 miles, when skirmishing began, it was in a very thick wood, the 8th was thrown out as skirmishers. We advanced over half a mile in the wood, when we found the Regt and marched by the flank to an open lot to the right—beyond us about 1000 yards the Rebels were drawn up in a line of battle—we advanced three or four hundred yards—halted and commenced firing. I do not know how long we were on the field—for

---

[3] Sermon on the Mount, Matthew 6:34

myself I fired over 60 rounds, the first time that I have ever expected to dispose of that amount of ammunition. We had five wounded in our Co., one I am afraid mortally. In the Regt we lost some 12 or 15 killed and 70 or 80 wounded, but there is some consolation, we burned the bridge and destroyed the railroad. There were only one or two Regts engaged beside ourselves.

"Not unto us. Not onto us—but unto Thy name be the Glory of our safety"[4]

Brooks

It was close to four and a half hours that the 8th CT was hotly engaged, as the Confederates, on a hill by the Richmond and Petersburg Railroad tracks across a ravine, poured in musket and artillery fire. Total Union losses that day were 345, with 184 Confederate casualties. Union forces once again failed to press a substantial numerical advantage and fell back to their ever-growing defensive line across the peninsula, giving Confederate forces more precious time to bring in reinforcements. Apparently, Grant's orders to act quickly had fallen on deaf ears.

When tracing the path of the 8th CT during the Bermuda Hundred campaign, I was disappointed to find so little remaining. The most disappointing was the Port Walthall location, which now has a gas station and convenience store, with a wildly busy truck depot behind it. Trucks were racing by in all directions and I had to watch my step. I finally found the dirty, graffitied sign in the bushes near the road. As I was taking pictures of the sign, a trucker pulled over, got out, and proceeded to empty his travel urine bottle in the grass not ten feet away from me! My thoughts immediately turned to the relatively pristine battlefields of Antietam, hoping that those in charge realize how fortunate they are to not have a place like this!

---

[4] Psalm 155

Camp 8th Conn. Vol. Near Petersburg, Va.
May 8th, 1864
Dear Brother and Sister,
I am not going to write a very long letter,-from the fact that I do not feel very much like making crow's marks.

Very likely you will hear through the papers of the fight we had yesterday. Our regiment lost 75 men killed and wounded. We stayed on the field until we had fired all of our ammunition (60 rounds per man). It was rather warm work but God brought us through safe. We start tomorrow running on another scout,-it will be my birthday,-a grand celebration of my 21st year.

The movement up this way has worked admirably and if things go on as well as it has, we shall do better than I ever expected to.

But I am not going to write more. My love to Orlando and Nellie. Kiss the children for me. Remember that I am in the hand of God,-and that His will be done.

May God bless you and yours is the prayer of your brother   Albion D Brooks

From Albion's perspective, he apparently thought things were going well and they would "do better than I ever expected to." If only!

May 11 Wed Eve
We started again early in the morning of the 9th marched without much opposition to within about two miles of Petersburg tore up the railroad too—we have one man killed and two or three wounded among the latter was Thomas[5]. He is the third bedfellow of mine who has been wounded and yet unworthy me has been spared. We stepped out one night—a night spent in cold and expecting the rebels—there were two alarms but they did not amount to much—we arrived back to camp the 10th well tired only.

Very large mail to day—but not anything for me—my 21 birthday—the 9th—spent expecting to have a fight with the Rebs.

The Battle of Swift Creek occurred on May 9—Albion's 21st, and unfortunately, his last, birthday. Often in war, a speck of land for which men were willing to fight to the death one day would be quickly abandoned the next. Such was the case with Port Walthall Junction, as

---

[5] Albert H. Thomas, Co A 8th CT, Enlisted October 7, 1861, wounded May 9, 1864, appointed Commissary Sergeant July 1, 1864.

Beauregard sent his troops south to Swift Creek, just a few miles north of Petersburg.

Finding the enemy gone, Union forces headed south along the Richmond and Petersburg Railroad, and the Richmond Turnpike toward Swift Creek—but not before seeing the grotesque, bloated corpses of their unburied comrades, scattered about the terrain from the previous battle, swelling in the sweltering 100-plus degree temperatures.

When the two armies met, the Union initially pushed the Confederates to the south side of Swift Creek. A general stalemate ensued, with one notable exception—due to some confusing orders on the Confederate side for a change, two South Carolina regiments crossed the creek and made a pointless advance on a strong Union position. They were driven back with heavy losses, but the Union troops did not pursue. The battle continued in the form of occasional artillery and skirmishing, but neither side was inclined to cross the creek for a major engagement.

Swift Creek didn't look too swift during my visit in 2024.

Meanwhile that day, five Union gunboats went up the Appomattox River to attack Fort Clifton. Unfortunately, the U.S. Navy had yet to figure out how to raise their guns to shell elevated positions. Conversely, Confederate gunners had no problem shooting down on the gunboats. After sinking one ship and almost causing another to run aground, the remaining gunboats retreated back to City Point.

Fort Clifton was intact, the bridges across Swift Creek remained standing, Petersburg was safe for the present, and to the Confederates' surprise, the next day they found the entire Union force had left Swift

Creek and once again went back to their *defensive* positions across the Bermuda Hundred peninsula. Apparently, the concept of a swift, aggressive *offensive* campaign was alien to the Army of the James.

Perhaps Albion was suffering some survivor's guilt, as he states that three of his bedfellows had been wounded, "and yet unworthy me has been spared." Unless one has been in combat, I don't think it's possible to fully understand the trauma of seeing a close friend badly wounded and suffering, or losing a close friend—sometimes several in the same battle. For all his previous talk of God protecting him from harm, in recent diary entries he had written that "<u>I wish not to know what</u> is coming," and that he prayed for victory, "Even though it may be my lot to be one of them who shall fall."

Indeed, the bell was about to toll for Albion Brooks, as he had only 23 more days to live.

May 17, James River near Petersburg, VA

We started from camp again May 15th (I believe this should be the 12th) *early in the morning. We marched about 4 miles when skirmishing commenced, we advance about a mile driving the enemy's skirmishers before us.*

~~Shot~~ [6]*Camped for the night in a fine wood, it has rained more or less all day so that we were soaked. It rained considerably during the night. In the morning we made coffee and then advanced about a mile and half did not meet with much opposition, we camped through the night on the edge of a wood and we made quite a breastwork of rails and in the morning we made coffee and then advanced again, about a mile beyond were the Rebel earth works.*

We did not meet with much opposition. They left all the out works and we turned them against them. We went out on picket that day. Were released about 4 o'clock PM next day—that night was quiet. Were roused up about three o'clock in the morning and stood ready—it was very foggy. About four o'clock the rebels drove in our pickets on the right and for an hour the fighting was heavy. They drove back the right of all of the line. About five o'clock they attacked our Brigade. It was so foggy that we could not see the Rebs so that they were upon us before we knew it. We were on the rough(?) side of the ditch in the crossing over the Company became

---

[6] Albion Brooks wrote the word "Shot" and then crossed it out. As a very religious man who was troubled by having to work and fight on the Sabbath, his conscience also bothered him with the thought of killing. Was this a simple mistake, or was he about to talk about shooting someone, then changed his mind?

separated and broken up. Co A fell back to a brick house at a level part of the CO., and were released to hold the position. The Rebels drove our Brigade back of our skirmish line but did not undertake to come farther, we stayed out on picket until about 5 o'clock where the rebels commenced to advance, we fell back, the whole line had fallen back and after being relieved by another line we all started for camp—arrived here about 8 evening—we were whipped but if it had not been for the fog then we should have a different story to tell.

I never was in a place where I heard the bullets whistle quite as much as they did there—but God brought me through—we, Co A lost two men wounded   Brooks

The Fog of War: The Battle of Drewry's Bluff

Historians often write about the fog of war—a metaphor for the clouded judgment and perceptions that occur during the stress of battle. However, during the Battle of Drewry's Bluff on the morning of May 16, 1864, the confusing fog of war was literally caused by fog!

The lead-up to the battle began the morning of May 12, as the 8th CT, along with the 18th Corps and part of the 10th Corps, headed north along the Richmond Turnpike. The day was spent in skirmishing, with the Confederates continuing to fall back to the north. May 13 saw more of the same, with the Confederate forces retreating to a line of earthworks.

As Albion mentions, the weather had turned from extreme heat to rain, and more rain until they were all "soaked." They marched in mud, slept in mud, and had no tents or rubber blankets to shield them from days of rain.

On May 14, the Union troops found that the line of Confederate entrenchments had been abandoned, so they commenced to occupy them. Nothing occurred on May 15, which gave everyone time to rest. They would need every ounce of strength for the next day. While Butler had no plans for a major assault against Richmond, and was only testing the rebel's strength and defenses, Confederate General Beauregard had very definite plans—destroy the Army of the James.

The Confederate attack was set to begin at 4am on the morning of May 16, but the fog was so impenetrable it was difficult to see someone standing just a few feet away. After delaying almost an hour, when it became clear that the fog wasn't going to clear any time soon, orders were given to advance. Confederate General Ransom's division attacked the Union right, on the east side of the Richmond turnpike. Though initially making progress, the Confederate troops were slowed by the fog, and by the telegraph wire that Union soldiers had cleverly strung between tree stumps as trip wires. The Confederates became entangled in the wire, and then became sitting ducks for the heavy Union musket fire that poured in.

According to Albion, about 6:30am, the 8th CT at the center of the Union line—whose right flank was exposed to the turnpike—came under attack. They were soon taking fire from the front, to their right, and to their left. As Albion stated, "It was so foggy that we could not see the Rebs so that they were upon us before we knew it."

Captain Henry Hall of the 8th CT described the ferocious assault, with vicious hand-to-hand fighting, as the two sides were "firing, bayoneting, and clubbing each other face to face… The rebs stood in line twenty deep not fifteen feet in front of us…In five minutes they were on three sides of us."[7]

As the 8th CT was about to become completely surrounded. They held on as long as possible and then fell back. While official reports were very critical of the 8th CT's retreat, the men fighting in the fog that day knew they would be captured, or worse, had they tried to stand their ground any longer.

As the morning wore on, there followed a general Union retreat. However, things could have been worse for the Army of the James. The dense fog was just as confusing and detrimental to the Confederate soldiers who became lost and wandered off in the wrong directions. The 1st Virginia, coming upon an unoccupied Union camp where coffee was still brewing, stopped their advance for a cup of the precious commodity, and to rummage through the camp to see what else they could find. Confederate commanders had numerous problems of their own, and failed to press their advantage.

While it was a Confederate victory, Beauregard was angered that the Army of the James was able to retreat to their defenses relatively intact. He believed that with the proper execution of his plan, they could have destroyed Butler's army. Perhaps without the fog they would have, but then as Albion stated, had it not been so foggy, the Union also "should have a different story to tell" that day.

The Battle of Drewry's Bluff was a surprisingly costly few hours—4,100 Union casualties, and 3,000 Confederate casualties. Among the Union losses were 1,388 men taken prisoner—a notable example being General Charles Heckman, who thought he was rallying his troops in the fog, only to discover to his horror that it was the 7th Virginia regiment!

---

[7] Letter from Captain Henry C. Hall, 8th CT, to his brother and sister. Liska and Perlotto, page 152

Heckman's attempt to pretend to be a Confederate officer didn't last long. Taken prisoner, he was exchanged a few months later and returned to duty.

The Halfway House, so called as it is about halfway between Richmond and Petersburg, was General Butler's Headquarters during the battle, and a location to which the 8th CT and their brigade retreated. Today, it is a restaurant.

The 8th CT returned to camp and once again traded their muskets for axes and shovels, continuing to fortify the defensive line—which would prove to be something of a line of confinement for the Army of the James after the battle of Ware Bottom Church on May 20, 1864.

Though not well known, this was a significant engagement, in terms of both casualties and results. Union losses were about 900, with about 600 for the Confederates. It was a victory for Beauregard, sending Butler's men back behind their defenses, and allowing the Confederates to begin their own line of defenses, known as the Howlett Line. The situation was described in *Grant's Memoirs*[8]:

> *Previous to ordering any troops from Butler I sent my chief engineer, General Barnard, from the Army of the Potomac to that of the James to inspect Butler's position and ascertain whether I could again safely make*

---

[8] Grant, Ulysses S., *Personal Memoirs*, Chapter XLVIII, www.gutenberg.com

an order for General Butler's movement in co-operation with mine, now that I was getting so near Richmond; or, if I could not, whether his position was strong enough to justify me in withdrawing some of his troops and having them brought round by water to White House to join me and reinforce the Army of the Potomac. General Barnard reported the position very strong for defensive purposes, and that I could do the latter with great security; but that General Butler could not move from where he was, in co-operation, to produce any effect. He said that the general occupied a place between the James and Appomattox rivers which was of great strength, and where with an inferior force he could hold it for an indefinite length of time against a superior; but that he could do nothing offensively. I then asked him why Butler could not move out from his lines and push across the Richmond and Petersburg Railroad to the rear and on the south side of Richmond. He replied that it was impracticable, because the enemy had substantially the same line across the neck of land that General Butler had. He then took out his pencil and drew a sketch of the locality, remarking that the position was like a bottle and that Butler's line of intrenchments across the neck represented the cork; that the enemy had built an equally strong line immediately in front of him across the neck; and it was therefore as if Butler was in a bottle. He was perfectly safe against an attack; but, as Barnard expressed it, the enemy had corked the bottle and with a small force could hold the cork in its place.

The Bermuda Hundred Campaign was effectively over, and Beauregard could now send thousands of troops to help Lee at the ensuing battle of Cold Harbor. However, based upon Barnard's report to Grant, portions of the Army of the James could also now be sent north "by water to White House" to reinforce the Army of the Potomac. Albion's date with destiny was rapidly approaching.

May 21 AM
We have been cutting wood for two or three days past, the rebels seem inclined to bother us some but they have not done much harm. We have a very good line of fortifications, many—received a letter yesterday from William. Be with us God.

May 21 PM
It has been quiet today. The men have had soft bread to day—and what they most needed—rest! Another day would do good. Many souls to day have given their farewell to this earth and have gone, we trust, in a better brighter world—many today have answered the last Roll Call. Many

who for three years have worn the army blue have put them off and put on brighter and purer robes. They have had crowns of gold put on their heads

The roar of the cannon never ever will disturb their quiet, but what is to come—we know not—I have been kept, how much longer He alone knows, but Thy will be done. Brooks

"How much longer He alone knows." Albion Brooks had 13 days to live.

Camps at Somewhere and Nowhere, May 21/64
My Dear Brother and Sister,

I will just drop a line to let you know that I am still in the land of the living. Rebel balls and shells have not, as yet, come in contact with this poor body of mine, and if lying close to the ground will save me—you may be sure of giving me welcome again.

But then—here I am this Saturday morning—in the line, one of the Union and Rebel batteries are settling a small difficulty—and once in a while—the rifle speaks, yesterday two Reg. chums fell in a Rebel battery—lost about 200 men—and had to fall back. We have a good line of works now—they have kept the brigade busy cutting down the woods front of our line.

Your unworthy brother gazes with much more <u>feeling</u> at the blisters on his hands than with pride in very truth we have worked considerably and I think that we have a strong position which the Rebel army cannot take without much trouble.

The last two weeks have been weeks which we all shall remember from time to come. Mind we are not in the Army of the Potomac—but in proportion to the members engaged, there has been about as hard fighting here as there. We have lost about 130 in all since we landed at City Point and stand a good chance of losing as many more.

It is a poor place to die here. With no hope of having one's bones laid in New England soil—but then we hope to give them a place this summer. The feeling among the troops here is quite good, though we have not the confidence in General Butler that we should have in some others.

But I must close—give my love to Orlando, Nellie, and kiss the children for me. Tell them to write. I do not have time to myself. Now we work a great deal of the time, and fight, or expect to. The others please pray for us. That God will give us the victory—then He will prepare those, who before another month shall have passed—will be laid in a soldier's grave—may God bless you and yours, in the prayers of your most affectionate brother, Albion D. Brooks

Direct via Fortress Monroe

P.S. I sent some money the other day to William. I wish that Angie if she has time, would make me some shirts—the same as those you sent—make them <u>very</u> large so they will not shrink so small, and take the pay out of the money I sent. Albion

It was difficult to read Albion's opening paragraph of this letter, "I will just drop a line to let you know that I am still in the land of the living. Rebel balls and shells have not, as yet, come in contact with this poor body of mine, and if lying close to the ground will save me—you may be sure of giving me welcome again." As we will see, *not* lying close enough to the ground is exactly what caused a "Rebel ball" to "come in contact with" his "poor body" and his sister would never again give him welcome.

May 22 Sunday Eve
Not such a Sabbath as we should have had at home—though there has not been much firing—but enough to remind one that we are in the midst of war—for some reason on this I feel rather sad—not that coming events cast their shadows before—but the sights of the last week have left such a sad feel, recollections which time cannot efface—My God how many have gone—and not have had hope in flesh. B

The bloated corpses of his comrades, the fierce, hand-to-hand fighting, the loss of friends, the brutal heat, the relentless rain, the disorienting fog, the mud, the blood—it's no wonder Albion was feeling sad, with "recollections which time cannot efface." For someone who still carried the emotional scars of Antietam, the horrors of the Bermuda Hundred Campaign must have opened old wounds, and no doubt cut new ones deep into his heart and mind.

Wed Eve May 25/64
Rained eve—cold, disagreeable, it is such a day that makes one homesick—and wish to see the faces of those at home—but there it is part of the soldier's life—to do and to die is what we may expect, and hardship, toil and death are among the things for which we must be prepared.

It has been quiet here for the last week—all of the force are at work on breastworks, which with busy prepared to meet an attack keep us busy about all of the time—"He that dwelleth in the secret place of the Most High shall abide under the shadow of the Almighty."
Brooks

"…to do and to die is what we may expect, and hardship, toil and death are among the things for which we must be prepared."

Albion's usual optimism had definitely taken an even darker turn during this campaign.

Perhaps the most succinct, albeit scathing, summation of the Bermuda Hundred Campaign was written by Alan Nevins in *War for the Union 1864-1865*:

> *At one time or another, Butler, W. F. Smith, Gilmore, cavalry commander August V. Krautz, and Rear Admiral S. P. Lee, delayed movements, muffed opportunities, and failed miserably. Tempers became ragged, everyone blamed everyone else, and everyone was to blame. The Confederates under Beauregard scraped together troops from here and there and managed, with the help of Federal asininities, to hold Richmond, Petersburg, and the vital communications between, while at the same time penning up the much superior Army of the James.*
>
> *A comedy of errors and general ineptitude, combined with a skillful Southern leadership to prevent a Northern success, one that might have obviated ten months of siege at Petersburg.*[9]

On a personal level for Albion Brooks, the failure of the Bermuda Hundred Campaign was to be a fatal failure. It meant that rather than occupying Petersburg or Richmond, or as close to Richmond as possible, he would be sent to Cold Harbor, where he would be dead within a few days.

---

[9] *War for the Union 1864-1865*, Alan Nevins, Konecky and Konecky, NY, 2000, page 48

21
The Final Days of Life

So, this is it.

The last few days of Albion Brooks' brief life—spent in battle, and marching, and exhausting tree cutting, and building fortifications. Due to Butler managing to bottle up the Army of the James, negating its offensive capabilities, Grant was free to pull 16,000 men of the 18th Corps from the defenses on the Bermuda Hundred peninsula and add them to the meatgrinder of his Overland Campaign, which would ultimately see a staggering 55,000 Union casualties and 33,000 Confederate casualties.

On May 28, Albion and the 8th CT left their camp about 5pm, and after a few hours of marching, reached the Bermuda Hundred Landing. Before dawn the next morning, they boarded "a thing—species unknown," as Albion referred to the ship with his trademark wit. The vessel was the barge *John Haswell*, which was towed out into the river, where it then left for White House Landing.

James River
Sunday May 29 on board—a thing—species unknown
We left our camp yesterday afternoon, marched to the landing, embarked this morning about 5 o'clock and here we are on the bull track (?) 200 less in numbers in every other respect very well. We have lost 10 men from Co A—but He that brought me through so many—brought me through all this campaign. We expect to go—rather we have no idea as to where we are going—but I should not wonder if we went into the Army of the Potomac—for myself I do not care much—only I should like very much to settle down in camp and security a little.

The 8th seems to go over the same ground twice—we have so far at least. There is many things to be seen twice, but I rather not have but one sight.

Sabbath day with all thy thoughts,
and yet in what a place.
In what surroundings
to hold communion with one's God.

Brooks

With the losses continuing to mount, it's no wonder Albion was yearning to "settle down in camp and security for a little," but that was not to be. In fact, it would be quite the opposite—the epitome of the old saying

"Out of the frying pan, into the fire." He also mentions that "The 8th seems to go over the same ground twice...but I rather not have but one sight." Albion is making a joke out of it, but how true this was for soldiers everywhere who would take, retake, and re-retake the same ground, or would march back and forth and back again. It must have been demoralizing that after years of war, soldiers often didn't seem to be making any progress, and nothing to show for their sacrifices and suffering—other than the staggering loss of friends and comrades.

The suffering would continue for Albion and the 8th CT on their journey to White House Landing on the overcrowded barge.

Albion's Last Diary Entry
May 31, White House, VA
(3 Days until Albion's Death)

We arrived here last night about 6 o'clock. We had one of the most uncomfortable journeys that it was ever our lot to have—but like everything it had an end, and here we are ready to join the Army of the Potomac or anything else which Uncle Sam may see fit to give us to do.

We have not had a mail for three days—I expect a "good lot" when it does come. It is a splendid morning—the trees are leaving out and everything looks so different from what it was one or two days hence—the war, what misery has thou caused—what misery here. What pain in the hearts of those we love in our New England Homes, but "He that tempers the wind to the shorn lamb"[1] will do all things for the best.

Albion's last diary entry was almost prophetic:
"...like everything it had an end."
"What pain in the hearts of those we love in our New England Homes."

The same day as his final diary entry, he wrote his last letter to his beloved sister Emily, and Clayton.

White House, VA, May 31/64
My dear Brother and Sister,
You see that we have changed course. I cannot write but just a word—we can hear Grant's cannons and probably will be moved in a few hours.

---

[1] Generally believed to be a quote from the Bible, it is actually from the novel **The Life and Opinions of Tristram Shandy, Gentleman**, by Laurence Sterne, published in nine volumes between 1759 and 1767.

Give my love to all—we are expected to move every moment. My health is very good, and I hope for the best—May God bless you and yours in the prayers of your affectionate brother   Albion Brooks

Of all Albion's many letters, diary entries, and essays, these would be the last words he ever wrote. There would be no time for anymore writing as the 8th CT was soon on the march, and then went straight into battle, but like in so many other instances throughout Albion's army life, there was a screw up in the orders.

Grant had wanted the 18th Corps to join his forces gathering at the small town of Cold Harbor, VA, which like Gettysburg, drew in both armies due to its several crossroads. A successful Union cavalry engagement took place there on May 31, and Grant hoped to have the 18th Corps be in Cold Harbor and ready for battle the morning of June 1. However, somehow the wrong orders were sent, and the 18th Corps was misdirected to New Castle, a small ferry town on the Pamunkey River. As soon as they arrived in New Castle, they were informed that they were at the wrong place and got back on the hot, dusty roads and resumed marching, this time to Cold Harbor.

Rather than being fresh troops ready to fight in the morning, they didn't arrive until 3pm, worn out from the long, hot march, after having gone many miles out of their way.

As Albion didn't have the chance to write the details of June 1-3, the following is Captain Charles Coit's official report:

GENERAL: I have the honor to forward the following report of the operations of my command since June 1, 1864:

At 6 a.m. June 1 we left our bivouac, 12 miles from White House Landing, Va., marching with the column toward New Castle, Va. During the afternoon we halted near the enemy's lines, Cold Harbor. After resting about an hour, we formed in line of battle, the left of the brigade resting on the right of the Sixth Corps, our position being between the Tenth New Hampshire Volunteer on the right and the One hundred and eighteenth New York Volunteers on the left. In this line we moved forward to the support of the advanced line, halting 100 paces in the rear of that line. About 7 p.m. the advanced line having been withdrawn to the right, we advanced, crossing an open field in our front, and moved into the woods beyond, where we constructed temporary breast-works, and, having ascertained through scouts sent out that the pickets of the brigade to the right and left of us did not connect, by direction of Captain Clark, assistant adjutant-general, pickets from our right were posted to cover our front.

Our loss during that day was 2 killed and 4 wounded. Before daylight the next day, June 2, we were ordered to relieve the Fortieth Massachusetts Volunteers, who were occupying the front lines to our right, forming on the left of New Hampshire Volunteers. During the day, under a heavy fire, we completed a breast-work which had been commenced on this line within 200 yards of the enemy's works. Our loss this day was 1 killed and 6 wounded.

> CHAS. M. COIT,
> Captain, Commanding Eighth Connecticut Volunteers[2]

A simple line by Coit just stating the facts, "Our loss this day was 1 killed and 6 wounded." All things considered during the long, bloody Civil War, just one killed would be considered very fortunate. Unfortunately, Albion Brooks was that single statistic.

According to Brooks' family history, Albion was in one of the forward rifle pits on the morning of June 2, taking fire from four Mississippi regiments a relatively short distance away. Uncomfortable from laying low in the same position for so long, he raised up just a little to stretch, when a bullet tore into him. According to the official Casualty Sheet, he was "Wounded in groin"—the bullet coming in the left side of his body and exiting just above his right hip.

Albion must have known. In that instant it took that piece of hot lead to tear completely through his body, he must have known.

Albion Brooks' brief life had come to an end.

---

[2] *Numbers 259. Report of Captain Charles M. Coit, Eighth Connecticut Infantry, of operations June 1-9. HDQRS. EIGHTH REGIMENT CONNECTICUT VOLUNTEERS. Cold Harbor, Va., June 11, 1864.*

22
The Death of Albion Brooks

Early on the morning of June 2, 1864, Albion Brooks lay mortally wounded in a forward rifle pit under enemy fire at Cold Harbor, Virginia. There are no known accounts describing how Albion was carried back across the battlefield, most likely over Beulah Church Road, to the field hospital at the church, nor is it known how long it took to extract him from the front lines under fire.

At the start of this book was the heart-wrenching letter Chaplain Moses Smith wrote to Reverend Thompson. The letter is almost identical to the one the Chaplain wrote to Emily and Clayton, but this one had more details. It was delivered to Emily and Clayton by a friend of Albion's. One can only imagine the shock the news of Albion's death brought, and "What pain in the hearts of those we love in our New England Homes."

Emily had loved him as a brother, and when orphaned, cared for him and loved him like her own son. She had fed him, clothed him, educated him, protected him from a harsh world when he would otherwise have been alone. War leaves one powerless to protect their loved ones, and for all of Emily's fervent prayers, she could not protect Albion. She could not stop that Mississippi soldier's .58 caliber bullet, composed of 1.14 ounces of lead, from ripping apart blood vessels, organs, and muscles inside of her smart, kind, affectionate little brother. And she could not be there to hold his hand, soothe his pain, and bid him farewell.

18th Army Corps Hospital on the field June 4, 1864

Mr. S. C. Kingman,--Dear Sir:--In an engagement near Cold Harbor, June 2d, your dear friend and brother, Albion D. Brooks was severely wounded. As his Chaplain, I was happy to be with him. The ball, (a bullet) struck him in the abdomen, on the left side, and passed through, coming out above the hip. It was supposed the wound was mortal, but we knew it would be for his comfort to do all possible.

He seemed to rally during the day, (he was wounded in the morning) rested well at night, and yesterday morning thought he felt better. I was with him much of the time. I left him during a part of the afternoon to visit the regiment which was still in the front and on returning found him sinking. About a quarter before nine o'clock last evening, (June 3d) he quietly breathed his last.

He was perfectly conscious to the end. He spoke of his wound several times to me as we were together, but never with any anxiety. He said that God's will was right, and he could trust all to him. He seemed perfectly resigned, desiring, if permitted, to see his friends and labor for God, but leaving all for God to determine.

A little before his death he said, "I am going," and then slowly added, "Lo, I am with you always, even unto the end," and soon closed his eyes and breathed more and more slowly until he ceased. He was very much appreciated and beloved by all the company, of which he was Orderly Sergeant. The officers and men send their sincere and truest sympathy to all his friends.

Probably no man in the regiment has been more ready to help me in my work, or more efficient from my first entrance upon it in the regiment. He recited to me in Latin and Greek, last spring, before the commencement of his active campaign, and often expressed the hope, that he should be allowed to serve his Master in active life. We regret his loss to the army, and to the world.

To you, we cannot add to the knowledge of his worth. May you be comforted in the assurance that God's will is best, and that you may hope in confidence that he is only "gone before." He is early released from earth to dwell with God.

We have buried him here by this hospital, marked his head board distinctly so that it can be readily found, if any friend should wish to visit it.

We are about 3 miles from Gaines Mills, on the direct road from old church to Meadow Bridge, some 10 miles from the White House.

I am in the midst of many wounded and dying, and can write no more.

Respectfully yours,
Moses Smith.
Chaplain 8th CV

How many times I have replayed this scene in my mind—Albion surrounded by his friends and Chaplain Smith, amongst a sea of "many wounded and dying" after the horrific losses of June 3, when over 6,000 Union soldiers fell in the span of an hour. Looking pale, in pain, yet clinging to his faith that he was in God's hands, knowing that only moments of his young life were left, finding the strength to say, "I am going." Then, with his last breaths whispering the phrase he used over and over in his writings, "Lo, I am with you always, even unto the end."

Albion did not cry out, "Why me?" He did not say that God had abandoned him. He did not lose his faith when death was imminent. He died as he lived, true to his beliefs. As the following relates, Albion Brook's faith "manifested a power controlling his heart and life."

Alfred Waud sketch of "June 2nd Positions in Cold Harbor, rifle pits."

Connecticut War Record
July 1864
Camp of the 8th Regiment, Conn. Vols.
Chesterfield Co., VA., June 20, 1864

After discussing all the losses suffered by the regiment during the previous three weeks, the correspondent wrote the following, and appears to have been present at Albion's death:

Of these last I must say a few words respecting one, whose loss is felt by us all. I refer to Albion D. Brooks, Orderly Sergeant of Company A. In early life he gave himself to Jesus Christ, and hoped to become a minister of His Gospel. At the commencement of this war, he was studying to prepare for that work. But the call of his country seemed to him the call of God. Like many a noble youth he left the school for the camp—Classics for the Tactics and Manual of Arms.

Unlike too many in our army, he did not leave his piety at home. He entered the army to serve God, and he did serve God. In the tent, on the march, in the trenches, in the fight, in the hour of death, he manifested a power controlling his heart and life.

We think that he only found his congregation and was preaching in the army sooner than he would have entered the pulpit, if he had remained at home. When the regiment reenlisted, Brooks was prompt to enroll himself among the veterans; but even then he did not relinquish the hope of earlier days, but still improved his leisure hours in camp, pursuing Latin and Greek.

He was wounded on the morning of June 2d, and died on the evening of 3d. He suffered severely, and keenly felt the disappointment of life cut short, but often said, "God's will be done." Once the messenger was evidently near, he looked up to us who stood around him and calmly said, "I am going." Then closing his eyes he slowly repeated, "Lo, I am with you always, even onto the end." Thus he left us; and we felt that even amid the roar of cannon and the groans of the dying it is good for the Christian to die.

"He has fought the good fight, he has kept the faith."

It was difficult to read that "He suffered severely, and keenly felt the disappointment of life cut short." After a tumultuous early life of loss and heartache, never having a stable homelife for very long, and two and a half years enduring the cruelty of war—the last month of which had been a constant strain, physically and mentally—he was not even given a quick, painless death.

From Captain William Hawley, Head Quarters, 3rd Brigade, 2nd Division, 2nd Army Corps, 14th Connecticut Regiment, to Reverend Thompson, June 7, 1864:

>...*My chief reason for writing today is to communicate to you the sad news of <u>Albion</u> <u>Brooks</u> death - Learning that the 8th Conn. was in the 18th Corps. which joined the Army of the Potomac recently, I rode almost a mile & a half this morning to visit Albion & Capt. Hoyt - I found that poor Albion had met a soldiers death, that I should see him no more on Earth again - He was shot through the body on the 2d of June & died on the 3rd - Capt. Hoyt, who is in the Brigade Staff, expresses the greatest regret at the loss of Albion, he had the entire charge of Capt. H's Co. and was acknowledged to be the best orderly in the regiment, always prompt and faithful in the discharge of his duties and a brave and gallant soldier - He had been recommended for promotion, and if he had lived would probably soon have obtained a Lieutenants Commission - He was one of the few, who though under so much of the evil influence of army life, did not fall into <u>one</u> bad habit of the army - On the other hand his Captain told me he was a <u>better</u> boy than when he left home - His life is an example of a Christian patriot that is truly noble - Not many have rendered such faithful service to their country as a soldier as he, not many Christians have been so devoted & true to God, as this noble boy has been. Under all the trying circumstances of his life as a soldier - It is sweet to know that he is now far from all the sounds of war & at peace with the Savior, whom he loved so well...*

Albion did not have the luxury of a funeral and probably nothing more than a blanket in which to wrap his body, if even that. His official records in the National Archives indicates what he was wearing when he was buried—including the boots he had custom ordered from Clayton and Emily. At least his body was spared the indignity of being stripped of clothing and shoes, and his belongings stolen, as happened to so many soldiers did who died on the battlefield.

Inventory of the effects of Albion D. Brooks 1st Sergt. Late a member of Captain Henry M. Hoyt's Company A of the Eighth Regiment of Connecticut Volunteers…he died in Hospital, at Near Cold Harbor VA on the 3rd day of June 1864 by reason of Wounds received in Action June 2nd 1864.

INVENTORY

Flannel sack coat 1
Pairs trousers 1
Pairs flannel drawers 1
Flannel shirts 1
Pairs boots 1
Pairs socks 1

I CERTIFY ON HONOR, that the above inventory comprises all the effects of 1st Sergt. Albion D. Brooks, deceased, and that He was buried with his effects.

Lieut. Morgan, Commanding the Company
STATION: Bermuda Hundred
DATE: June 18th 1864

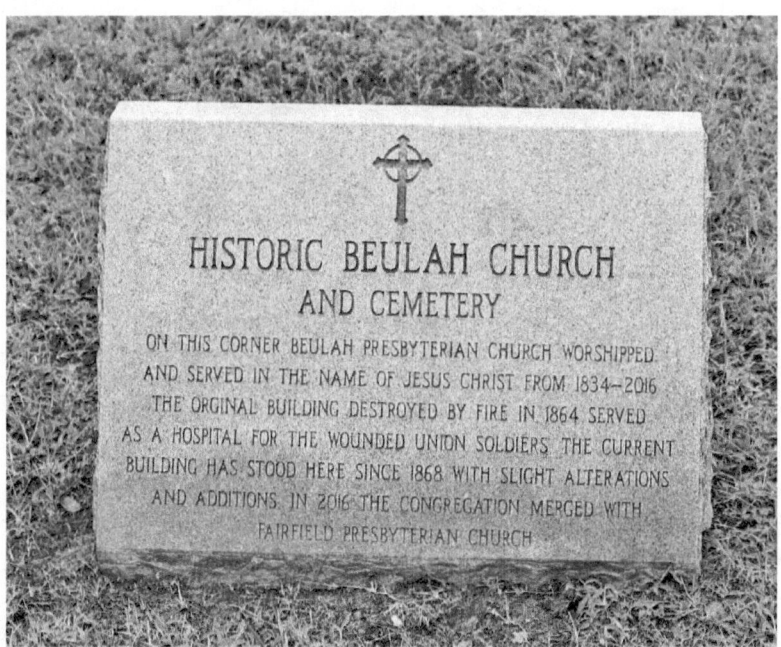

A monument at Beulah Church in Cold Harbor which indicates that this was the site of a Union field hospital. This is most likely where Albion died.

A section of another Alfred Waud sketch from Cold Harbor. Note the "Stretchers, men going to the hospital."

The face of death is the same wherever it occurs. In this Matthew Brady commissioned photo at Antietam, an unburied Confederate is next to a fresh Union grave. A crudely cut board has the soldier's initials and regiment. Albion would have had something similar.

23
In Pursuit of My Dead Brother

One can only imagine the shock and grief amongst Albion's family and friends at the news of his death, but it must also have propelled them to take quick action to recover his body and bring him home. Albion's brother, William Brooks, was ready within a few days to travel to Cold Harbor. No doubt Emily also wanted to go, but with four young daughters to look after—one of which was just two months old, Clayton was the wiser choice to accompany William, or so it seemed.

The following are just five of the known diary entries of William Brooks:

June 10, 1864, Friday

Left Bridgeport on Friday, the 10th of June. Called on Mr. Thompson - former pastor of my brother, Albion. He was much affected to hear of the death of my brother. He gave me and Clayton letters of introduction to Mr. Stewart. Brother Clayton concluded not to go any farther and at the depot left me. I felt somewhat sad – alone - in pursuit of my dead brother. I reached Philadelphia at 9:30 and took a lodging at the Chestnut House.

In March of 1862, Rev. Thompson had left the South Church in Bridgeport to become the pastor of the 21st Street Dutch Reformed Church in Manhattan. That month he also joined the New England Soldiers' Relief Association at 104 Broadway, where he tirelessly cared for the wounded and dying throughout the remainder of the war. William and Clayton no doubt traveled from Bridgeport to New York on June 10 and met with Rev. Thompson there.

William states that Rev. Thompson "was much affected to hear of the death of my brother," yet it isn't clear if this was the first he had heard about Albion's death, or whether he had already received the letters from Chaplain Moses Smith. As the plan was for William and Clayton to continue to Washington, D.C., "the letters of introduction to Mr. Stewart" must have been for someone who could help in the recovery of Albion's body.

I felt shock and heartbreak as I read William's following lines:

Brother Clayton concluded not to go any farther and at the depot left me. I felt somewhat sad – alone - in pursuit of my dead brother.

In this time of deep grief, when William could have used a helping hand and a friendly face, why on earth would Clayton abandon him at the depot? Clearly, William did not expect it, and it was a decidedly emotional blow to his already low spirits. He would now have to try to locate Albion's body in a war zone, get it exhumed, and arrange for its transportation back home—alone.

June 11, 1864, Saturday

Saw Mr. Boardman and obtained Commission to come on and remain 2 weeks. Left Philadelphia at (?) reached Washington at 6:30 P.M. Met a Mrs. (?) and little daughter going to visit husband and father. Aided them as much as I was able. Went up to Harewood Hospital with them – then bidding them goodbye left them.

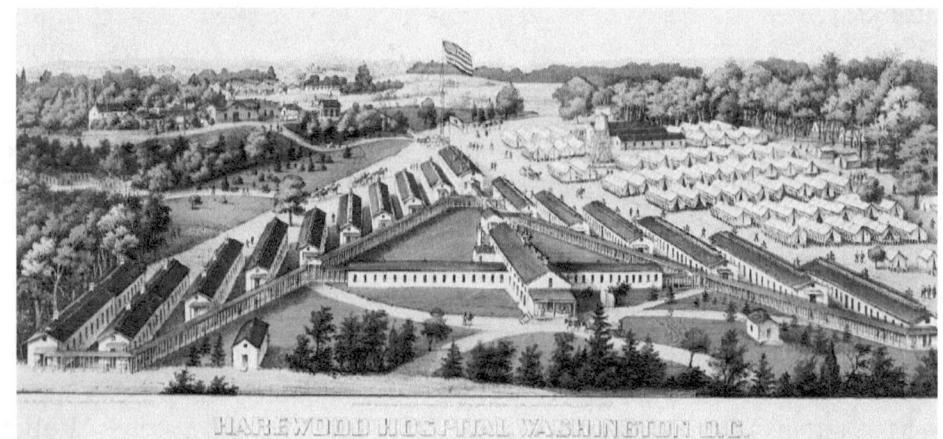

Harewood Hospital was specifically built as a pavilion-style hospital to care for the large numbers of wounded. 1864 lithograph by Charles Magnus.

As the Cold Harbor campaign was still active, it may not have been possible to travel any further than Washington, D.C. at this point. Even if it was possible, it was certainly not prudent. It is no surprise that William went out of his way to help the woman and her daughter to visit her husband, as it's exactly what Emily or Albion would have done, as compassion ran deep in the Brooks family.

June 17, 1864, Friday

Felt poorly in morning - trouble in bowels. Went to St. Paul's Congregational Church, distributed papers, tracts, etc. No cases of special interest. One poor fellow died. I do not know whether he had any hope in Christ. He was conscious and they said out of his head and so I had no chance to know of his Spiritual Condition. In the P.M. went to the Baptist Church Hospital - some low cases - one or two dangerous. In the evening went to the Soldier's Rest. Had a very pleasant time. Found a number of Maine boys from Heavy artillery and Cavalry.

One man I found from Massachusetts who was seeking an ear. He had been a very wicked man - but his wife a pious Godly woman. She had prayed for him - but he had not given heed to her entreaties. When he was at home on his thirty day Furlough he drank and treated his wife harshly - telling her to go away and not pray where he could hear her. One night he came home a little tight. He said, "I told my wife that I did not want her praying about me. I had not long been in bed before she came and kneeling down commenced praying - at first to herself, but soon out loud."

"At first," he said, "I was angry. Soon I was forced to get up and leave the woman. I could not help thinking what a wicked wretch I was. But now I want to go home and kneel down and pray with her. I don't know what she would do."

Thus after 9 years of prayer for her husband, she is answered, "Ye shall reap in one season if ye faint not."[1]

Went into a colored church.

June 18, 1864, Saturday

The day has been a very pleasant day, somewhat cooler than yesterday. Visited my hospitals - found the patients about the same - nothing of particular interest. Ate some ice cream - not very good.

The headline here: Ice cream on a hot summer's day in Washington, D.C.—no easy feat without electric refrigeration. Actually, ice cream goes way back in Washington circles, and with George Washington himself, who purchased an ice cream maker in May of 1784 for Mount Vernon. Jacob Fussell began manufacturing ice cream in Pennsylvania in the 1850s, and opened an ice cream factory in Washington, D.C. in 1856. Ice cream was given to hospitalized Union soldiers during the Civil War, and according to Walt Whitman, it was the first time many of them had tasted the cold, sweet treat we all now take for granted. Unfortunately for William, the ice cream he ate was "not very good."

The following is his last known diary entry from this time period, and regrettably no further mention of the search for Albion's body is made. There is some evidence that William continued to Cold Harbor sometime after his two weeks in Washington (see next chapter). If so, he was unsuccessful in locating his brother's grave. It is not known if there were subsequent unsuccessful attempts in 1864 or early 1865 by William or other family members or friends. Regrettably, Albion would have to wait to finally go home.

---

[1] Galatians 6:9, "And let us not be weary in well-doing: for in due season we shall reap, if we faint not."

William begins the diary entry with favorably describing a "Colored Hospital," and then some preaching at a few locations with less than enthusiastic attendees.

June 19, 1864, Sunday

After eating breakfast went with Brother Buck and distributed papers to the prisoners in two prisons, then to Colored Hospital. Found in good shape - patients doing well and making fine looking soldiers. Saw men learning to write and read and reading etc. Their order was good and they presented a better appearance than most any hospital I was ever in.

At one P.M. Preached in jail opposite our rooms, then assisted Brother Leas at the Baptist Church. Not very good attention here, - next at the Methodist Church. Few present. I spoke from "Behold I stand etc." Then to Washington Hall, had two short services, Brother Leas one and I the other. Returned and Brother Leas left for the Front via Washington. Am intending to go to King Street Hospital though my head aches and I feel about sick.

At the end of that diary entry, William then records the words of a dying soldier, Jacob Wentworth. It is one of the most poignant things I ever read, and brings tears to my eyes with every reading.

"I willingly lay down my life for the life of the Nation"

Jacob Wentworth of New Milford, Litchfield County, Connecticut, was mustered into service with the 19th Connecticut Infantry on August 11, 1862, at the age of 39. He left behind a wife, Ann, brothers, sisters, and his father.

The 19th CT Infantry became the 2nd CT Heavy Artillery on November 23, 1863, and served in the defenses of Washington, D.C. It was a relatively easy and safe assignment—one which brought ridicule from battle-tested soldiers in the field—but that was to change dramatically in May of 1864, when General Grant needed infantry soldiers to replace his heavy losses. Several artillery units around Washington, D.C. were plucked from their comfortable forts and sent into action. The 2nd CT Heavy Artillery was one of them, and was transferred to the 6th Corps of the Army of the Potomac, where it quickly saw service in Grant's Overland Campaign.

The bloodiest day that the 2nd CT HA experienced was June 1, 1864, at Cold Harbor, VA, when the regiment led the charge against the Confederate's line near the Cold Harbor Road, manned by a North

Carolina brigade. The Union forces broke the line, but a subsequent counterattack drove them back.

Lewis Bissell of the 2nd CT HA wrote in a letter to his father on June 2, 1864:

The men began to fall and oh! The storm of leaden rain that poured into us cannot be described. The roar of musketry was terrible, but not so awful as the cries of the wounded.[2]

Monument to the 2nd CT HA at Cold Harbor.

No ground was gained, and the losses were horrific—323 casualties in about an hour, which was an estimated 2% of the entire male population of Litchfield County, Connecticut! Among those casualties was Jacob Wentworth, who received a serious leg wound and was brought to a hospital in Alexandria, Virginia. On June 19, 1864, Albion's brother, William, who was visiting the wounded, recorded Wentworth's words in his diary.

Words of a Dying Soldier to His Wife, and Church and Friends
June 19, 1864 Sunday

I enlisted in the service of my imperiled country because I love it and wished to do my duty in serving it. As a result of my enlistment, I have been

---

[2] *The Civil War Letters of Lewis Bissell: History and Literature Curriculum,* Olcott, Mark; Lear, David, The Field School Educational Foundation Press,1981, p. 245-246

mortally wounded at the battle of Cold Harbor on the 1st day of June, and since then I have been a great sufferer.

Yet, I do not regret that I enlisted to fight the battles of my country. I willingly lay down my life to save the life of the Nation. Let my country survive the onsets of this wicked Rebellion—though I suffer and go from my home and friends to a premature grave.

To the Church of my choice and Christian friends in general, let me speak a word.

Be true to your Country and your Country's God. Stand by the Constitution. Study and obey God's word. Sustain the institutions of the Church. Attend the preaching of the word, the social meetings, family and social prayer. Maintain deep and personal piety. Be active in your endeavors to train your children for God, to win souls—to gain hearers.

But I must speak once more to her whose fortunes have been linked with my own, and who is dear to my heart—but whom I am not to see again.

My Affectionate Wife—all your fond and cherished hopes of my recovery have been cut off. I am to leave you in lonely widowhood to battle the ills of life, husbandless and alone—nay, not alone, for He whom you serve and who has promised to be the widow's God, will be with you. Live near to Him. Cast all your cares upon Him, for He careth for you. Let the loss of your husband lead you to cling closer to Jesus. That He will bear your burdens, soothe your sorrows and supply your wants. He will never leave or forsake you.

I must now bid my wife, my father, my brothers, my sisters, and all my relatives and neighbors an affectionate and final farewell.

My peace is made with God. I am resigned to His will. I have a strong bright hope of heaven and wait with patience for Jesus to take me home to rest.

Jacob Wentworth died the following day.[3]

I continued reading Lewis Bissell's letters regarding Cold Harbor, and two pages later, my blood ran cold when I saw the following:

"The next morning I helped carry Brooks off in a blanket."

Could he possibly mean Albion Brooks, who was wounded that morning of June 2? What were the chances? There must be other Brooks in the 2nd CT HA, and how would he know anyone in the 8th CT?

Further reading brought up some tantalizing connections. One of Lewis Bissell's tentmates was Will Plumb, brother of Sergeant Seth Plumb of the 8th CT. Bissell wrote that Seth Plumb came to visit them on June 4,

---

[3] Wentworth is buried in the Alexandria National Cemetery, Section A, Grave 2253.

and he also makes several references to the 8th CT, including the fact that they were only camped about half a mile away at one time. So, there is a slight possibility that he knew Albion Brooks.

The search of the entire roster of the 2nd Connecticut Heavy Artillery revealed that no one had the first or last name of Brooks. However, Bissell's own Company A had Andrew Brooker, who during the charge of June 1 was wounded by shrapnel in both legs and several other places in his body. Unable to retrieve their wounded due to heavy fire, Brooker lay on the battlefield all night and wasn't carried off until the next day. He died June 6.

So here are the possibilities:
1. Bissell's nickname for Andrew Brooker was "Brooks."
2. Bissell made a typo and meant to write that he "helped carry Brooker off in a blanket."
3. Whoever transcribed the letters[4] mistakenly wrote Brooks, although two pages later correctly wrote Andrew Brooker in Bissell's casualty list.
4. Admittedly, this is the least likely, but while helping carry the wounded on the morning of June 2, 1864, in addition to members of the 2nd CT HA, he also helped carry Albion Brooks, whom he knew through his connections with the 8th CT.

I have often wondered how a seriously wounded Albion was removed from the rifle pit, under fire, and brought to the field hospital. Bissell's letters offer a tantalizing possibility, but without the original letters, it is one I can't possibly prove—and perhaps not even then. I tend to think Bissell had his hands full with the 2nd Connecticut's dead and wounded, but just maybe…

In any event, Bissell's vivid descriptions of the awful moans of the wounded, with no water to give them, no stretchers to carry them, and no coffins in which to bury them, paints a terrible picture of the morning of June 2, 1864—and the real slaughter didn't occur until the next day.

At the very least, we can surmise it was a dangerous and dreadful job retrieving the horribly wounded men from the battlefield under fire. It was also an excruciating journey for those wounded to be jostled around on a

---

[4] There is some indication that Bissell's son, Carl, transcribed at least some the letters. There is also a mention that part of the grant Olcott received was used to transcribe the letters. I have tried contacting descendants in an attempt to locate the original letters to see them for myself, but so far have found them either deceased or with disconnected phone numbers.

stretcher—if one could be found—or worse, in a blanket, over uneven terrain, only to be dropped at an overcrowded and understaffed field hospital, with little chance of finding any relief from their incomprehensible pain and suffering.

Then, if your suffering mercifully ended and you were placed in a soldier's grave, it was a hastily dug hole with no coffin and little ceremony.

I suspect that our modern, sheltered minds cannot truly comprehend what transpired at Cold Harbor, or indeed at any battlefield past or present. We can only rely on the precious few written words of those who were there, and the long rows of grave stones that punctuate their stories.

Cold Harbor National Cemetery
LOC HALS VA-4-4

24
Albion Goes Home

Over the long course of my research, I have had some wonderful conversations with National Park Rangers who have always provided valuable knowledge. One phone conversation with a ranger at Cold Harbor—who was amazed at the wealth of information I had found in the form of Albion's letters and diaries—said it was unlikely that Albion's body would have been located and transported all the way back to Maine after the war. He asked if I had proof that it had been found and moved, and was I certain that the grave stone in Kingfield was not simply a memorial, with no body beneath it? Wooden grave markers were subject to the elements, and rain and snow could quickly rot the wood or make the writing on it illegible.

At the time, the only "proof" I had was that I knew it in my heart, and my only certainty was that I could feel it in my bones—neither of which, unfortunately, are valid citations. I think many historians have been there and done that—knowing with every fiber of their being after years of research that something was true, but lacking that one document or artifact to validate it.

Within minutes of that phone call, I was on the phone with the Town Hall in Kingfield, Maine, trying to find out where the burial records were for the Riverside Cemetery. Much to my dismay, it appeared that no one knew where they might be, or if they even still existed. Newspaper searches in both Connecticut and Maine yielded no results for the poignant story of a brave Connecticut soldier's remains being returned to his Maine hometown by his loving family. I was beginning to lose hope when I decided to go through the photos I had previously taken of the material in the Connecticut Museum of Culture and History collection.

It turned out that a very important letter was right under my nose, or at least on my computer hard drive. While it wasn't exactly the smoking gun of evidence, it strongly supported that feeling in my heart and bones that Albion's remains had indeed been found and retrieved:

Office Post Commissary, Richmond, Va., August 10, 1865

Mr. S.C. Kingman
Dear Sir,
Having learned of the desire of many of the friends of the late O. S[1]. Albion D. Brooks, Co. A, 8th Conn. Vet. Vols and being well informed of

---

[1] Orderly Sergeant. Documents always refer to Albion as 1st Sergeant.

the circumstances connected with his death and burial, I take the opportunity of giving you such information as will lead you to the recovery of his remains if you desire.

I am a member of the same "Co." but have been some time on detached service, and knew nothing at the time his brother was inquiring to learn of him, and being one of three who buried his remains with a head board at his grave which remains in the same condition as when I left them, for I have visited the spot on two different occasions this summer.

Should you, sir, propose to come on, or send for them, I will render all assistance in my power. You will find me at the Post Commissary on 7th Street, with Capt. D. D. Mott, Richmond, Va.

Remember me with kindness to Capt. H. M. Hoyt.

Very respectfully
Your obedient servant
Alfred Howes

This was one of those "wow moments" for which every researcher dreams. Granted, it was not an exhumation or transportation document, but what a wealth of information it provided, and by "one of three who buried him," and may have been one of the friends who stood by him as he died!

- Alfred writes that he "knew nothing at the time his brother was inquiring to learn of him," which certainly implies that William Brooks was in Cold Harbor asking for information to help locate his brother. Of course, the enquiry could have been by letter, but in my opinion, William was there in person, as were "many of the friends" also trying to locate Albion's grave.
- Alfred also informs Clayton that Albion's "head board at his grave which remains in the same condition as when I left them, for I have visited the spot on two different occasions this summer." The wooden head board had not deteriorated in the 14 months since it was placed there, and was still quite legible. And, Alfred Howes was certain of this as he had personally visited Albion's grave not once, but twice, and just recently that summer.

These were the kinds of friends Albion had, friends who cared enough about him, even in death, to visit his grave, and take the time to write to his family and offer any assistance necessary to aid in recovering his remains.

Naturally, I wanted to know more about Albion's friend, Alfred Timothy Howes. He was born in Hawley, Massachusetts in 1832, one of 12 children! The 1889 *Record of Service of Connecticut Men* curiously lists Howes as having enlisted in Montgomery, Mississippi on September 20, 1861. As of yet, I do not know how or why a Massachusetts man enlisted in Mississippi and ended up in a Connecticut regiment.

Howes appears to have survived the war without any notable wounds. In 1866, in Adams, Massachusetts, he married Harriet Melvina Roys (1833-1911). They had two daughters, a son (who died in infancy) and adopted another daughter. The 1870 census finds Howes in Newfield, New Jersey, working as a carpenter. He lived to the ripe old age of 91, dying on May 5, 1923, and is buried in the Rose Hill Cemetery in Newfield.

Back to Albion—further research revealed this important record of Albion's burial in Kingfield, although the regiment is wrong, and maddeningly there is no date of burial. I asked the Kingfield Historical Society about this, and was delighted to find that the person to whom I spoke, knew local historian B. Moore, and said she had done very good work going through the original burial records for the area in the 1980s and created a new index.

So, in 1986, at least, the original burial records did exist for the Riverside Cemetery. While there is no date of burial, a record would not have been created if an actual burial had not taken place. That was welcome news!

Accession #	5027				
Surname	First	Middle		Maiden	
BROOKS	Albion	D.			
Born Day, Month, Year	Died: Day, Month, Year	Age Year Mo. Day		Military Service	
	3 Jun 1864	21		Sgt. 1st Me. Co. G	
Name of Cemetery	Street or Route	Town		County	
Riverside		Kingfield		Fra	

NAME	BORN	DIED	AGE Yr. Mo. Dys.
died at Cold Harbor, Va., Civil War			

Submitted By	Date	Source of Information:
	Jun 1986	B. Moore

There was also this record online[2], which again, unfortunately has no date of burial.

Last Name	First	Middle Init.	Address		Serial No.
rooks	Albion	D	Kingfield, Me. (Franklin County)		
Date of Birth	At			War	
1843				Civil	
Date of Death	At		Cause		
June 3, 1864		Cold Harbor, Va.			
Date of Burial	Cemetery			Section No.	Lot No.
	Old Village			B	52
Grave No.	Book No.	Page No.	Next of Kin		
Date of Enlistment	At		Date of Discharge		Branch of Service
Rank		Type of Marker or Stone			
		Upright stone. Flag.			
War Record					
Additional Comments					
Source: No A. G. O. Rec. in Me.					

Finally, in Agnes Thompson's unpublished family history, *A Maine Family*, I found the following on the last page regarding Albion:

After the long war was over, Clayton and Emily went to the spot where he was buried. They had his body taken "down East" to Maine where he lies buried beside his father in Kingfield, Maine.

Game, set, match. Both Clayton and Emily went to Cold Harbor, where presumably Alfred Howes directed them—either in person or with explicit directions—to Albion's grave. What a moment that must have been for Emily, who had been both a sister and mother to him, seeing his name on a piece of wood over a partially-sunken mound of dirt, close to where he had suffered for a day and a half, and then "quietly breathed his last." I hope Emily was not present as Albion's bones and tattered clothing were dug out of the ground, and she never saw the boots in which he was buried—the same boots she had custom made for him.

Whatever the somber and gruesome details of the exhumation may have been, the important thing is that, due to the care of his fellow soldiers, and the love of his family, Albion was finally brought home.

---

[2] Maine.gov, Veterans Cemetery Records, 1676-1918, from the Adjutant General's Office Records in Maine.

25
If I Had a Time Machine

Who can forget the classic 1960 science fiction film *The Time Machine*, based on the brilliant H.G. Welles' 1895 book? And what red-blooded, post-apocalyptic woman wouldn't want handsome actor Rod Taylor time traveling into her backyard?

Welles' time machine, which looked like a steampunk Santa's sleigh on steroids, had a dial to tune in the date to which you wanted to go, and it would take you there in resplendent Victorian style. Of course, rushing headlong into an uncertain future is nothing short of terrifying and dangerous—just ask any Morlock—and perhaps heading into the past is also fraught with unforeseen dangers, but at least there is some assurance that much of past history is documented, and can give the time travelers some framework in which to navigate.

So, what would I do if I had a time machine? That would take another book to fully explore, but basically, I would visit the building of the ancient sites of Gobekli Tepe, Stonehenge, and the Great Pyramid, chat with Chaucer and Shakespeare, attend concerts by Bach, Mozart, and Beethoven, and Benny Goodman at Carnegie Hall in 1936, and a thousand other things.

If I had a time machine, I would also turn the dial back to around September-October of 1861. I would make my way to Bridgeport, Connecticut and find out where Samuel Clayton Kingman lived and knock on his door. I would explain that I had important business with his brother-in-law, Albion Brooks.

What a moment that would be, to meet Albion in person! To hear his voice! Once I recovered from what would undoubtedly be a shock—or maybe I would have gotten over that shock factor having already met Chaucer and Shakespeare—I would get down to the nature of my business, because this was not a journey in which to have a pleasant conversation; this was urgent, life or death business.

I would tell Albion enough about his life and family to prove that I knew a great deal about him. I would assure him that I admired his patriotism and desire to serve his country, and his deep faith that resigned him to whatever fate might befall him if he enlisted.

Then, in no uncertain terms, I would tell Albion, "DO NOT ENLIST!" I would bluntly tell him that he would be killed if he enlisted and that it would not be the best thing for him—obviously—or his future grieving family and friends.

I would tell him that someone of his good nature and abilities would better serve the world by *being alive* in it, and doing good for countless people for decades to come.

I would tell him there was a Mary B. somewhere in Connecticut whom he should marry and raise a bunch of wonderful children. He should become a clergyman, or an author, or a teacher, or all of the above, to educate, inspire, comfort, and uplift parishioners, students, and everyone around him. He could be a significant force for good in the world, and that if he enlisted, he would go to an early grave in the ground of a brutal—and ultimately senseless—battlefield.

Albion would be stunned. He would be confused. He would struggle to comprehend what was going on with this strange woman who came out of nowhere and seemed to know everything about him and his entire family. He might think I was an angel of God come to save him. He might even think the Devil himself sent me to trick him. He might think and feel countless things, but would he listen?

Would he believe that the best course of action was to stay at home or go to Europe and live the life for which he studied and dreamt of living, and that it was the best way to honor God? Or, would he steadfastly maintain that he had a duty to his country, and if he had to sacrifice his life, so be it, as it was all part of God's plan. Or, would he have been drafted anyway, and still suffered the same fate?

I don't know, but I would give it my best shot to dissuade him, because I believe with all my heart that the loss of Albion Brooks was a particularly tragic loss to the world, even in a war where so many young men became casualties. Perhaps the few who read this book will agree, and be inspired by Albion's story and do some act of kindness in his memory.

However, even so, it will all pale in comparison to what he could have accomplished in life with the power of his words and the force of his heart and faith.

Perhaps I am biased—maybe just a little bit—but then, what should one expect after devoting more than 30 years to the pursuit and study of a man who died about a century before I was born? Many people have told me there is some powerful karmic connection behind it all. Maybe, but maybe the qualities of the man alone were enough to pull me down those decades-long rabbit holes.

Albion was smart. He was funny. He was brave, honest, compassionate, trustworthy, and yes, even kind of handsome. Albion's faith was unshakable even to his dying breath. Everyone loved him and spoke highly of him.

He had a difficult and tumultuous childhood, constantly moving, never knowing his father, losing his mother, living in poverty, taken in by his poor, but loving, sister, but rather than making him embittered and cold toward the world, he considered himself blessed and grateful for what he did have.

Then, just as he finally had a stable and loving home in Bridgeport, the Civil War broke out and he suffered countless hardships and horrors in the army, and in the end, made the ultimate sacrifice due to a rebel bullet tearing through his body, lingering in terrible pain for 36 hours before "quietly breathing his last."

How does Albion's story *not* pull on your heartstrings? How does this young man *not* impress himself on your heart, mind, and soul? How do you *not* want to jump into a time machine and travel back to the fall of 1861 and shout in Albion's face, "DO NOT ENLIST!"

Of course, H.G. Welles' imagination is not reality. There are no time machines—but I still suspect there are Morlocks lurking somewhere—and we can't alter the past. However, we can most definitely influence the present to improve the future, and hopefully, the story of Albion Brooks, and the obsessed author who doggedly pursued history, can do just that in some small way.

Thirty years ago, I read a few words about a forgotten Civil War soldier, and from that moment I felt the great weight of an obligation and responsibility to tell his story. It was not on the same scale as the call of duty to God and country to which Albion so nobly gave his life, but it was a call, nonetheless. And one to which I devoted more years of my life than Albion lived.

The journey has been a mixture of sadness and joy. To immerse yourself into another's thoughts and feelings, losses and struggles, hopes and fears, is to lose part of yourself. Being Albion's biographer was a unique form of self-inflicted torture, which was not the first time I did this to myself, and god help me, it may not be the last biography I write, although I doubt I have another 30-year run left in me!

Would I do it all again? In an historical heartbeat! For all the time, effort, and expense of this journey, like Albion, I feel blessed. It was an honor to get to know him, and a privilege to tell his story. I feel a great sense of contentment—and no small relief—that this project is complete. Which is not to say I'm not still hoping for more letters and diaries to turn up, but the task I set upon myself long ago is now printed and bound and in your hands.

One final thought—had Albion survived the war, became a clergyman, had a family, and lived a quiet, but ordinary life, would I still have written this book? Could it be, that with his early, tragic death, he set into motion something that will have an even greater and more widespread influence?

Albion would simply say it was all part of God's plan, and after all, who am I to argue with that?

The End

Appendix A

Other Soldiers

The Thompson Collection included seven letters to Samuel Clayton Kingman from soldiers in the field from November 1861 to July 1864. I personally found it impossible to *not* include these previously unknown letters, from basically forgotten soldiers. All of these letters deserve the light of day to tell the stories of their lives and locations, and perhaps help researchers.

Lt. Daniel J. West, 6th CT

In April of 1861, Daniel J. West of Bridgeport, CT, enlisted in the Union Army, becoming Sergeant of Company H of the 1st Connecticut Regiment V.I. for a term of 3 months. Mustered out at the end of July, he quickly re-enlisted in August of 1861, this time for a term of 3 years, becoming 1st Lieutenant of Company I of the 6th CT Regiment V.I.

West was wounded in the leg[1] on October 22, 1862 at Pocotaligo, South Carolina—a failed Union attempt to destroy railroad tracks and bridges on the Charleston-Savannah line. On July 18, 1863, he was wounded again and captured at Fort Wagner[2]—a failed Union attempt to take the Confederate fort resulting in 1,515 Union casualties to just 174 Confederate losses. He was imprisoned at Macon, Georgia, but the *Connecticut Men of the Civil War* does not list the date of his parole, although West was discharged from the army in March, 1865[3]. A pension record dated August 21, 1886 lists him as "DEAD."

Port Royal, South Carolina
November 25, 1861
Friend Kingman,
I believe that you requested that I send you some relics from this part of the country if I met with any. I send you a Secesh pistol. This pistol, together with about 30 cannon, several tons of ammunition and other valuables stores, were taken after the battle here on the 7th Inst[4].

---

[1] According to the *Hartford Courant*, October 30, 1862, page 2, West was wounded in the "leg, slightly."
[2] The *Hartford Courant* on July 28, 1863 lists West as "wounded and missing."
[3] The *Hartford Courant* of April 11, 1865 states, "First Lieut. Daniel J. West, 6th C.V., has been honorably discharged."
[4] "Instant" refers to the current month, so November in this case.

Knowing that you are a good judge of Firearms, I trust that you will at once perceive that this is one of the best—London Manufacture and has all the modern improvements combined,-making a weapon of great perfection. The stock is a beautiful specimen of Southern mechanism.

But it is useless to expatiate the merits of the article, as they are apparent to all who have examined it. General Sherman has endeavored to purchase it for a Holster Pistol and when I refused to part with it, he threatened to bring the subject before the War Department in order to keep it out of the hands of the government. I send it to you. I think that Connecticut should have the honor of owning this weapon. If you can see fit to present to the Historical Society of Connecticut, you can do so.

Things are all quiet here. Some of our boys (three companies from this Regiment) went over to the mainland yesterday. They had a skirmish with the Rebels and drove them back. I haven't heard the full particulars yet.

I should very much like to hear from you, if agreeable.

Lieutenant D. J. West

P. S. If you should write, direct to
Port Royal, South Carolina
Company H 6th Regiment, Connecticut Volunteers

P.S.   *December 14, 1861*

I undertook to write you and send the pistol about a month ago since but I couldn't get it through. I am going to try again today. Nothing of importance here. Our Company is to be taken for an Artillery Company to man Fortifications here. We can hear heavy cannonading in the direction of Tybee. Don't know how they are going along but hope to hear of the taking of Pulaski before long. Hoping that this article will suit,

I remain Yours Truly
Lieut. D. J. West

- Where is this pistol today? Did it make it to the historical society, or did General Sherman finally get his hands on it?
- In April of 1862, Union artillery pummeled Fort Pulaski with their new James rifled cannon, forcing the fort's surrender and cutting off the important port of Savannah from Confederate use.

Captain William S. Marble, 7th CT

William S. Marble was born in Connecticut in 1838, and before the war, worked at the Wheeler & Wilson sewing machine factory, so he may have known Albion, who also worked there. He enlisted as a sergeant in Co. H of the 7th CT V.I. in September of 1861, was promoted to 2nd Lieutenant on July 1, 1862, and to 1st Lt. April 4, 1864.

Marble was severely wounded in the shoulder at Bermuda Hundred on June 2, 1864—the same day Albion was wounded. While recuperating, Marble got the devastating news that his younger brother, George E. Marble, age 20, had died of typhoid on July 24, 1864, after serving just 7 months with the 1st Connecticut Heavy Artillery. George is buried with his parents in Manchester, CT.

Marble was mustered out of the 7th CT on October 24, 1864, but then just one month later received a commission to be captain of Company I of the 7th CT. At Fort Fisher in January of 1865, command of the regiment during the attack fell upon Marble, who subsequently wrote the official report on the action.

Apparently admired by the men of his former Company H, they presented him with a stunning Tiffany sword, which came up for sale in recent years.[6]

William S. Marble[5]

Marble survived the war and an 1880 census listed him as being single, and a machinist in Philadelphia, PA. Sometime in the 1880s, he married Tillie Ricker, a woman 26 years younger, not born until 1864, the year he was wounded and his brother died. Marble passed away on August 18, 1893 and is buried in the Philadelphia National Cemetery.

Hilton Head Isle Port Royal, S.C.
December 11, 1861
Sir
I have written to Laughton a number of times, but have received no answer. Monday, I saw Lieutenant West [see previous letter in this section]

---

[5] Photo by Stephen Hand Waite (1832-1906), 271 Main Street, Hartford, CT. Waite would also take what the *Hartford Courant* (April 16, 1862, pg.2) called "an admirable photograph" of Frederick Douglas during his lecture tour in Hartford in 1864. Waite was friends with John Greenleaf Whittier and Ralph Waldo Emerson, and when he retired from photography after 50 years, he was the longest practicing photographer in the country. He collapsed of heart failure on his back porch while putting food in his ice box and died soon after. https://www.digitalcommonwealth.org/search/commonwealth:c247f1192

[6] The sword was listed for $14,440 at www.horsesoldier.com. It was subsequently reduced to $10,800 and is no longer for sale, so it was either withdrawn from sale or was purchased. (Unfortunately, not by me.)

and he told me Laughton was very sick. Will you please write and let me know how he is getting along?

Yesterday our Company went over to Dufuskie to visit the Plantation of one of Mr. Stoddard. We found it one of the most beautiful places we ever saw,-the most beautiful flowers, orange and the Magnolia all in full bloom. The house was deserted, the family having left at the time our troops landed at Hilton Head. The house was furnished all splendid. The furniture we brought back with us, also the Crockery and other things. After the furniture was taken out, I was left in the house with two men to see to the packing of the crockery. We found a five-gallon Demijohn[7] of Splendid Madeira Wine and you can guess we were not long in taking a fine swig of the Crather.[8] I filled a quart bottle and set it aside to bring away with me. Then we put the Demijohn back where we found it. Just then the Major and Surgeon came in and found my Bottle and they took a swig. The Demijohn the Major took charge of. We also got honey, chickens, geese, and turkeys. The negroes were all tickled to see us, making hoe cakes and boiling eggs for us.

I got about 20 good nice oranges. I wish I could send you one or two. Will you write as soon as convenient and let me know how all the Boys are at the Shop. Give my respect to Mr. Larkin, also remember me to friend Laughton.

Yours in haste, William S. Marble
Direct to me: Co. H 7th Regiment Connecticut Volunteers
Hilton Head, Port Royal, Beaufort District, South Carolina

P. S. I have got money but no stamps, so you will have to pay postage. There is not a stamp on the island.

John Stoddard had married Mary Mongin of Dufuskie, whose family owned the 770-acre cotton plantation named Melrose. The house—which the Union army apparently pillaged—was originally built in 1770. After the war, Stoddard divided much of the land into 12-acre parcels which he sold to the freed slaves.

Frank Taylor, 48th NY

Franklin[9] Bentley Taylor was born on December 6, 1843 in either Sharon or New Preston, CT. Like his father, he was a carpenter when the

---

[7] A large glass bottle with a narrow neck holding several gallons, often carried in a wicker basket.

[8] The transcription has a question mark with the word "Crather." There is no known word. A Krater was a Greek drinking vessel, so perhaps Marble was making reference to that?

[9] The 1860 Bridgeport, CT census lists his name as Francis.

war began, and at the age of 18, he enlisted in Company E of the 48th New York V.I.[10] Taylor survived the war and the 1870 census lists him as having the rather exciting profession of being a detective in New York City. He died on April 20, 1899, a widower, while living at 137 West 112th St. He is buried at the popular Mountain Grove Cemetery in Bridgeport, CT.

Headquarters 48th Regiment
Fort Pulaski, Georgia
August 11, 1862

Photo courtesy of RobM

Friend S.C.K.,

Thinking that you would like to hear a little from this department, I thought I would spend a little time in writing to you. While I am writing, there is a rebel steamer laying off the Fort; she has just come down with the flag of truce bringing a lady and her little boy. Today the monotony of garrison life was disturbed by the appearance of a Rebel steamer coming down the Savannah. The third Rhode Island artillery took their positions at the guns, and anxiously awaited the moment that they might try their skill in gunnery.

When within about three miles of the Fort, we distinguished a flag of truce on her bow and the Confederate flag floating over her stern. She steamed down within a mile of the fort, which the Colonel thought was as near as he wanted her to come, and so gave orders to fire a shot across her bow. This being done the steamer hove to and waited for us to send a boat aboard.

The tugboat <u>Thomas Foulks</u> being here, the Colonel sent one of our Lieutenants and the Adjt. to carry out General Hunter's orders, which is to detain all boats that come from Savannah with flags of truce, for some reasons unknown to me. The officers on the steamer, not liking that way of doing business, put about and tried to run away. Orders were given to the artillery on the Fort to sink her. After firing about twenty shots, not one of them taking effect, I am sorry to say, she got out of the range of the guns of the Fort.

Our tug then ran into the dock and received on board a six pound field piece and went in pursuit of the Flying Rebel, gaining rapidly on her. When within range, two shots from the field piece brought the rebels to a standstill. The tug brought her down opposite the fort, where she now lays

---

[10] His father, Nelson, was born in New York, so perhaps there were still family ties there which led Frank to enlist with a New York regiment.

awaiting the orders of General Hunter. There is a rumor going the rounds that an attack on Savannah is to be made soon.
  From a Bridgeport boy F.B.T.
  Frank B. Taylor

  Paper is scarce and no postage stamps here. They won't take money in payment for letters.

Not a flattering portrayal of the 3rd Rhode Island Artillery. However, this was quite the exciting break from "the monotony of garrison life!"

Speaking of artillery, apparently Taylor was something of an artist, with an interest in artillery, as his letter included the following wonderful illustrations.

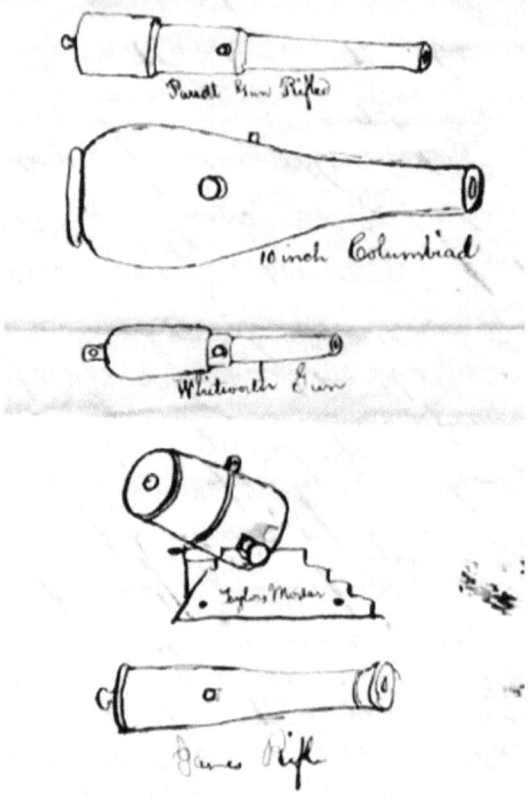

William B. Curtis, 10th CT

Newbern, North Carolina
August 24, 1862
Kind sirs,
  We received your well-filled box some time ago while on picket duty 10 miles from Newbern.

I should have written to you before but could get no paper and ink. Yesterday we were relieved and returned to camp.

We are very much obliged to you for the things. The dried meat and fish were excellent.

I received your letter in due time, also the paper which I thank you very much for. I am well as are most of the boys at present.

Remember me to the Shop boys.
Yours with respect,
William B. Curtis

The Wheeler and Wilson Manufacturing Company, for whom Clayton worked, had obviously sent a box of food to one of their "Shop boys," William Curtis, who had enlisted with Company K of the 10th Connecticut in October of 1861. The 10th CT was in Burnside's North Carolina Campaign, and at the Battle of New Bern, the line of battle was the 8th CT, 5th RI, and then the 10th CT, so perhaps he and Albion were aware of each other's presence on the field.

Curtis, like Albion, was promoted to Sergeant in 1862 (July 13), and also reenlisted at the end of 1863. He was wounded at Darbytown Road during the bloody Petersburg Campaign. On October 13, 1864, Union forces were probing a new Confederate defensive line, which they failed to take. It was another of those "minor" engagements that are all but forgotten and gained no ground, yet resulted in about 450 Union casualties.

Curtis' injuries must have been serious, as he was discharged due to disability nine months later on July 18, 1865. After the war, he was married and worked in a factory[11] in Bridgeport. He died at the age of 51, on February 24, 1893, and is also buried in Mountain Grove Cemetery. His grave stone spells his name as "Curtiss," but this is the only record of that spelling I have found.

Photo courtesy of RobM

John H. Smilie, 24th MA

The following letter, also from New Bern, NC, was from John Henry Smilie of Company H of the 24th Massachusetts, which was in that same front line of battle at New Bern with the 8th and 10th CT. He filed for a pension on

---

[11] The 1870 census is difficult to decipher, but it looks like it was a brass factory.

November 9, 1863, so perhaps he had been disabled through wounds or illness.

Born on January 25, 1828, the 1860 census indicates that the 32-year-old Smilie was a "cordwainer" (shoemaker) in South Reading, MA, which was a center for shoe factories. In 1851, he had married Clarissa Kidder and had two children. In 1860, they were divorced, and the reason given was "for criminality."[12] I had no idea what that meant as it could have all sorts of implications, but discovered that the polite, 19th century term for adultery was "criminal conversation." The only question in this case, is which of them was doing the "talking?"

Smilie then married Charlotte Sweetser in Boston on April 6, 1864, and they had two children. The 1870 census shows he was still living in South Reading, MA, and Smilie's occupation was…a dentist!

The 1889 death certificate of Clarissa Kidder Smilie lists her as the "widow" of John Smilie, so he died sometime before that, although no document has yet been found with the information of his death.

Newbern, N.C. Oct. 3rd **[1862]**
Friend Kingman,

It is just one year ago today, since I was sworn into the service of Uncle Sam, and I wish I was out of it. I tell you there is some fun in a soldier's life, but more out of it, but there are two years more.

I should like them to glide away as quick as a telegraphic dispatch but they won't, the days are something like Parson Emerson's sermons, D----d long: the nights are short to me for I go to bed about 10 and getup about 5. We have hard boards to sleep on, there is no soft side to the boards here.

I received your letter, also one from Abner[13]. Books and pencils. I can't find out the price of anything. I wrote to know what they cost for they were for my Captain,-the pencils and drawing book.

I got some relics for Abner but the Provost Marshal confiscated them. I paid $3.00 for one book for him. It was all written with the pen in 1630. It was a valuable chemical work. Tell him that I will try to get him some papers,-those I can send.

As to my revolver, if anyone wants it, sell it if you can. Get $12.00 or more. It was owned by General L. O. Branch and is a good revolver. It ought to bring more, but I will let it go for that. If Thomas Parker gets a chance to sell it, let him dispose of it and pay you the money.

---

[12] *Boston Evening Transcript*, April 26, 1860, pg. 4
[13] Abner Augustus Kingman, 1830-1917, another of Clayton's long-lived siblings. Abner was a printer in Boston.

I don't want the money but I thought now would be a good time to sell it, as a good many are going away to war.

I am very thankful for the postage stamps. I want you to send me some more next time you write, $1.00 worth and charge me for what you have sent. Thomas Parker will deliver you this. He is one of the lucky kind,-got his discharge. I am one of the unlucky kind, bound to see it through or go where I can't see.

Give my best respects to Abner A. K. Tell him that I won't forget him and as soon as I get my eyes on anything, my hand goes on to it instantly for him.

Write soon,
Yours, J.H. Smilie
One of the invincible 24th

- Excellent analogy: "I should like them to glide away as quick as a telegraphic dispatch but they won't." People don't write like that anymore.
- "…the days are something like Parson Emerson's sermons, D----d long." I don't know who the long-winded Parson Emerson was, but you could probably insert the clergyman of your choice into that amusing statement.
- As a former R&D Chemist and lifelong science geek, I fairly swooned over the description of the handwritten, 1630, chemistry book he bought for $3! Where is that book today!?
- Of course, the 800 lb. gorilla in the letter is the revolver he is willing to sell for $12. The revolver of Confederate General Lawrence O'Bryan Branch. The man who was a U.S. Congressman, turned down a cabinet position as the Secretary of the Treasury, enlisted as a private, became Colonel of the 33rd North Carolina, and became a Brigadier General. The same Confederate Brigadier General who was with A.P. Hill's Division, who on September 17, 1862, rushed from Harper's Ferry to Antietam in time to turn back the final Union attack (in which Albion was a part). The same Confederate general who, after the battle, was chatting with several other generals when a Union sharpshooter spotted the cluster of high-value targets and fired his rifle—hitting Branch right in the face and killing him instantly. Can you imagine the value today of Branch's revolver? Smilie doesn't explain how he came upon it, but as Branch was at the Battle of New Bern, that is the most likely location.

- While there were a lot of Thomas Parkers in the Union Army, it is probably safe to assume this was Thomas E. Parker, also of the 24th Massachusetts, Company E.

Corporal William Krapp, 23rd CT

William Krapp was yet another of the sewing machine factory "Shop Boys." He enlisted on August 30, 1862 with Company I of the 23rd Connecticut V.I.

There are a few transcription questions by Agnes Thompson in this letter, and I was unable to find the original to try to figure them out.

Histoire de la guerre civile en Amérique Atlas. Paris, 1890
http://hdl.loc.gov/loc.gmd/g3701sm.gcw0080000

Lafourche Crossing, April 7th, 1863
Dear Sir,

I thought I would pen you a few lines hoping they may find you in good health. I, myself, am in very good health at present. Have not seen a sick day since I have been in service. We are stationed on the Opelousas and Great Western Railroad, some 55 miles.

We are stationed at the Headquarters of the Regiment and have a very easy time of it. The duty is not much. We are stationed here with Company E to guard the railroad bridge from being burned by bands of citizens, guerrillas. We are alarmed very often by picket firing and expect to play our hand before long if things do not go right at Brashear City. (By the way, the railroad runs to Brashear)

General Weitzel[14] is in command of this department and his Brigade was ordered to Berwick some fortnight ago on account of the Rebels receiving heavy reinforcements in men, guns, and Boats, one of them being the Queen of the West. (those of ours being greatly inferior to her) Were ordered to fall back to Bayou Boeuf [?] with the Brigade to wait for more reinforcements, -which they have received some 3 days ago, making the number of men some 25,000. They came from Baton Rouge. They were Grover's Zouaves [?], Emory Brigades and another which I do not recollect (the Conn. Battalions 12th, 24th and 25th are with them) Perhaps before this reaches you we may hear some stirring news. The place to be attacked is Franklin and Patterson villages where the Rebels are stationed with heavy force at Franklin. Franklin is where the great salt works are by which the Rebels supply themselves with salt, and Boeuf [?] as it is a direct route from Port Hudson to Texas. And the enemy get their supplies by this route. Berwick is situated on a Bay of the same name. It is a small village and has been occupied by our forces ever since the railroad came in our possession. It is situated on an island and is a beautiful place to be stationed at.

The *Queen of the West* had a storied career. Built in Cincinnati, Ohio in 1854, she was converted to a ram ship in 1862 and played decisive roles in the First Battle of Memphis and at Vicksburg. Captured and used successfully by the Confederates in February 1863, she was ultimately destroyed by Union ships in April 1863.

The country is in utter ruin. The cane fields are left standing from last season and it cannot be used for anything. Most of the plantations are confiscated by the Government and their agents are gathering the

---

[14] The life and career of Major General Godfrey Weitzel cannot be condensed into a footnote. He may be best known for accepting the surrender of Richmond.

molasses and sending it to New Orleans as fast as possible. They say this is the loyal part of the state. It is only because our forces occupy it that they are Union. Most of the darkeys have run away from their masters and help is scarce so they are only going to raise corn and potatoes and pork so they can have something to live on for the next year. The inhabitants say they nearly starved when our forces took possession of these parts. (They ought to have stayed away a little longer)

The weather is quite warm now; the spring is far advanced and everything is in bloom and looks beautiful. The Regiment is in very good health at present. We have lost only 2 men by a sickness.

Soldiering is a lazy life and a dog's life. We wish, all of us, that this cursed War was over and everything settled satisfactory to both sides. But we hope the North will not give one Peg to the Copperhead Party. I suppose by this time the election for governor was decided. I hope the Old State of Connecticut was not the first to back down. We soldiers are afraid that Seymour has been elected, but hope not as we think him to be a dangerous person to the cause of our rights and Country.

Since my last writing there have been heavy reinforcements passing. Every day there have been about 4 heavy trains loaded with troops. It would seem that they intend to do some fighting before long as they must have a force of 30,000 men at the Bay. The morning of the tenth General Weitzel crossed the Bay and the rest passed over during the day. They have a long pontoon bridge for the purpose of Crossing the Artillery,-the troops crossing on gunboats. I expect that they have commenced the attack.

General Banks takes command in person of all the forces there. It is hardly thought that the Rebels will make a stand but will retreat to the Bayou unless they have had reinforcements.

I think it doubtful myself for it is of too much importance to lose without a struggle. Today is Sunday and the boys are writing their letters as the steamer leaves Tuesday the 14th.

I will have to close now to be in time. I hope this letter will find you in good shape and the rest of my shopmates. Tell Warner to turn Abolitionist. Tell Smith to stick out for I believe he is right. I can tell a good deal about the treatment of the darkeys by their masters but can't do it in writing. When I get home, which is not far off, I can tell better. The report is, and we expect, that our time is out on the 30th day of June.

I suppose you're doing a good business yet. According to accounts I hear that business is very good. I must close now as it is getting dark. Give my best wishes to all and excuse my poor writing. Answer this. Tell Smith, Hoven, Zramen to all write and all the rest. Give my respects to Mr. Larkin and to Dewhurst.

Yours truly
William Krapp

Directions: William Krapp
Company I, 23rd Connecticut
New Orleans
19th Army Corps Louisiana

William Krapp was mustered out on August 31, 1864, after just one year of service—a year in which he had "a very easy time of it." Not all Civil War service was created equal.

He married a woman named Myra, and had a daughter, Kittie. He passed away on

Photo courtesy of RobM

March 33, 1899, at the age of 58, and is also buried in Mountain Grove Cemetery in Bridgeport, CT.

George A. Parkington, 2nd Independent Battery, Connecticut Light Artillery

This was one of those puzzles of transcription. Agnes Thompson had written that this letter was from "George A. Rukington." I could find no one of that name—or any variation—in the soldier's database, and with no regiment listed, I was at a dead end. For a while.

Not giving up, I found the original letter to see if I could decipher the name. After staring at it for quite a while, I asked Bob to take a look to see if he could make any sense of it. We ruled out a capital "B" as the writer had written in "Bridgeport." Bob saw that the capital "R" in "Remember" wasn't similar to the first letter in the last name, either. He suggested that it might be a "P." With that possibility in mind, it suddenly dawned on me it could read "Parkington."

Within seconds, I was on the soldier's database and gave a resounding cheer when up popped George A. Parkington, 2nd Independent Battery, Connecticut Light Artillery. A quick check of the regimental history showed that they were indeed in service near New Orleans during the time the letter was written. If you've never struggled with a tough research nut to crack, and then cracked it, you can't imagine how satisfying it is to reveal a hidden piece of history, or a person long forgotten.

So then, once I had a name, more digging revealed that George Amasa Parkington was born in Sharon, CT in 1837. He married in 1859 and at the start of the war was yet another of the "Shop Boys."

Algiers, Louisiana, July 8th, 1864
Sir,
While I was at Brashear City, Louisiana, I gathered a small collection of insects etc. Mr. Whitney was making us a visit and I thought it might be acceptable to you, as I knew you were fond of such things. I shall try and get a better collection before I come home.
The boys are all well and things are going along finely. I often think of you and long for the day to come when I can return to old Bridgeport, but I do want to see the War closed first and I shall try and do my duty as a soldier while in the service.
Remember me to all especially your wife and children.

Yours
George A. Parkington

Parkington survived the war and it seemed likely he would have returned to the sewing machine factory, but the 1870 Bridgeport census indicated he worked at a grocery store. The 1880 census stated he was a clergyman. Machinist, soldier, grocer, clergyman—how did that happen? Fortunately, I found his 1881 obituary[15] which is summarized below:

Rev. George A. Parkington
To many in this city and in other places will come with sorrow the tidings of the death of Rev. George A. Parkington, who died at his residence in Fair Haven yesterday afternoon about six o'clock. For some time he had been lingering in a very enfeebled state. A number of weeks ago he was prostrated with pneumonia, which brought him very low, and typhoid symptoms supervened accompanied with great physical prostration.
The deceased will be deeply mourned. He was a very lovable man, affectionate, kind and warm hearted, winning people to him and retaining their friendship, while as a preacher he was magnetic, sympathetic and popular, with a ready natural flow of language and a rare gift for entertaining and interesting. He was a self-taught man. He was in early manhood an inspector at the Wheeler & Wilson manufactory, Bridgeport. He left that business when his country called its sons to arms for the Union. He enlisted in Captain Hotchkiss' battery...He went out as a bugler and having some knowledge of pharmacy was soon made hospital steward. He had embraced religion previous to the war...and he and others

---

[15] *New Haven Morning Journal-Courier*, February 2, 1881, pg. 2.

were engaged in active religious work among his comrades in camp. Upon his return, place was made for him again in the factory. After a time he engaged in the grocery business with Deacon Brown, of the Washington Park M.E. Church, the firm being Brown & Parkington.

He worked in his grocery business for some time, but was encouraged to pursue the clergy:

...passing very successfully the requisite examinations. He entered the ministry in 1872."

Parkington was minister in several churches in Connecticut, his last being the East Pearl Street M.E. Church in Fair Haven.

Parkington had a relatively brief, but fascinating life—obviously a man not afraid to take chances and make major changes in his life. Perhaps the Civil War taught him that life was too short to delay following your dreams.

The monument to the 2nd Independent Battery, Connecticut Light Artillery, Gettysburg. Many thanks to Michael Worden for taking this picture for me.

When next you visit Gettysburg, look for the monument for the 2nd Connecticut Light Battery on Hancock Ave., 0.3 miles south of the large State of Pennsylvania Monument. And for all those Civil War trivia geeks, here's an interesting fact—this battery was the only Federal battery at Gettysburg to have 14-pounder James Rifles and 12-pounder howitzers.

Appendix B
The Brooks Family

The following is more of the fictionalized family history by Agnes Thompson, which includes actual letters.

A Maine Family

"Father wanted us to learn all we could. He always said that knowledge is the key-stone of power, the thing that raises us above the animals," George [the son] said sadly.

"So he did. I hope that we can manage to keep you both in school," said the young widow as she left the room.

"I think I remember him best in school," murmured William, the 10-year old. "I can see him now sitting at his desk on the platform in the front."

"I wonder who will get the wood for the fireplace now that father will not be there anymore," said George.

"Sometimes he would let us write on the blackboard after we had helped carry the wood in," William added.

The boys cried softly. After all, they were only 10 and 12-years-old and no one was looking at them.

"He didn't like it when we climbed on the seats to look out of the windows," said William.

"Or forgot to carry in the drinking water," added George.

"It sometimes seemed to me that when we were spelling he gave us the hardest words," William said.

"He was pleased when we spelled down the older boys, even if he would never say so," added George.

In the kitchen, the two girls were also thinking of their father and their future.

"Aunt Abigail says we will probably have to move in with grandpa and grandma Eustis in Jay," said Pamelia. Pamelia, 17, and Emily, 16, sometimes called their stepmother Aunt Abigail. She was the sister of their mother and they had known her as "Aunt Abigail" before she became their stepmother. "Perhaps we will have to go and work in the Mills."

"I don't want to work in the Mills," said Emily. "Father helped me prepare for the examinations and I have references for Carthage and Jay. I hope that one of them will take me. I want to be a teacher like father."

"I hope that you may do so," said Abigail. "But they may already have someone else, and they may think you too young. We will have to cut our coat to fit our cloth."

"I think we can make more money working in the Mills than teaching," said Pamelia. "Besides, I don't think they will hire you at Jay or Carthage."

"Let the girl be," broke in Uncle Nathan. "It is well that she is interested in education. We will see what happens."

It was January 10, 1845, a cold blustery day. The Brooks family had just returned from burying George Brooks, the husband and father. Pamelia, Emily, George, and William were children of the first wife, Anna. Albion, the son of the second wife, Abigail, was just two years old.

George Brooks had been a teacher at Kingfield, Maine, from 1824 to 1838, when his first wife died. The family had moved to Carthage, Maine, where he was teaching at the time of his death.

The bereaved family moved to Jay and lived with the grandparents, Deacon and Mrs. William Eustis. The Eustis's had fifteen children, five of whom were still living. Five of the fifteen children died in infancy. Raising children in Maine was not easy. Abigail, the young widow, was their youngest child. And Hannah, sister of William, a blind spinster, also lived with the Eustis's.

In the fall, Emily did not get a school, but with the encouragement of Uncle Nathan, went to a boarding school in Farmington. She wrote her brother William about the school and her hopes.

Farmington, September 13, 1845
Dear Brother William,

I like it here better than I expected. I wish you and George were here. I want a slate very much and if you will lend me yours and your geography and atlas if it is Smith's, I shall be greatly obliged. Please ask mother if she will not fold them in a paper with my rubbers and send them up by the first opportunity.

There are about 80 scholars here now. The school will be 12 weeks or a little longer. I mean to try my best now, and I shall be quite somebody I rather think, and so can you, dear brother, if you'll only try. There is a magic power in this little word and I hope we shall both be under its magical effects.

I have no thought of going to the Mills now unless pecuniary affairs oblige me to. I mean to learn something, to teach somebody's children somewhere. I wish I could get a school somewhere so that I could board with you, but then we can not have all our wishes supplied, and we must make the best of this world, take as it comes, and if we cannot see each other to talk, we'll make our agent a pen to do it for us.

I hope much of you, brother. It affords me pleasure to think you have made so much good improvement of your means. I want you to think what

you had better do, calmly and rationally, and then do what you decide is for the best, and it will be right, perfectly right, you never can do anything wrong when you act thus, so don't be alarmed.
Your sister
Emily E. Brooks

This, from the 16-year-old Emily to her 10-year-old brother. And, in the years to follow, the pen was often the agent used to keep members of the little family in touch with each other. As long as she lived, Emily was to advise and help her sister and her brothers.

George and William, back in Jay, were doing their best to overcome the difficulties of getting an education. The finest gift their father had left his little family was the appreciation and the desire for education. There were many chores about the Eustis home; wood to be chopped and animals to be fed. The school was about 5 miles away. The boys had to get up early, do their chores before breakfast, and then walk the 5 miles to school.

Abigail sent Emily news of the family when she could find time to write.

Jay, December 30, 1845
Dear Emily
When I look around and see how are our family is scattered, it seems I shall never see you all together again. I received a letter from Pamelia at Lowell. We thought she was in Hallowell and were all astonished, but "good on her head." I wish you were there with her working, making "money to kill," as she said. She plans to write you to come up there soon. If you have any notion of going, I want you to come down here first or get out to Carthage. We all want to see you and hear you sing some of those lively songs.

Perhaps you will say, "I have got along without you," but I don't care for that. A friend is a good thing but I want to be something more, a mother.

George is at the neighbors' now and goes to school. He is well. William is here, a bed and asleep. Albion grows like a pig. Mrs. R's son has gotten a girl. You have lost him.
Your mother
Abigail Brooks

Emily did go to work at Lowell. School terms were short and money was scarce. The wages seemed very desirable. A friend at Carthage wrote her.

Carthage, Sept 12, 1846
Ever Dear but Distant Friend,

I have thought of you so much lately that I cannot help hoping that you are coming home this fall. I do not wish to advise you but think it would be better for you to come and go to school or teach this winter. I do heartily wish that you would. "But," you say, "I don't thank you for your concern about me. I can take care of myself without any of your help." And so you can, rather too well to suit my pleasure and enjoyment. You must do as you think proper.

But I cannot bear cannot the thought of you keeping yourself shut up there when you can do so much good by teaching, and I fear that it may shorten your days in depriving yourself of the enjoyment of liberty and freedom. I feel anxious concerning your health, and Pamelia's also.

Yours truly Ng Storm

Pamelia Brooks Nichols

Pamelia and Emily were joining many daughters of New England farmers when they went to work in the Mills. These young women with energy, perseverance, and ambition, for almost half a century, from 1810 to 1860, formed the great body of Mill employees. They had something of the pioneer spirit, a willingness to venture into a new industrial world, and confidence in their ability to live in that world with dignity and self-respect. They lived in strictly supervised corporation boarding houses.

John A. Lowell and Patrick T. Jackson were largely responsible for the excellent living conditions in the Mills of New England. Lowell had visited England and seen the Mills of England. One factor he considered important in overcoming the competition of England was the educational and moral superiority of the New England population. Much attention was given to the physical and moral care of employees. Libraries, lyceum programs, and evening courses were provided for them. The employees, themselves, put out a paper, "The Lowell Offerings." Encouragement was given in music and in church attendance.

Many of the girls, like Emily, interspersed the short term of teaching with Mill work. They managed to pay off family mortgages, helped brothers through school, or collected dowries for themselves.

Pamelia returned to Maine and went to work in the weaving Mill at South Berwick. It was popular to write in verse and she wrote to Emily:

South Berwick, Maine, June 20th 47
Dear Emily
Your letter, Emily found me well,
Making money in the Mill.
The first two weeks my average pay
Was one shilling six pence every day,
Since then I've wove with greater speed,
By which more wages I have made.
Besides my board for three weeks since,
I've made three dollars, thirty-five cents.
By this you see I do as well
As you can do in the cotton Mill.
My health is good, my spirits light,
My heart's at ease, my prospects bright.
The news from Jay you wished me to tell
Is, Mother writes that they are well.
Our grandparents are failing, they say,
Aunt Hannah's the same as when we came away,
Mother thinks we had better go home
Ere Grandfather and Mother are laid in their tomb.
For they wish to see us ere they go
The way of all that dwell below.
Mrs. Gordon and I new dresses have bought,
Gingham, muslin, checked and wrought,
A black lace veil and flowers by the way,
To make my market while I stay.
And now, I should like to know
If you, in Lowell have found a beau.
That cough, which is so "loud and rough"
It is, in itself, I'm sure, enough
To make you leave the cotton mill,
And in some other place to dwell,
Where you can breathe the pure fresh air,
And of that blessing, health, have your share.
Now my advice to you why give,
For you to go where you can live
And not in Lowell work and stay
'Til life and health have passed away.
And now, Dear Sister, fare thee well
'Tis from my heart I wish you well.
It rains today

So I say
This is from your sister Pamelia
May you bloom like the rose,
Have plenty of beaus,
And walk in the way,
That is heavenly

The death of their grandfather, Deacon William Eustis, on August 25, 1847, called Emily back to Jay. Here, with the help of Uncle Nathan, she got a school and taught in the fall. There were 42 scholars from 5 to 12 years of age. She received two dollars a week and her board. Now, at last, she was doing what she had always wanted to do.

Emily alternated between teaching and working in the Mills with a short stint as a bookkeeper for a newspaper, *The Atlantic Corporation*. There was little field of employment for educated women. A few months turn as a school mistress was not a very remunerative occupation and there were many who combined teaching and Mill work. From the small amount Emily made, she managed to send money to her brother and her grandmother.

Lewiston, March 19, 1849
Dear Brother William,

I suppose you are all out of patience waiting for the treasure which this letter will carry to you. Pamelia said that you wanted it very much and I felt bad that I could not send it to you but we were not paid until this afternoon. I hope you have not been too disappointed.

I want to see you and Brother George very much. I am glad that George is going to stay and work on a farm for I think it will be better for his health than it would be in the Mill.

Pamelia said Aunt Hannah was not so well as when I left. I hope the pleasant spring air will revive her. How bad we should feel were we blind as she is, and could not see the blue sky and light clouds as they float over our heads in this pleasant season. I shall send grandmother some money next payment which will be a week from Saturday. I suppose they are making sugar now.

Tell mother if she wants anything that she cannot conveniently get, to send me word and I will get it for her.

As for little brother Albion, I hardly know what to say to him. I hope he will be a good boy and then everyone will love him, but I shall whether he is good are not. That thimblefull of kisses he sent was very acceptable.

Yours affectionately, Emily

The year 1850 brought changes. Abigail remarried and she and Albion went to live in Kingfield. William hired out to Colonel Wheeler in Weld, Maine. While there, he studied, taught, and united with the Congregational Church under John S. Wheelwright, in addition to working for Colonel Wheeler.

The Brooks children got their education at the time when public secondary education in New England lagged. Academies, run by highly educated men, usually ministers and idealists, largely took care of secondary education. It was traditional that all the brightest children should attend them, and the boys, at least must be prepared for college. If a boy or girl recommended by the elementary school teacher could not raise the little tuition involved there was usually someone in the community who would loan them money. The masters wasted no time on students who could not do the work. In a sense it was a golden age of education. The aristocratic tradition of education remained, but attached no longer to birth, and not yet to wealth.

Both George and William prepared for college through these schools, working part of the time and going to school part of the time.

North Jay, Maine,
Dear Brother William,
I have received a letter from Emily. She is well and earning two dollars and quarter per week clear from board. She and Pamelia are both at Lawrence working in the Mill. She wants me to go up there this spring and I think I shall unless I work for Elias H. Lake. I asked him thirteen dollars a month for six months. Do you think that is enough? I shall not go to Kingfield this spring as the season for moose hunting has passed. I have been cutting all the remainder of the woodpile for the past few days. I have it almost conquered.

I understand that you are having a private school at Weld. I am glad to see your mind is spent on knowledge. Knowledge is the key-stone to power; it is knowledge that raises men from the level of the beasts to a position but one lower than the angels of heaven.

Yours in haste, George H. Brooks

In Lawrence, Emily joined the congregational church. At church she met her future husband, Samuel Clayton Kingman. He was learning to be a machinist at the Lawrence machine shops under Aretus Blood. He lived not far from the corporation boarding house where Emily and Pamelia lived. Both Clayton and Emily attended the "Ladies' Reunion of the Central Church" designed to "promote personal acquaintance and works of charity." Each meeting was opened by the reading of Scripture and prayer, and closed with prayer and singing. The members had to pay at least three cents at every meeting…

…Emily stayed at the Mill for a while, then went to care for Pamelia, who had married and was to have a baby. Late in 1852, she got word that Abigail was very ill and she went to Kingfield…

Times in New England were hard. Everyone was interested in California. With several companions from Bloomfield Academy, William sailed from New York on the *North Star* in 1855. He hoped to make money in the gold fields to complete college. He worked hard. When they had a dry spell and there was was not enough water to mine, he went into the mountains and helped build a reservoir. In two years he had enough money to return. He entered Waterville College (now Colby College) and eventually graduated.

George had completed one year of Bowdoin College. He too, felt the urge to go to California and he left a few months after William. He got the western fever and did not return to New England.

A letter from George, now rarely heard from, to his sister, Emily:

Horsetown, California, January 3, 1861

My dear sister,

I had thought I should write to no one in the States until I could return and look the world in the face, but your kind letter has opened the seal of fountains of other years and the memories of the past, crowding into my mind until they seem like realities of the present.

I am still in Horsetown, reading some law; and Justice of the Peace for the township; was elected last month one of the Associate Judges of the Court of Sessions. I do not drink strong liquors, play cards, and am a Union Democrat. I have a very pretty lot here in town on which I have some twenty-five fruit trees, most of which will bear this year. I have a small, neat house on it, two rooms, and furnished according to the fashion of this country. I am not married. More than that, I do not expect to be until I am able. Should that time ever come, I shall return to New England, although I candidly confess that the lady I loved has long since been a bride. Yet I believe in the old proverb, "There are as good fish in the sea as have ever been caught."

I suppose I should not know at Albion now if I should see him. Tell him to study and improve his mind, for the time is fast approaching when men of mind and nerves will be wanted. And tell him should his country call, there is a time to fight as well as a time to pray, and that the safest way in the hour of danger is to keep your eye on the enemy, and then you won't be shot in the back. I tell his this as one who has known some dangers. Your brother, George H. Brooks.

But George probably did not get to gather all the fruit from his twenty-five trees. The Civil War broke out and he enlisted in Company "H" of the 1st Infantry Regiment of California at San Francisco on August 1, 1861. Company "H" was the first of the California volunteers to be mustered in. While this army of the west did not engage in the big battles of the east, its men served longer, all fought as bravely, and died as valiantly as any in the east.

George Brooks

Back in Connecticut, Emily and her husband had two young daughters. When Clayton was called up to go in the army, Albion begged to take his place as he was single and young. So Albion Brooks was mustered into company "A" Eighth Regiment, Connecticut Volunteers.

William graduated from Waterville College with the class of 1862. He helped to organize company "E" 16th regiment, Maine volunteers, and was mustered in as the First Lieutenant, August 16, 1862.

So the three Brooks brothers were all in the United States army, George from California, William from Maine, and Albion from Connecticut.

This was the family history Agnes Thompson wrote of her ancestors, but while she also wrote of the death of Albion, what of the other Brooks children?

Two of George and Anna's daughters who died young were: Katherine 1831-1833 and Anna 1835-1840. They are both buried with their parents and Albion at the Riverside Cemetery, Kingfield.

Pamelia, born in Kingfield in 1828, worked in the mills until 1851 when she married John B. Nichols (1821-1904). They had two daughters, Mary, 1854-1884, and Lizzie, 1855-1878. After Pamelia's death, John remarried (Philena Eaton 1822-1892) and had two more children, neither of whom lived long: Alonzo 1861-1866, and John 1864-1865.

From her letters, Pamelia appeared to have the same wit, compassion, and intelligence of her siblings. She died of "consumption," a.k.a. tuberculosis, possibly contracted during her years in the mills, and exacerbated by breathing in all the harmful fibers, causing those "loud and rough" coughs. Her obituary read:

Pamelia Brooks Nichols, at East Haverhill, Massachusetts, September 3, 1857, died. Mrs. Pamelia A. Nichols, 29 years old. She united with the Baptist church during the "revival" three years since, then has adorned this profession by a Holy and consistent life. During the first part of her sickness, her mind was somewhat distressed by doubts and fears, which soon vanished, giving place to calm serenity and bright expectations of future Glory. Cheerfully she resigned her husband and children into the hands of God, and waited the "Father's bidding." A few hours before she expired she exclaimed, "I am standing at the gate of Heaven and long to enter," and ere long this we trust that she has crossed its threshold and mingled her voice in the music of heaven.

On September 5, 1858, the recent widower, John Nichols, wrote to Emily:

Dear Sister, I received a note from you a short time since. In reply to the same I would say that I was quite pleased to hear that you were well and getting along so finely.

Well, with me is far different. Almost everything has gone wrong since Pamelia died. My health is pretty good and that is all. I suppose I ought to be thankful for that. I have had no one to talk to or that could sympathize with me in the least which made me feel very lonely and my loss more keenly. Pamilia was a dear wife and I think she had a superior mind. The children will miss her example and precepts in their education. Finally, the like I may never expect to see again.

Another kind, smart Brooks gone too soon.

One final word from John Nichols, who lived a life of tragedy, watching two wives and all four children die. John apparently couldn't even catch a break and have a quiet and peaceful old age. At 74-years-old, he wrote a letter to Emily from East Haverhill, January 18, 1895:

I am stopping with Eliza and Ann this winter. Eliza fell down the stairs and struck her head. Has been sick all winter.

The nurse and I have watched with her for six weeks. Rather hard for old folks like me. She came out to the kitchen Thanksgiving for the first time. Is now getting along finely for a person of ninety. In February next

Ann is eighty-eight and is quite deaf and almost blind which makes it very bad to take care of.

I sometimes look back and wonder what I have done to have two old maids thrown on my hands to take care of. I am not aware that I have been so much worse than others. However those that Know, more is expected of them.

John died at age 83 of heart disease and dementia.

George Henry Brooks was born in Kingfield in 1833, and was what people would call a character, and a character who led a life of adventure. George, without a doubt, deserves a book of his own—but one Brooks biography at a time, thank you.

However, he is too juicy a character to gloss over in a couple of paragraphs, so here he is in a nutshell, followed by excerpts from his letters.

After a relatively quiet life in Maine working on farms and going to school, he headed for California, stricken by the same gold fever as his brother William, who had preceded him a few months earlier. While he never hit the "Mother lode," he did okay for himself for a while.

He then practiced law, became a Justic of the Peace, and an Associate Judge. When the Civil War began, he was quick to enlist in the 1st California Infantry in August, 1861, and had many adventures in the Southwest. After the war, the Brooks family lost touch with George, and it would be 51 years before they found him. In the words of Wilson Brooks, William's son, in letters he wrote to family members in 1905:

I know you will be pleased to learn that after 51 years of separation from the family, George Henry Brooks has been found. He lives in Shafter, Presidio County, Texas, and is at the present time 72 years of age, hale and hearty. After being mustered out of the army in 1864, he went to Santa Fe, New Mexico and spent a year in hunting.

From 1868 to 1869 he drove cattle in and out of Texas.

In the fall of 1869, he went to Presidio County, Texas, and has resided there continuously ever since.

From 1869 to 1874 he lived at Presidio, Texas, where he was a stationary engineer.

From 1874 to 1890 he resided at Ruidosa, where he ran a mill.

From 1891 to 1893 he resided at Marfa, where he was County Assessor.

Since 1893 he has resided at Shafter, where he has worked in the silver mines and ran an ice plant.

At the present time he is County Surveyor of Presidio County, to which position he was elected in 1902. He is still a Democrat.

On July 8, 1878, at the age of 45, he married Ygnasia Reza, cousin of Don Louis Terrazas[1], Governor of the state of Chihuahua, Republic of Mexico. His wife at the time of her marriage was 16 years old.

They have seven fine children living, all of whom are a credit to the family.

George (age 72) and Ygnasia (43) Brooks and their seven children, from a baby to adults. Shafter, TX, December 6, 1905.

I don't even know where to begin with all of this, so I will just add some excerpts of his letters.

North Jay, May 1, 1851
Dear Brother William,
...I suppose that you have heard of Abigail Eustis's marriage? It was a rather sudden affair, anyhow.

Well, that is a not exactly glowing congratulations to the bride. This was the marriage of Albion's mother with Abisha Landers in Kingfield. Interesting, he doesn't call her Abigail Brooks, as she did marry George's father.

I thought the following displayed more of the Brooks wit:

---

[1] An influential politician and businessman, friend of President Benito Juarez, was once in a confrontation with Pancho Villa, and owned ranches totaling over 7 million acres.

North Jay, July 20, 1851
Dear Brother William,
...*I suppose that you think I am loafing yet, but it is not so. I have been to work some time and my fingers are so stiff that I can hardly hold a pen to write or let go of it after I do get a hold of it. I am at work for Mr. Colimon Hyes (?) I have twenty dollars for five weeks. It is a very good place to work, but like other places, you have to work.*

The following was George's way of telling William he was teaching school again. Given that he had on occasion written in Latin to William, he could be thankful this was at least in English. His opinions of the tiny town of Carthage and its children are none too flattering.

South Carthage, February 9, 1853
Dear Brother,
Without doubt you will be somewhat surprised to learn that I have conveyed my earthly tabernacle once more to this remote, woebegone section of this terrestrial ball and that here I am swaying the scepter of petty despotism over a few ragged urchins; but such is the truth and once more I am engaging in the laudable pursuit of enlightening the minds of down-trodden humanity.

The following is one of several letters he wrote to Emily and Clayton from California, where he was goldmining, which apparently suited him "quite well."

Horsetown, February 29, 1856
Dear Sister and Brother,
After a hard day's work I find myself seated with pen in hand to write you a few hurried lines,-few indeed they must be for the mail closes in a few minutes.
I presume that though my letter may be short, it may have some interest to you, if nothing more than to know that I am alive and well and enjoying myself as well as I can which is quite well.
...I am very sorry to hear that Pamelia's health is so poor but I hope that she will recover and that I shall have the privilege of seeing her again, although it may be some time before I shall visit that part of the country again...
... Business is quite good here now and the mines, as a general thing, are doing well, but, after all, there is a good deal of humbug about California. Some are doing well, others nothing, some are making their hundred dollars a day, while hundreds are not making a hundred cents a

day. But, after all, I think that a man can, if he will, make good wages here any time, but the fact is there are many who, unless they can make the biggest kind of pay, will not work. It cannot be expected that men who will not work for three or four dollars per day but had rather lay around stores and gambling houses, will ever make a great deal unless they are very lucky.

... I presume that Albion is getting to be a large boy, and, of course, a smart scholar. You must try and give him a chance but still it will be better for him to break his own road as much as he can. I did it and perhaps I ought to have gone on as I started but to tell you the truth, Emily, my health was giving way, and had I continued in my college course, I think by the time I had got through I should have been a good graveyard subject.

How different I feel and look now, stout and hearty: I look as though I could stand any hardship.

As my sheet is getting filled I must close. Please to remember me to all friends. My love to Albion.

Horsetown, March 12, 1856

Dear Sister and Brother,

As I have a few leisure moments this evening, and nothing to disturb my mind, being alone in my camp, I hardly think that I can better improve them then in penning you a few hasty lines, although I have no news in particular to write except that I am still enjoying good health and serene of mind and well maybe happy.

Could you just step into my old camp and see me with pen in hand and a huge pipe in my mouth before a table covered with books and papers, while a good fire sparkles in the big stone fireplace. I think you would agree with me that I am enjoying myself to the extent of human desires. I would give considerable if you could just look into our camp and see how we live here in California. I think it would make all your eyes stick out some.

I have been camping alone for some time passed until within a day or two. Day before yesterday a fellow came here and wanted to stop with me and, of course, my generous disposition would not for a moment harbor the thought of refusing him, so he is stopping with me now.

Last night we were talking about Atlantic matters and with Yankee inquisitiveness, I asked him from what state he was and he told me he was from Massachusetts. Of course, I then asked him from what town and he said South Reading. Upon inquiring still more, I found that he formerly lived close by to Mr. Kingman and was well acquainted with Clayton and all of his folks. We were old friends very quickly. His name is Eaton, but he goes here by the name of Tom. I guess that he used to be rather wild when he was at home, but he is a first-rate fellow now and steady too. He is going home soon (to see his wife that he married eight weeks before he came out here.)

...Well, I suppose you want to know how I am making it, not big, I can assure you. I just weighed our day's work (two of us) and we had fourteen dollars and a half. That is rather more than the average pay however. I hope to strike it one of these days, as the Dutchman says, "by de bushel," but don't expect to, quite as big as that.

As I cannot think of anything else to write I will give you the prices of some articles of provisions. Flour is selling here at four dollars per [?], Potatoes ten cents per pound, butter 75 cents; beef, fresh 18 to 20 cents; molasses good at $1.50 per gallon; pork fresh 25 cents; salt 30 cents; ham 30 cents and everything else in proportion. It has cost me this past winter about twelve dollars for rubber boots alone, and I have not got a pair now that are good for anything. Thus, you will see that a person must make something to live here.

... My love to all of your babies and all, including the rest of mankind and the people generally.

Considering Emily had made $2.25 per week teaching, $14.50 worth of gold in one day was quite good—except the cost of food and supplies was equally high. The following shows that George was very much in the "wild west."

Horsetown, October 14, 1856
Dear Sister and Brother,
... As you see, I am still in the world-renowned town of Horsetown, and am still engaged in the honest occupation of a miner. My health is good, never was better, my weight of about 160 pounds. I used to weigh at home from 140-150.

The diggins are very good here and I am doing very well at present. I expect William will be here soon,-shall know in a few days.

...A few nights ago a man was killed in this place in a fray with another. I was just about to go to bed when I heard the sharp report of a pistol in the street. I sprang out and ran off down the street where I found a man lying on his back and the blood gushing from his neck where he had been stabbed. He only said, "I am a dead man."

I stooped down and felt for his pulse but could distinguish no motion. I, then, with two or three others, took him up and carried him into a doctor's office where he expired in a few moments. He was the one who fired the pistol, but which did not take effect. The man who killed him has been arrested, but will get clear, I think. Such is California.

Horsetown, Jan. 3, 1861
Dear Sister,
... You said you were growing old. Yes, it must be so, although I remember you only as I saw you last, some seven or eight years ago, and probably should we now meet, we should pass each other unrecognized; for a glance into the glass tells me that Time has not passed me unheeded, but has left his impress upon my brow; but the same heart beats within my breast now that throbbed there eight years ago, and I trust the time will come when I can obey the dictates of my heart and repay many kindnesses thought to be forgotten of which are still fresh in my memory,

After this letter, George apparently ceased writing to his siblings, and after the war they lost track of him and didn't even know if he was dead or alive for half a century. George passed away in Shafter, TX from typhoid at the age of 77. What a life he had!

The reunion of Brooks brothers William and George (3rd and 4th from the left) after over 50 years, in Glen Ellyn, Illinois in 1905. They were the only surviving Brooks siblings at this point.

William Eustis Brooks was born in Kingfield in 1835. According to family history, his Grandmother Eustis was "greatly disappointed because he did not want to be a cobbler." Fortunately, he had higher ambitions and had a long, illustrious career as a clergyman.

First, however, there was his gold fever, which he treated by going to California in February, 1855, with friends Augustine H. Wyman[2] and William H. Bigelow[3]. While not striking it rich, he did earn enough after two years to pay for his college education, which was quite an accomplishment.

Apparently, he left home rather suddenly, as he announces his arrival to Emily and Clayton in the following letter from Columbia, California, April 8, 1855. Another bombshell is that he is engaged:

What, what does all this mean? Columbia, California? Dear brother and sister—from whom can this be? What, William? How can he be there? I thought he was in Bloomfield attending school, but no, he has gone to California—left his studies—left or given up getting an education. Yes, he must, else he would not have done so. Well, I am sorry, sorry for I hoped he would grow up to be a man useful in the community. What could have been the reason? Why did he not let us know of it? Why did he leave us?

These and similar exclamations I seem to hear you offer as you get this letter and open it. I expect you will feel somewhat surprised when you receive this if you have not heard before that I have left Bloomfield. I somewhat expect you have heard ere this that I have left Bloomfield as Miss Ann H. Wyman partially promised to write and let you know. I seemed to hear you say, "Who is this Miss Wyman he speaks of?" She is a young lady whom I met in Bloomfield and have, as the saying is, chose her to be the companion of my life, and as such, if nothing happens to the contrary, introduce her to you.

And, as a sister, you will, no doubt, be anxious to see what kind of a choice I have made. But I well know, as well as you, that I am not the person to describe her. But this much I will say, that she has ever been a girl of virtuous habits, of a kind, open, frank disposition and of lively feelings. At times she may be called rude by some. She has I hope found the "Pearl of great Price" and attained pardon through the blood of Christ. She had not when I left joined any church since it has not been

---

[2] Augustine H. Wyman, 1837-1916. The 1880 census from Skowhegan, Maine lists him as the part-proprietor of a broom factory, who was partially disabled from being "poisoned by shaving soap." I have not, as yet, delved into that mystery!

[3] William H. Bigelow, 1835-1890. Served in the 16th Maine. After the war he was a school superintendent in Maine and then a special agent for the post office.

many months since she has hope in the mercy of God. She has dark eyes, dark hair (not black) light skin and full rosy cheeks.

If she does not write to you, I should like to have you correspond with her so you can as I think you will like her if you ever get acquainted with her. I hope one day you will. It may be that you will think she had some influence in my coming here but she did not know what I was thinking of till I had pretty well made up my mind to come, and though she did not oppose my coming, neither was it her wish to influence me to go.

And the reason that I came out here was this: I found if I went on with my studies I should get deeply in debt and I thought it would be better for me to get something to go to school where I wouldn't get deeply in debt. And, after thinking it over, I concluded to come. And here let me tell you that it is my intention is to go on with my studies when I return.

I know it was a very difficult step, coming out here, from what I expected, but I hope it will be all for the best. I have been here nearly two weeks. I have not as yet done much but soon expect to. I with some others have taken of a claim now and shall, if nothing prevents, go to work in the morning.

I am in hopes that I may get in some pretty good places so I can go back as soon as possible to resume my studies.

Columbia where I am now is quite a village and is one very corrupt place. I never saw so little regard to God's holy day as is here. Business goes on more briskly than on any other day and all the places of amusement are in full operation. There are two churches in this place and I find it pleasant to go to the houses of prayer and to seek sanctuary of my God. I find in need of religion in the heart here and I hope you will continue your prayers to God in my behalf.

Columbia, California. The churches are in the background.

I have not much more to write now. I want you to answer this as soon as you can and direct to Columbia, Tuolumne County, California.

Please tell me where George is and what he is doing. How does Pamelia get along? Write all about the family. Tell Albion to be a good

boy and learn fast. Kiss little sister for me. I must close now wishing you for the present goodbye.
Affectionately yours, William E. Brooks

Apparently, something happened "to the contrary" with the sometimes "rude" Ann H. Wyman, as she and William never married. Perhaps she was none too happy with his decision to suddenly leave her to go to California, and didn't want to wait years, or perhaps have him never return.

The following letter from William to Albion from Columbia on September 16, 1855, indicates that Emily hadn't answered his last letter from May.

Dear Brother Albion,
As Emily does not see fit to answer the letter I wrote to her long, long ago, I will try to see what effect it will have on you.
Now, you will write, won't you? Yes, I know you will. Well, Albion, how do you do? What are you doing? How are you enjoying yourself? I expect that you have got to be a great big strapping boy and that I should hardly know you.
But I hope you grow in goodness as well as in size and that you try and learn something new every day of your life, and that, above all, you learn how to love, serve and obey that being who has said, "Remember now they Creator, in the days of your youth, before the days of trouble come, and the years approach, when thou shalt say, "I have no pleasure in them." Do you ever think of Him who came here on earth that you might have life eternal? Do you ever pray to Him and ask him to guide, keep and direct you? If you have not, you will now begin, won't you?
Perhaps you would like to know how I am getting along. Well, I am happy to tell you that I am getting along well. I hope that if I continue to have as good luck as I have had, I may be able to return in a year or so and go on with my studies. I want you to tell me all, how you get along, how much you go to school, what you study, how you like it, etc. Now, be sure to.
My health has been and is good and I am enjoying myself finely. We have good meetings which I attend; also Sabbath Schools and I attend them also. Besides the books we have in the Sabbath School, there is a circulating library of 1000 volumes containing of Histories, Travels, Biographies etc. So you can see that I have all the books to read that I can

ever get time to. I have got a first rate fellow to live with. His name is Albert G Leyhton (?)[4]. We keep "old Bachelor's Hall."

Would you like to have me tell you what kind of a house or cabin we have? Well, I will tell you. It is made of logs and is some 20 feet long and 12 to 14 feet wide. We have a fireplace to do our cooking by and I can tell you we live well. Would you not like to slip in and take tea with us? If you will, you shall be welcome.

You doubtless know that George has come out here. I have not seen him but I had a letter from him a short time ago. He was well and in good spirits. If he has not written to you and you write to him, direct to "One Horse Town, Shasta county, California."

Now, dear brother, I want you to be a good boy, study and grow up to be a wise, useful, and intelligent man. Remember to gain an interest in the Savior first as you have one friend "that sticketh closer than a brother and who will never leave nor forsake you, but will ever be near you to own and bless you and will, at last, if you do his will, take you to live with Himself."

So, in the midst of all the vices that the "corrupt" mining town of Columbia has to offer, William Brooks reads books, goes to church, and quotes the Bible. Why does that sound familiar?

William's letter to Emily from Columbia, dated July 15, 1856, is apparently in response to her reaction to the news that his fiancé had dumped him for another man. And Emily had given birth to her second daughter, Mary.

I am glad to know that your health is better than it was and that you all are doing so well. You want me to send a name for little sis. Well, I will send one and if you will call her by it, I will send her a two dollar and a half gold piece. Ellen Josephine. The first is the first name and the second the middle name of two sisters I know in Bloomfield whom I think a great deal of. Their names are Ellen M. and Emily Josephine Leighton.

I was surprised that you should think I should be cast down at the great loss as I should judge, you think that I have met with. I am no such fellow as to come down at such a thing as this be assured. If I never meet with anything worse, I shall be glad.

Anna has got a good smart man I think from what I have learned and I hope she will be happy. Do you think I had better return when I get

---

[4] This could be Leighton, or possibly a transcription error of his old friend and mining partner, August Wyman. Agnes Thompson placed a question mark at that name as she wasn't sure what it was.

enough to go through college and not wait to get more at the risk of not going?

Think it all over and see how I should be and not have anything but myself to begin life with as it were. I was 21 last June and I think now I can come home next spring with enough to go through with or I hope so.

I want and am determined to get an "education" and I must though I sometimes wonder as to the use to put it to. I have always had a great desire to be a doctor and I seem to think more of that profession then any author and once, a short time ago, made up my mind to be your regular M. D. But I hardly know where my duty lies.

Please give me your opinion.

My partner tells me to have you call the baby "Arvilla" and I have no objection if you like it better.

George is willing to do his part with me in sending Albion to school and if you will just tell us the sum, I guess we will help him along. Please give my best respects to your husband and tell him I would be most happy to have him write in your letters. I always conclude I am writing to both of you when I write to one.

I would like to have him express his opinion in regard to my fittest course to take.

I must close now so good bye.

Your affectionate brother, William.

First, thankfully Emily chose not to call her daughter Arvilla! Second, it was surprising to learn—at least I was surprised—that William had originally intended to be a medical doctor. Finally, I found it quite heartwarming that both he and George wanted to pay for Albion's education. What a generous family, these Brooks!

William's wife, Angie, and sister Emily.

Of course, William did return to Maine and, as promised, graduated college. After the Civil War, rather than go to medical school, he graduated from Yale Theological Seminary in 1867. He was ordained and installed as pastor in the Congregational Church in New York, and Albion's friend, Rev. Alexander R. Thompson preached the sermon at the event.

In 1874 he moved to New Haven, CT to be pastor of the Congregational Church there. In 1880 he became president of the Tillotson Collegiate and Normal Institute in Austin, Texas for five years—not knowing his long-lost brother was also in Texas. Then came the moves to churches in Chicago, IL, Muscatine, Iowa, Benton Harbor, Michigan, back to Chicago, back to Maine, and then finally Connecticut, until poor health caused him to retire in 1906.

William Brooks.

He had a long, happy marriage to Angie Richardson Wilson, and they had five children. Unfortunately, the son they named after Albion, died at age 5, but the others lived to adulthood and provided many grandchildren. It was on Christmas Eve, 1906, at the Cambridge, Massachusetts home of his son, Clayton, that he "became fatigued" with the festivities with some of those grandchildren. "Some time during the night he was stricken with apoplexy and never recovered consciousness, passing away the evening of December 26, 1906." The official death certificate lists the cause of death as a cerebral hemorrhage, with "Chronic Endocarditis" and "Chronic Nephritis" being contributing factors.

There were many tributes to William from friends and colleagues across the country. The following are some excerpts from one of his oldest friends, Augustine Wyman:

I formed an acquaintance of my ever dear friend, William Eustis Brooks, in 1850. We were together a great deal from that time in what was then the Bloomfield Academy, Maine, until February, 1855, when about the 20th of that month we started, with three other young men, for California.

We sailed from New York on the steamer "North Star" about February 23d. Somewhere off the coast of Florida we had a severe storm, otherwise our journey to San Francisco was uneventful. We arrived there about March 22d. We crossed the Isthmus by the Nicaragua route.

We made no stop in San Francisco, taking the first boat to Stockton. From there we went by stage to Columbia, called the Southern Mine.

William and myself, before leaving Bloomfield, entered into an agreement whereby we became partners. In all the time, until he came home, we had a common purse. I know we had implicit confidence in each other. We each spent what money we wanted and never had a reckoning between us. We both went to California for means with which to go to college.

We arrived at Columbia the last part of March and commenced mining at once, prospecting and taking up a claim, and buying two or three others. We owned two claims adjoining. I cannot say how long William was in that camp, or when he started for home. It is my impression he was in California less than two years. I know he bought a ticket to go on the steamer "Central America," but some good guardian angel communicated to him he had better wait and go on the next steamer, which he did. You know it is said there are many things in heaven and earth we do not understand. The steamer "Central America" was wrecked and all on board were lost[5].

... When we would have no water to wash out the gold, on such time William went into the mountains to work building a reservoir. I was told when he had an opportunity he would go out into the woods and make speeches to imaginary audiences and thus prepared himself for his future work. Those who said this predicted to me someday he would be a great orator.

His whole life in California and everywhere he was clean and manly. He was always to be relied on, so it could be truthfully said of him, as one of old, "Nature might stand up and say to all the world, this was a man."

All who became acquainted with him when a boy spoke in his praise, saying he was a fine boy, and a good boy makes a good man.

His comrades in the army, some of whom I am acquainted with, all speak highly of his integrity.

I hope I may clasp his hand again in the Better Land.

I say to his sons and daughter, as their father's chum, partner and friend, they will do well to emulate him in his many virtues, so that nothing but happiness may await them in their future of life.

Fine praise indeed. William Brooks was someone that made lifelong friends, devoted himself to helping others, preached the faith in which he steadfastly believed for his entire life, fought bravely for his country, and was a devoted husband and father. As I previously stated, William Brooks lead the life which Albion should have also had, if only he had lived.

---

[5] The *S.S. Central America* sank in a hurricane off the coast of South Carolina on the evening of September 18, 1857. The loss of life was 425 out of 578 passengers and crew, and an astounding 30,000 pounds of gold, which would be close to 1 billion dollars today. This large loss contributed to the financial Panic of 1857.

Then there is Emily Eustis Brooks Kingman, born in 1829 in Kingfield, Maine, the unsung hero of this book—or at least someone whose praises can't be sung loudly enough. By the age of 16, letters showed that she was very smart, fiercely independent, and confident that she would "be quite a somebody," just on the strength of her own talents and courage—and all this in the mid-19th Century when women had little chance of any sort of advancement.

In terms of compassion, and acting upon it, when Abigail fell ill, Emily was the only one who went to Kingfield to care for her. Emily was the only one who stepped up to take Albion. When Pamelia was having a baby, and then later when she was ill, Emily was the only one to drop everything and go to care for her for months.

Emily once took in a homeless boy from the streets of Bridgeport, and offered to give him a home and an education. After just over a week, however, the boy chose instead to steal $10 from her purse and run away. But hey, she tried! (And I would like to say this was the stupidest decision this boy would ever make, but I suspect he made any number of poor choices in what most likely was a brief and violent life.)

Clayton and their five daughters adored Emily.

Albion thanked God for giving him such a sister.

I wish I had the time and space to reproduce all of her letters, especially those back and forth to Clayton before they were married, but that, too, is worthy of a book of its own.

She passed away after a long illness on November 3, 1900, at the age of 71, in their home in Washington, Connecticut. I would like to think that if there is some afterworld, Albion was the first to greet her with open arms.

Emily Brooks Kingman

Appendix C
The Kingman Family

Samuel Clayton Kingman outlived all the Brooks siblings, not passing away until May 22, 1922, at the ripe old age of 92! His many accomplishments are listed in his obituary from *The Bridgeport Telegram*, June 1, 1922, page 10:

> **Samuel Kingman, Former Resident, Dies in Florida**
> *Inventor for Wheeler & Wilson Co. Gave Many Gifts to Church*
> *Was 92 Years Old*
> *Served on School Board Here and Was Active in Civic Life*

Samuel Clayton Kingman, a resident of Bridgeport for many years, died Sunday at the home of his daughter, Mrs. Ella Thorpe of Saint Augustine, Fla., at the age of 92 years.

Mr. Kingman reached his 92nd birthday anniversary on May 15, and was remembered with many messages of friendship and good cheer from friends in the North. He had been in ill for three months and for the last few days of his life remained in an unconscious condition.

For a number of years, Mr. Kingman spent his summers at Washington, this state, with his daughter, Mrs. Joseph I. West, and his winters in Florida, with Mrs. Thorpe.

Mr. Kingman was a native of South Reading, Mass., now Wakefield, the son of Samuel Kingman and Sarah Ring Pope. His father was a highly esteemed citizen of Wakefield, being a public-spirited man who served the nation, the state, and the town in various offices of trust.

Mr. Kingman was born May 15, 1830 and graduated from the high school, being the valedictorian of his class, and editor of the school paper, the "New Era." At the age of 18 he went to Lawrence where he learned the machinists' trade. He spent a year in the service of Col. Andersen at Richmond, Va.[1]

Mr. Kingman was prominent in his work with the Wheeler and Wilson Manufacturing Co. at Watertown, Conn., and became known as an inventor. He invented and patented many machines for facilitating the manufacturing of the sewing machine needle.

Mr. Kingman was married to Miss Emily Eustis Brooks in 1853 at Haverhill, Mass., a descendant of Governor Eustis. For 37 years they lived

---

[1] Joseph Reid Anderson was a general in the Confederate Army during the Civil War.

in Bridgeport where their family of five daughters grew up. They lived in a handsome residence at Washington Park.

The older generation of Bridgeport friends will recall his many benefactions to the poor, and his gifts were many. The bell of the Park Street Church to which the family belonged, was presented by Mr. Kingman in memory of his wife's brother, Albion Brooks, killed at Cold Harbor, June 3, 1864. The clock and communion table of this church were also his gifts.

During the Civil War he was an active member of the Christian Commission, visiting the boys at the front many times in that connection.

In the state militia he went from a private to first lieutenant, commanding company E flying artillery.

He was an expert marksman and owing to his fine shooting was tendered in 1876, the position of inspector of rifle practice on the staff of the colonel of the fourth regiment C.N.G.

After his removal to Washington, Conn., in 1890, he still retained an interest in Bridgeport, but became deeply attached to his adopted town, and on different occasions showed his public-spirited citizenship. At one time he presented the town a fire truck and the use of a building as its quarters.

His chief sport was rifle shooting and he held many medals.

Samuel Clayton Kingman, c. 1920, the oldest Mason in Connecticut at age 90. He did appear to love to dress up in uniforms.

During his long residence in Washington, he was a member of the First Congregational Church and his letters at the annual church roll call were looked forward to with much interest.

He was a Shriner and a Knights Templar, a member of the Hamilton commandery. At the annual gatherings last year of the Masonic Veterans Association in Meriden, Mr. Kingman, then the oldest one present, made one of the brightest speeches of the occasion.

The Kingman home in Washington, CT.

At one time Mr. Kingman was a member of the governor's staff. He occupied positions of trust and was an active member of the school committees of Watertown and Bridgeport and also of Washington.

He held friendly relations with ministers all his life, and was interested in their work.

He leaves five daughters. Mrs. Thorpe of Saint Augustine, Mrs. Frank Buckingham of Bridgeport, Mrs. Edward Buckingham of Lynchburg, Va., Mrs. Hiram C. Loomis of Chicago, Mrs. Joseph I. West of Washington, Conn., 14 grandchildren and 6 great grandchildren

The large Kingman monument in Mountain Grove Cemetery in Bridgeport, CT. Emily's headstone is under the left arrow, Clayton, the right. Their daughters and their husbands are buried around them.

William Warren Kingman, born in South Reading, MA in 1832, was yet another of Clayton's siblings. He served in both the 50th and 8th MA. As these letters were in the collection, it was worth reproducing them here to see where he was during the war.

To Clayton from his sister Lucy, shortly after William was mustered in, November 1862.

Friday morning. One of our neighbors had a letter from a soldier at New York and he wrote that William was quite sick.

The doctor vaccinated[2] him last week and it has made him sick and a number of the other soldiers.

We shall try to send some things to him tomorrow. Father brought that letter that Albion wrote with the others that Orlando sent and we thought you might want it so we send it to you.

Lucy

We have all got bad colds.

Marietta[3] had a letter from William this morning. He said he was better and the boat is ready for them. and they may go South any time. My love to all.

Camp Banks, East New York, L. I. November 25th
Dear Brother Clayton,

I now take my pencil to write you a few lines to let you know where I am and how I am. I am now in East New York, Long Island on the Union course.

As Father is going out to see you, I should like to have you come out and see me. Father, I expect, will come. I should be very happy to see you with him. My health is very good except the toothache once in a while.

We came here last Saturday afternoon from New York. We were in the Franklin Barracks two nights. We marched here, 8 miles., with knapsacks and they were some heavy. I can tell you my back was sore enough when I got here. It is said there are about 40,000 troops in and about here in different camps.

It is a pleasant day and it seems good to see a pleasant day. It has been raining most all the time we have been out of Massachusetts.

We came by your place last Wednesday night or Thursday morning in the Steamer <u>City of Boston</u>. Of course, we could not see your place it was so stormy and thick. I saw the <u>Great Eastern</u>. It is a large boat.

---

[2] This was most likely a small pox vaccination, which was first created by Edward Jenner in 1796.

[3] William married Marietta Whiting on August 29, 1862.

Dear brother, I should like to have you write to me if you can get time to write to a Soldier. Give my love to Emily and the rest of the folks and Charley. Tell him to come and see me if he can tell him to write, sure. I will give you the directions.

William W. Kingman Camp Banks
Co. E. 50th Regiment M. V. M.
East New York, Long Island
Care of Captain Littlefield[4]

Baton Rouge, March 6, 1863
Direct to William W. Kingman
Co. E. 50th Regt. Mass. Vol. New Orleans, La.
Dear Brother,

By this time I guess you would like to hear from me. I am now at Baton Rouge on the Mississippi River. It is a very pleasant place and quite high ground, the first I have seen since I left New York. All along the river it was very low and swampy, full of dead trees.

It seemed like getting into a new country when we first saw this place and the hill we had to go up. When this place was taken by our forces a great many buildings were burned. Most of them were built of brick. I saw one that a cannon ball passed through, another was all riddled with bullets. Nearly all the folks left this place and houses, lands, many very neat houses are left desolate. We occupy one for a hospital, a very neat and snug little house.

A large part of the penitentiary was destroyed, a very large building. There is now a New York Regiment camped in the interior. It is very warm in here in the daytime, but at night it is some cold and the boys are apt to take cold, and they do. I have a bad cough. It is a poor place for sickness. Some of the boys are sick with Diarrhea. I have had it for more than four weeks but it is better now.

It is raining some today. Shall not have much drilling to do in the rain. We have to work here when we drill in Brigade Drills from 2 in the afternoon till 10 at night, double quick most all the time or a large part of it.

We are in the 3rd Brigade under Brigadier General Dudley[5] of Boston. He is the brother of Marthy Dudley that taught school in South

---

[4] Samuel Furbush Littlefield, 1826-1905, was a tin plate worker before the war, and a hardware merchant after. Born in Wells, Maine, married in Wakefield, MA. Died at his home at 20 Chestnut, St., Wakefield, MA of a cerebral hemorrhage at age 79.

[5] Nathan Augustus Monroe Dudley, 1825-1910. William refers to him as an "old chap," but Dudley was only 38 at the time, just seven years older than William.

Reading a number of years ago. He is a gay old chap and a good General. I wish we had more such men as he is. We are under marching orders now and are likely to start any time. We are going in the direction of Port Hudson to see if the enemy are throwing up any works in the woods. There are any quantity of rebels all around us, and a large force, it is said, outside our pickets. Our Cavalry have been fighting quite often and bring prisoners in.

We shall go in a large force when we go and shall be gone some days I think. We shall have some hard marching to do. We have got all our stuff packed and the quartermaster is ordered to pack all his stores.

I hear from home quite often. Folks are all well.

I shall have to get this franked and you will have to pay it at your Office. I would not do it if I could help it but we cannot get any stamps for any money. Some have paid as high as 10 cents for one. They are not kept in this place at all.

I must close this letter as the soup is ready. Give my love to Charley and wife, your wife and children. Write to me if you get time. It would be thankfully received. I am well and remain

Your brother W. W. Kingman

The letters next pick up after he was mustered out of the 50th MA, but reenlisted with the 8th MA.

Baltimore, Maryland August 1, 1864
Dear Brother,,
I thought I would drop you a line today. I suppose you knew that I was again in the service of my Country, and for the period of 100 days. That was what we were mustered for. Nearly one week has passed and we are in this place some five miles from the city in a splendid grove and on a hill overlooking the city. We can see it from here. I never saw a better or pleasanter camp ground than this.

We passed over that portion of the railroad that the Rebels destroyed: One place, Gunpowder Bridge, they are all in good running order now. They were in this grove but as they did not have any guns, they could not shell the city. They could have done a good deal of damage if they had had guns. I think they are somewhere in this State so we are looking out for them.

The 20th Pennsylvania left here this morning for Fort McHenry. It was a splendid Regiment, 1500 strong. Ours is 1000, mostly veterans. We have got good officers: Littlefield is our Captain, Jason H. Knight[6], 1st

---

[6] Jason H. Knight, 1838-1894 was a shoemaker from Wakefield, MA.

Lieut., James Burdett[7] 2nd. They are first-rate men and well-booked up. I did not think I should be nailed again but as the camp was ordered out, I thought best to go with them, one week, today, of our 100 days. I hope I shall have a chance to see the city of Washington. I have long wished to see that place. Probably I shall be some disappointed.

We had a hard old drill yesterday (Sunday) an inspection with all of our troops. Made some of us grunt with our load.

One thing, they do not come very often, not more than once in a month. We have a splendid Brigade and very large. It is said we are in a Brigade to be stationed in or near the city of Baltimore. I had as leave stay here as to go anywhere else. You must excuse this dirty sheet. I can't keep it clean any way, - so much dust all the time. There has been no rain of any amount a since I left home for the camp.

There are many sick now and off duty. They may be sick and they may not be. I know some play it to get out of duty. I should like to have you write to me and send me a paper if you can. Direct to me Co. E., 8th Regt. Mass. Vol., Baltimore, Maryland, care of Capt., S. F. Littlefield.

Our living is the same as before, salt horse. It will take some time to get used to it. I saw James Carter. He came out here to see us. He lives in Baltimore. He carried out a lot of letters the boys had written. We have a good deal of leisure time, - getting berries and games of all kinds. We have a good deal of spirit as well as singing.

I was very sorry I could not have seen Angie when she was at Father's. She went away the day I went home. Give my love to Emily and the children. Has Charlie gone to war yet? Hope he will not have to. It is a hard life but it must be done by some-one or down goes our country in the dust.

Write to me when you can. I must close these lines now as I have got to go out on a 2-hour drill. Remember me to all. I remain your brother

W.W. Kingman

Co. E. 8th Regt. Mass. V.M. Baltimore, Maryland, Care of Capt. Littlefield

Baltimore, Maryland August 26th 1864

I received your letter of the 21st and was very glad to hear from you and that you were well. I am glad business is so brisk with you but I am

---

[7] James A, Burdett, 1837-1886 was born in Providence, Rhode Island. He was a "shoe finisher" in Wakefield, MA when he died of Bright's Disease (kidney disease) at age 49.

sorry there are so many young men that stay at home and are able to do military duty.

If I had stayed at home a while longer I should have gone for one year. The bounty was large, 925 dollars, quite a lift for a poor chap like me, but now I get state pay and government making for 3 months 108 dollars, ten days more on to that.

There is no chance of getting any money until the Paymaster gets here, and there is no telling when he will be here.

Marietta sends me a little now and then, so I do not get entirely out. Now if you would let me have a little change now, I will pay you when I get home and get paid off. I don't like to borrow, but I don't want to ask Marietta every time I get out, shall do without it before I will do it. Fruits are not very high out here. I can buy peaches at 50 cents a box, Bartlett Pears were high being 4 pears for 25 cents, - quite small at that. We can get milk at 10 cents a quart, cakes and pies in any quantity, so you see we can get along with money. Our rations are mostly salt pork and coffee, soft bread and fresh meat 3 times a week, but that makes us sick when we eat it. Our cooks make a soup of ours. Mother could make a better soup with pork than we get here.

I hope we shall not move from here. Hardly think we shall go from here now. Our boys are all well except Sergeant Carter and he is not very sick. My love to all. I hear Lanny is going out to Connecticut. I had a letter for him yesterday.

I remain your brother
W.W. Kingman

Baltimore, Maryland, September 21st, 1864
Dear Brother,

I received your kind note with the money. I should have written before but did not do it. I hope what you just sent me will last until my Time is out. Some of our Boys in Camp have reenlisted and got their Bounty and spent all of it, $350.00. They are off and in the guard house nearly all the time. Some feel rather blue about it as they have got to go for a year on no money, - spent it all.

Etta is or has been sick for some time past but is some better now. My health is good.

I thank you very much for your kind offer. I hope I shall not need it. I want to clear $100.00 (one hundred dollars) by this operation and must be prudent of money. All our boys are well. It is almost roll call and I must close soon. Received a letter from home today. Mother was well I believe.

We have only 4 days to serve. Then I want to go home and VOTE FOR LINCOLN. How they will be licked this fall (McClellan I mean) We want such peace as report says Sheridan has done. My love to all, Emily and the children.

I remain your brother
W.W. Kingman
Excuse mistakes and half sheet of paper.

After the war, William returned to Wakefield, MA, and continued being a shoemaker. His wife died in 1879 at age 35. He married another woman named Marietta Colburn, in 1880. He died in Wakefield at age 70 of "vascular disease of the heart" at his home at 30 Pearl St.

Orlando Pope Kingman (1839-1885) was important to Albion, so his letters deserve some space here. They no doubt became acquainted when Albion spent those two years living in the post office in South Reading, MA. Orlando enlisted in August of 1862, with the 2nd Company of Massachusetts Volunteer Sharpshooters. Perhaps his older brother, Clayton's, marksmanship skills ran in the family.

Unfortunately, Orlando was never to fire a shot at the enemy, as a mysterious, lingering illness confined him to hospitals and convalescent camps for his military career. The following are all letters to Clayton.

This is a classic example of what it was like traveling to join your regiment:

September 1862
I have a chance to write and I will improve the opportunity. We are still here waiting but expect to go today and join the Regiment. I wrote my last from New York. That evening at 2 o'clock September 4 we took a boat for Amboy, New Jersey, thence by cars to Camden, then took a ferryboat, and after 10 minutes we arrived at Philadelphia at 1 o'clock P.M. There we were treated to a nice supper and then we marched through the city, took the cars to Baltimore stopping at Perryville and by ferry to Havre de Grace which is opposite across the Susquehanna. On the ferry boat and all along the way to Washington was a guard from the 18th Conn. regiment.

We arrived in Baltimore at 3 o'clock P.M. the 5th. (As we were riding along one fellow shot a pig out of the window with his revolver and killed it.) We stayed at Baltimore until 9 o'clock P.M. then took cars for Washington.

In Baltimore I took a walk to the Bible society and got me a Testament, as I gave the one I had away, and when I came out the squad of Cavalry was passing. The officer rode up to me and told me to fall in the ranks as he was picking up stragglers. I told him my company was across the street so I did join in. The Massachusetts 6th[8] was expected and all the stores were shut up as they thought there might be a row. (The 6th did not come through then). We arrived in Washington about 12 o'clock P.M. and I turned in on the platform of the Soldiers Retreat and slept soundly.

I went about the city the next day, to the Capital, White House, etc. Most of the boys were disappointed in the looks of Washington. In the afternoon we left to join our Regiment. We marched ten miles over the Aqueduct Bridge, over Arlington Heights, to Halls Hill where they were encamped when we arrived. The orders were to march so we had to keep on after resting a few hours.

We started at 1 o'clock Sunday morning, and at noon we stopped by Alexandria for 2 hours, then marched two miles further by Fairfax Seminary (which is now used as a hospital) and encamped. (We call it Camp Canada) Two of us pitched a tent of our rubber blankets (as we have no tents yet) and after making our coffee, I slept sound until awakened about 12 o'clock by the orders to fall in in line of battle. As we new recruits had no guns we stayed to guard the camp as the rest fell in,-as the report was that the Rebels were coming. (They were only a few miles off.) It was a false alarm. Stayed here two nights and then marched 5 miles more and camped near Fort Woodbury. I went all over the Fort from which there is a fine view of Washington. Stayed here two nights and the next day started for Maryland. About 20 of all stayed behind the rest and when we got to the bridge they would not let us pass, so we had to get a pass and so we are here in Washington waiting to join our regiment. We expect to today.

Has Charley[9] gone? I saw the 20th Conn. Regiment. I may come across the battery. How is business? I have seen no Chaplain in our Regiment but Sunday I was marching, stopped in a secesh field and got plenty of tomatoes and potatoes which we cooked and had a good dinner.

Is Charlie married? Write. Where is Mr. Thompson now? Have you heard from Albion? Guess he has been in battle lately. Asked Charley about my rifle.

---

[8] On April 19, 1861—the anniversary of the Battles of Lexington and Concord—the 6th MA left Philadelphia by train and arrived in Baltimore. They were met by secessionists throwing stones and bricks, who then opened fire. The 6th MA finally returned fire. Private Luther C. Ladd, just 17, was killed—the first Union soldier killed in action of the war. There would be 4 Union soldiers killed and 36 wounded, with 12 civilians killed in the Baltimore Riot.

[9] Charles Edwin Kingman, born 1837. Family history says he served in the army, but if he did, I cannot find with what regiment. He married Margeret Woodruff in 1862. The 1920 census listed 83-year-old Charles living in Needham, MA with his wife and 2 children.

Direct letters to me at
Washington D.C.
2nd Company Sharpshooters, 22nd Mass. Regiment
Care Captain Wentworth

We have Sharp's Breach loading rifles.
I must close to get this in the mail. Kiss Ella, Mary and Carrie for me and my love to all and Albion when you write. So good bye and remember your
Brother Orlando

Orlando guessed that Albion had "been in battle lately." Yes, it was called Antietam.

Orlando wouldn't be seeing any battles, as by his next letter he is already in the hospital, obviously being well cared for.

Post Hospital, October 19, 1862
You may have thought I was dead; but not quite. I am not well though. I don't know what the matter is. I am weak but there are some nice Ladies here that give me anything I want. One lady gave me crab apples, (they were large and nice) and milk and sauce and a nice blanket and anything that's needed.

Ladies come from Washington with wagon loads of things and give them all to the soldiers. They bring papers and distribute them around.

Have you heard from Albion? And where is Cooley[10]? And the battery? How is business at the factory? I want you to write and let me know all the news. How is Brown, Smith etc.? How are the ducks on the sound?

There is no news here. There are about 20,000 men here in camp. There's a splendid view of Washington and down the Potomac a good ways. Has the church got a minister yet? Where is Thompson? My respects to him. Those Thursday evening meetings,-do they keep up yet? Where is Charley? Is he married? Tell him to write to me. Love to Maggie and all inquiring friends.

It is very hard work sitting around doing nothing, sitting most of the time. But I must come to a close as it is supper time. I enclose 20 cents in stamps which I wish you would change for three cent ones as they are not plenty here and send them to me. The direction is:

---

[10] Henry Mather Cooley 1841-1914, 1st Sgt. 14th CT. Captured at Gettysburg, July 3, 1863. Was paroled (date unknown) and returned to the ranks. Survived the war, married, and was a machinist.

Post Hospital, Near Alexandria
Care Col. Belknap

Post Hospital Oct. 23, 1862

I received your letter yesterday, the 22nd and $1.50 and three stamps all right. I am greatly obliged to you as I can buy little things, sweet potatoes etc. What is the price of condensed milk there? It is $.50 a small can here. I tent with the cook for the sick and he makes puddings when he can get milk.

There is a nice lady here that gives me chocolate and dried apples and I stew them, so I get along first-rate. We have beefsteak every day, boiled rice and sugar every day and vegetable soup, but the climate here does not agree with me. My tent is near the brick house, close to where they cook. Yesterday I thought our tent would blow down, we had to brace it with ropes, and it blows now pretty hard, but we stood it.

... This camp is situated poorly. Water you must go almost a mile to get anything fit to drink and water is the principle thing and wood is scarce. Someone is buried every day here. No wonder, they are not half taken care of and some sleep on the ground.

The nights are cold here and days are getting to be. Where is Albion?

I do not expect to stay here long now. They are going to move this camp about a quarter mile soon.... I hope you have heard from Albion.

Post Hospital, Oct. 27th, 1862

... I received your letter yesterday (Sunday) and was <u>very sorry</u> to find you had been here and did not find me. I wish I <u>could</u> have seen you, but I hope to see you soon. I have sent to the Captain of our company for my descriptive list and I expect tomorrow for I sent for it a week ago to Sharpsburg, Maryland.

I can't tell how long it will take to come. A descriptive list tells how much clothing, pay, etc. The soldier has drawn.

I am pretty sure to get my discharge when I get my list. If I do not get it soon, I shall get the surgeon to write and then I shall get it.

11 A.M. 29th Wednesday

I have not got my list yet and I am going to write myself today to the Captain again. I shall not ask the Surgeon to write as he is full of business they all say. I ought to go home as I am running down. One man asked me if I had the typhoid fever. A man just put his head in my tent to ask me the time and he said, "You are failing fast," and I am.

New Camp Convalescence, January 5, 1863
Near Fort Barnard
Via Washington D. C.

I was examined as my name was on the list with some others of the 22nd boys on the 29th and today I have seen Dr. Curtis who said that he had sent you a note telling you what was to be done with me.

I do not know myself what is to be done with me.

Please write and let me know immediately. I am well as usual.

Convalescent Camp
January 21, 1863

I received your letter of January 13th and found that the doctor said that I was to be sent to the Regiment. I have not heard a word about it here. None of the others of the 22nd (some 25) who are examined have heard about it.

... They are building barracks: each holds two: there are about 50 built and 50 more will be built. I should go into one soon.

It is rainy and cold here today. The 19 Conn. has moved... Do you know Mr. James Sutherland[11] of Bridgeport in the company with Albion, the one Albion sold his watch to? Let me know if you do. He was here but has gone to Alexandria to the hospital.

I have been working in the post office today a little while helping the Post Master. I got the paper with a list of names of companies in it. I got a letter from Charles yesterday. He wants me to let him have <u>some money</u>. I have not been paid off so I can't let him have any.

... Love to all and when you write sending my love to Albion, the bully old soldier.

Convalescent Camp
May 16th, 1863

... The camp is beginning to look nice. The mud it is dried up in the grass and trees are green on the hills. The officers' tents are having gardens or flower beds and trees set in front. Yesterday we (the whole camp) had an inspection, formed in line, boots black, as at a dress parade. The barracks were also inspected. The straw beds were all taken out of the barracks and the men now have to sleep on boards. This is to keep away the "grey backs" [lice] which are plenty here.

George Parker of the 8th Conn. is discharged. I guess I shall send this letter by him. I enclose one for Charley with a ring in it.

They are forming an invalid corps here now, those that are not well enough to go to the field are put in it. They will be placed on guard in

---

[11] James Sutherland was discharged due to disease on March 26, 1863. However, he reenlisted with the 1st CT Heavy Artillery in January 1864 and was discharged in July, 1865.

hospitals, do private guard etc. I don't know whether their names will be struck off the rolls are not. The boys here that belong to the 38th New York, a two-year Regiment, they joined their Regiment about a fortnight ago. One of them was wounded at the 1st Bull Run in the hip and was a nurse in a hospital in Alexandria. Soon they were in the fight of Chancellorsville and he was shot dead. He was a fine fellow. His time was up the 1st of June[12]. I suppose Cooley's regiment, the 14th Conn. was there. I had a letter from Sergeant Cooley about a fortnight ago. He was well, had not been in any fight. I suppose our Regiment was in it also.

I had a letter from Albion some time ago.

Convalescent Camp, Near Alexandria, Va.
June 10, 1863

... It is a fine morning. We have had some warm weather lately. There are about three thousand paroled prisoners here. Some of the 17th and 27th Conn.: Sergeant North and a drum major who used to be in the city guard and Frank Foster and Leight of the old city guard.

Yesterday afternoon the magazine of Fort Lyons[13] blew up and killed quite a number. The surgeons from this camp all went over. Fort Lyons is about a mile from the old court where you came to see me. They have been examining all the men here for Invalid Corps. I was examined but sent to duty, i.e. back to office. The men that were wanted in office were not put on Invalid Corps. They were organized yesterday. There were quite a lot of them, four or five hundred.

... Where is Albion now? Is Sutherland there?

Post Office, Convalescent Camp
August 19th

I am pretty well now, although we've had some hot weather. The paroled men here expect to be exchanged soon. Do you hear anything from Henry Cooley? He was supposed to have been taken prisoner. We have prisoners come in here frequently,-deserters, they are closely guarded. Conscripts are coming on this way.

So Captain William Brooks has got well of his wounds. I am going to write to Albion soon.

---

[12] The Battle of Chancellorsville was April 30 – May 6, 1863, so this soldier died with only a month left of his service.

[13] On June 9, 1863, eight tons of black powder exploded at Fort Lyon, killing 25 soldiers and destroying thousands of rounds of ammunition. One witness described it as looking like the eruption of a volcano.

This was the last letter in the collection. At some point, after at least a year of being in hospitals and convalescent camps, Orlando finally came home. It seems as it would have been easier on him, and cheaper for the government, to send him home a lot sooner.

He was married in 1870 to Eunice Elizabeth Lyman, and they had two children. He was a machinist until his death in 1885 at the age of 46, and is buried in the Old Warren Cemetery, Warren, CT.

INDEX

21st St. Dutch Reformed Church, 243
7th U.S. Colored Infantry, 62
Admiral ship, 107
Alabama Regiments: 26th AL, 177
Alexandria, VA, 168, 247, 307, 309-311
Algiers, Louisiana, 272
Allen, Col., 74, 75
Allen, Orrin Sweet, 152
Amboy, New Jersey, 306
Andersonville Prison, 100
Androscoggin River, 51
Annapolis, Maryland, 7, 70-72, 88, 103, 115, 148, 163
Anne E. Thompson ship, 74, 75
Antietam Creek, 123, 124
Antietam National Battlefield, 129
Antietam, MD, 8, 11, 63, 64, 71, 94, 109, 117, 119, 121, 123-29, 132, 133, 136, 143, 145, 149, 168, 172, 206, 207, 210, 222, 231, 267
Apache, 183
Appomattox River, 224, 229
Aquia Creek, VA, 84, 112, 113, 116, 140, 147, 148
Armstrong, John, 197
Ashby's Gap, VA, 133, 135
Bahamas, 69
Baltimore, MD, 61, 70, 76, 118, 303-07
Banks, Gen. Nathaniel, 270
Banks, John, 94
Bar Harbor, Maine, 13
Barber, Sophronia, 94
Barnard, Gen. John, 228, 229
Baton Rouge, LA, 302
Battle of Cedar Creek, 94
Battle of Chancellorsville, 137, 311
Battle of Chantilly, 159
Battle of Cold Harbor, 8, 235-42, 246-50
Battle of Fredericksburg, 133-43
Battle of Manassas, 59
Battle of Memphis, 269
Battle of Okeechobee, 4
Battle of Plattsburg, 3
Battle of Reams Station, 130
Battle of South Mountain, 118
Battle of Trafalgar, 80

Bay of Fundy, 47, 48
Beaufort Harbor, NC, 90, 92, 99
Beauregard, Gen. P.G.T., 217, 224, 226-29, 230, 232
Benton Harbor, Michigan, 295
Bermuda Hundred, 215-32, 233, 241, 261
Berwick, LA, 269
Beulah Church, 237, 241
Bigelow, William, 290
Bissell, Lewis, 247-49
Blackberry Raid, 173-82
Blackwater River, 161, 214
Blood, Aretus, 280
Bloomfield Academy, 281, 290, 293, 295
Bogue Banks, NC, 92
Bogue Sound, 101
Boleyn, Anne, 166
Bolivar Heights, WV, 122, 126
Booly, Major, 193
Boonsboro, MD, 117
Boston, MA, 13, 42, 177, 302
Bosworth, Charles, 93
Bosworth, Sam, 93-6
Bowdoin College, 281
Bower's Hill, 213-15
Branch, Gen. L.O., 90, 266, 267
Brashear, LA, 268, 272
Bridgeport, CT, 4, 7, 12, 21, 23, 41, 42, 45, 47, 57, 59, 60, 62-4, 67, 77, 110, 116, 121, 122, 126, 127, 130-32, 146, 148, 162, 165, 166-68, 171, 173, 183, 185, 186, 190, 191, 201, 201, 205-10. 243, 255, 257, 259, 262-65, 271, 272, 297-300
Bristoe Station, 202
Broatch, Lt. William, 105, 116
Brook's Station, VA, 140
Brooker, Andrew, 249
Brooklyn, NY, 4, 171
Brooks, Abigail, 26-34, 48-52, 274-6, 280, 281, 285, 297
Brooks, Albion (nephew), 295
Brooks, Albion D., 1, 4, 7-20, childhood 21, 23, 25-33, 35-46; 47-52, faith 54, 57, 58; enlistment 59-67; 68-73, 80-

102, 105-20, 123, 125-30, 132-50, 153-55, 161-77, 181-93, 200, reenlistment 201-204; 205-234, death 235-242; 243-58, 275, 276, 279-82, 285, 287, 291, 292, 294, 296, 297, 299, 301, 306-11
Brooks, Angie, 126, 134, 143, 144, 146, 148, 162, 173, 189, 191, 219, 231, 294, 295, 304
Brooks, Anna (infant), 282
Brooks, Anna, 50, 51, 275, 282
Brooks, Clayton, 295
Brooks, Emily, 18, 21-38, 42, 45-51, 85, 91, 101, 110, 126, 129, 140, 146, 147, 155, 177, 184-6, 201, 202, 210, 211, 213, 218, 235, 237, 240, 243, 244, 254, 274-83, 286, 287, 288, 290, 292, 293, 294, 297, 298, 300, 302, 304, 306
Brooks, George and Anna, 51
Brooks, George E. (father), 25-7, 49, 50, 275, 282
Brooks, George H. (brother), 25-7, 38, 47, 50, 51, 60, 75, 174, 183, 184, 189, 191, 274, 276, 279, 280-2, 284, 286, 288, 289, 293
Brooks, Katherine, 282
Brooks, Pamelia, 21-3, 26, 27, 29, 38, 50, 51, 274-83, 286, 291, 297
Brooks, William, 21, 25, 26, 27, 37, 42, 46, 50, 51, 96, 106, 110, 111, 115, 119, 121, 122, 126, 127, 133, 134-137, 140-143, 155, 162, 174, 177, 183, 184, 185, 186, 188, 189, 200, 203, 206, 211, 218, 219, 229, 231, 240, 243-247, 252, 274-276, 279-282, 284-286, 288, 289-296, 311
Brooks, Wilson, 284
Brookville, MD, 117
Brown, George, 76
Buckingham, Gov. William, 153, 155, 167
Bulkley, John, 79
Bull Run, 167, 311
Burdett, Lt. James, 304
Burnham, Col. George, 167
Burnside's Camp, 7, 60, 63, 64
Burnside, General Ambrose, 60, 63, 64, 67-72, 74, 79, 81, 110, 113, 114, 116, 119, 134, 136-38, 140, 144, 145, 149, 161, 163, 164, 168, 176, 205, 211, 217, 218, 265

Burnside's Bridge, 119, 124
Burnside's North Carolina Expedition, 68-108, 149, 168
Burpee, Henry Loomis, 62
Burton, Abigail, 166
Burton, Alden, 166, 171
Burton, James, 163-72
Burton, John, 151, 166, 168, 169, 171
Burton, Mr., 121, 122
Butler, Gen. Benjamin, 216, 217, 226, 230, 232
Calhoun Cemetery, 63
California, 21, 40-2, 46, 281, 282, 284, 286, 287, 289-93, 295, 296
California Regiments: 1st CA, 183, 282, 284
1st Regiment California Vol. Infantry, 183
Cambridge, Massachusetts, 295
Canada, 47
Canton Center, CT, 94
Carlisle, PA, 9
Carolina City, NC, 84, 91, 97
Carrabassett River, 13, 21, 48
Carthage, ME, 13, 22, 26, 27, 29, 31, 36, 45, 47, 51, 274, 275, 276, 286
Central America ship, 296
Charleston, South Carolina, 106
Charleston-Savannah Railroad, 259
Chasseur ship, 72, 77, 78, 86, 87, 101
Chesapeake Bay Bridge and Tunnel, 84
Chesapeake Bay, 151
Chesapeake, VA, 214
Chesterfield Co., VA, 57, 239
Chicago, IL, 50, 295
Cincinnati, Ohio, 269
City of Boston ship, 301
City Point, VA, 216, 219, 220, 224, 230
Clark, Captain, 76
Clark, Thomas C., 79
Clemens, Thomas, 132
Coit, Capt. Charles, 212, 235, 236
Cold Harbor National Cemetery, 11, 250
Cold Harbor, VA 8, 11, 12, 13, 16, 49, 50, 62, 84, 207, 229, 232, 235-37, 239, 241-52, 254, 299
Columbia, CA, 290, 291, 292, 293, 295, 296
Congress ship, 109

Connecticut Museum of Culture and History, 17, 112, 251
Connecticut, 4, 12, 17, 18, 38, 41, 144, 150, 174, 175, 178, 181, 183, 184, 191, 192, 196, 197, 201, 256, 259, 260, 262, 265, 268, 270, 271, 273, 282, 295
Connecticut 8th Regiment V.I.: 7, 8, 12, 17, 18, 57, 59- 65, 71, 79-82, 88- 97, 100, 101, 104, 110, 109, 112, 114, 116-21, 123, 125, 126, 128, 129, 132, 133, 136-40, 143, 146, 147, 150, 152, 153, 156-58, 161, 165, 166, 168, 169, 171-78, 181, 183, 184, 186, 189-91, 196, 197, 201, 203, 204, 208, 209, 212, 215, 217, 220-24, 227-29, 233-35, 238-40, 248, 249, 251, 282, 310
Connecticut Regiments (other): 1st CT Heavy Artillery, 166-68, 171, 172 259, 261, 2nd CT Heavy Artillery, 63, 93, 171, 246-249, 2nd Independent Battery CT Light Artillery, 271, 273, 6th CT, 259, 7th CT V.I., 218, 260-62, 10th CT V.I., 264, 265, 11th CT, 208, 218, 14th CT, 57, 123, 125, 130, 131, 240, 15th CT, 196, 197, 16th CT, 111, 119, 122, 123, 125, 126, 152, 17th CT 5, 7, 169, 19th CT, 246, 310, 21st CT, 158, 197, 23rd CT, 268, 271
Conover, Dr., 197
Cook, David, 47
Cookville, NB, Canada 47
Cooley, Henry, 308, 311
Cornwall, CT, 63, 93
Corps of Artillerists and Engineers, 3
Crampton's Gap, MD, 118
Crosby, Fred, 212
Cuba, 42
Cumberland ship, 109
Curtin, Governor Andrew, 140
Curtis, William B., 264, 265
Cushing, Henry J., 142
Custis, Martha, 179
Damascus, MD, 117
Darbytown Road, VA, 265
Day, Fannie, 66
Day, Reverend Guy Bigelow, 66-7
Dayton, Captain, 75
Deep Creek, VA, 84, 209, 214, 217
Denehy, Carol, 65
Denehy, Jack, 65

Dismal Swamp, 84, 151, 184, 185, 186, 206, 214
Dix, Gen. John, 176-8, 181
Douglas, Frederick, 261
Drewry's Bluff, VA, 169, 226-27
Dudley, Gen. Nathan, 302
Dudley, Martha, 302
Dufuskie, S.C., 262
Dutton, Col. Arthur, 158
East Haverhill, MA 22, 23, 35, 38, 283, 298
Eastport, Maine, 47
Eaton, Philena, 282
Eaton, Tom, 287
Edgett, Handasyd "Handyside", 47
Elizabeth City, NC, 185
Elk Run, VA, 135
Elmira prison, 100
Emerson, Parson, 266, 267
Emerson, Ralph Waldo, 261
Emerson, Ruben, 43
England, 196
Eustis Family, 13, 51, 26
Eustis, Anna (Brooks), 27, 28, 51
Eustis, Deacon and Mrs. William, 26, 27, 51, 274, 290
Eustis, Hannah, 26, 27, 29, 31, 275, 278, 279
Eustis, Mahitable, 50
Eustis, Nathan, 26, 29, 52
Eustis, Sarah, 52
Evergreen Rest Cemetery, 199
Fair Haven, CT, 272, 273
Fairfield County, Connecticut, 166
Falmouth, VA, 114, 137, 144, 146
Farmington, ME, 275
Finger Lakes, New York, 2
Florida, 4, 39, 298
Fort Bartow, 81, 83
Fort Blanchard, 81, 83
Fort Brady, 4
Fort Clifton, 224
Fort Fisher, 159
Fort Gratiot, 4
Fort Howard, 4
Fort Huger, 81, 83
Fort Jessup, 4
Fort Leavenworth, 4
Fort Lyons explosion, 311
Fort Mackinac, 4

Fort Macon, 8, 84, 92, 96-101, 103, 106, 111
Fort McClellan, 152
Fort McHenry, 303
Fort McNair, 7
Fort Niagara, 4
Fort Pulaski, 263
Fort Sumter, 59
Fort Wagner, 169, 259
Fort Woodbury, 307
Fortress Monroe, 70, 72, 79, 84, 107, 116, 151, 192, 205, 216, 230
Fox's Gap, MD, 117, 118
Franklin, LA, 262, 269
Frederick, MD, 117, 118
Fredericksburg, VA, 85, 88, 89, 112-16, 126, 127, 128, 133-45, 148, 149, 168, 176, 182
Frost, Rev. D. S., 199
Fussell, Jacob, 245
Gaines Mills, VA, 238
Gardner, Alexander, 11, 114, 128
Garton-on-the-Wolds, Yorkshire, England, 47
Gaskin's Mill, VA, 135
George Washington ship, 219
Georgia ship, 152
Getty, Gen. George, 156, 158
Gettysburg, PA 5, 7, 88, 89, 142, 177, 178, 181, 193, 198, 210, 273
Gilmore, Gen. Quincy, 217, 232
Glen Ellyn, Illinois, 289
Goldsborough, Dr. Charles R., 117
Goodyear, Charles, 109
Grant, Gen. U.S., 207, 216, 217, 222, 228, 235, 246
Gray, Dr. John, 198
Great Eastern ship, 301
Guyon, Lt. Col., 193
Halfway House, VA, 228
Hall, Capt. Henry, 227
Harpers Ferry, WV, 8, 122, 125, 126, 267
Harewood Hospital, 244
Harland, Colonel Edward, 81
Hartford, Connecticut, 17, 60, 63, 65, 93, 105, 205, 259, 261
Harvard Medical School, 142
Hatteras Inlet, 72-80, 84-87, 107

Hawley, Capt. William, 57, 122, 127, 129-32, 240
Hawley, MA, 253
Heckman, Gen. Charles, 227-8
Henry VIII, 166
Hickman, Robert, 209
Hicks, Gov. Thomas, 61
Highlander ship, 75
Hill, Gen. A.P., 125
Hill, Gen. D.H., 181
Hill's Point Battery, 84, 155, 156, 158, 160, 164, 165
Hilton Head Isle, S.C., 261
Hingham, MA, 42
Hood, General John Bell, 119
Hooker, General Joseph, 153, 161, 162, 163
Horsetown, CA, 60, 281, 286, 287, 288, 289
Hotchkiss, Capt. Albert, 272
Howes, Alfred, 252-54
Hoyt, Captain Henry, 60-2, 71, 94, 95, 104, 105, 111, 144, 173, 174, 183, 240, 241, 252
Hull, England, 47
Humphreys, General Andrew, 139
Hunter, Gen. David, 263
Insane Hospital, Washington, D. C., 163-5, 169, 172
Jackson, Patrick T., 277
Jackson, Stonewall, 137
James River, 151, 210, 216, 225
Jay, Maine, 22, 24, 26, 27, 28, 36, 46, 47, 50, 51, 52, 274, 275, 276, 278, 279, 280, 285, 286
Jefferson Barracks, 4
John Haswell ship, 233
Jones, Charles A., 65
Jones, Charlotte, 65
Jones, Julius, 65
Keedysville, MD, 117, 119, 132
Kentucky, 162, 163
Kidder, Clarissa, 266
King, Lewis D., 63
Kingfield Historical Society, 49
Kingfield, ME, 12-14, 21, 22, 26-35, 42, 47-50, 203, 251, 253, 254, 275, 280, 281, 282, 284, 285, 290, 297
Kingman family, 17

Kingman, Carrie, 18, 49-51, 53, 149, 192, 308
Kingman, Charles, 302-04, 307, 308, 310
Kingman, Ella, 23, 149, 192, 298, 308
Kingman, Evelyn Clayton, 50, 51
Kingman, Katie, 213
Kingman, Lucy, 44, 301
Kingman, Marietta Colburn, 306
Kingman, Marietta, 301, 305
Kingman, Mary, 149
Kingman, Mary, 23, 192, 308
Kingman, Nellie, 212, 219, 223, 230
Kingman, Orlando, 44, 60, 71, 98, 99, 106, 111, 190, 191, 212, 219, 223, 230, 301, 306, 308, 312
Kingman, Samuel Clayton, 18, 22-4, 31-9, 42, 44-46, 50, 59, 60, 66, 71, 85, 86, 91-3, 102, 109-11, 126, 127, 129, 135, 146, 147, 177, 185, 186, 187, 188, 191, 201, 202, 210, 213, 218, 235, 237, 240, 243, 252, 254, 255, 259, 265, 266, 280, 282, 286, 287, 290, 297-301, 306
Kingman, Samuel, 42-5, 59, 135, 298
Kingman, Sarah Ring Pope, 42, 43, 298
Kingman, William W., 44, 60, 301-5
Knight, Capt. Jason, 303
Krapp, William, 268-71
Krautz, August, 232
Lacy House, 113-15, 137, 140
Lacy, Major J. Horace, 137
Lafourche Crossing, LA, 268
Lamb's Artillery, 3
Lamson, Lt. Roswell Hawkes, 159
Lamson, Lt., 157, 158, 159, 161
Lander, Abisha, 22, 27-32, 48-51, 53, 285
Lander, Kezia, 48
Lanesville, VA, 181
Lawrence, MA, 280, 298
Laytonville, MD, 117
Lee, Admiral S.P., 232
Lee, Dr. J. H., 197
Lee, General Robert E., 113, 116, 117, 151, 177-9, 202, 216, 229
Lee, William, 179
Leesborough, MD, 117
Lewiston, ME, 279
Lincoln, Abraham, 146, 167, 198, 199, 306

Litchfield County, CT, 63, 181, 247
Littlefield, Capt. Samuel, 302-4
Longfellow Mountains, 48
Longstreet, Gen. James, 151, 152, 161
Lovettsville, VA, 133
Lowell, John A., 277
Lowell, MA, 276-8
Lyman, Eunice, 312
Macomb, Major Gen. Alexander, 3
Macon, Georgia, 259
Maine Diner 14
Maine, 12-4, 18, 20-4, 25-7, 30, 32, 34-6, 42, 45, 47, 50, 51, 53, 142, 207, 219, 244, 251, 254, 274, 275, 277, 278, 280, 282, 284, 290, 294, 295, 297
Maine Regiments: 2nd ME V.I., 168, 16th ME, 111, 133, 140, 141, 142, 143, 282, 290
Manassas Gap, VA, 135
Manchester, CT, 261
Manhattan, NY 243
Marble, George E., 261
Marble, William S., 260-2
Marfa, TX, 284
Marsh, George H., 123, 124
Marsh, Lt. Wolcott, 105
Mary B, 206, 207, 209-11, 256
Marye's Heights, VA 138, 139, 143
Maryland, 7, 116, 117, 120, 121, 126, 132, 133, 142, 178, 213
Massachusetts, 13, 22, 27, 32, 253, 283, 287, 295, 301
Massachusetts Regiments: 2nd Company of MA Vol. Sharpshooters, 111, 306, 308, 6th Mass, 307, 8th MA, 301, 303, 304, 22nd MA V.I., 308, 23rd MA, 75, 24th MA, 91, 265, 268, 40th MA, 236, 50th MA, 301, 302
McClellan, General George, 12, 68-70, 74, 107, 110, 113, 132, 134, 140, 179 219, 306
Meade, Gen. George, 201, 202
Memorial Military Museum, 65
Merrimack River, 23
Merrimack, MA, 142
Merriman, Captain, 75
Mexico, 285
Middletown, MD, 117, 118
Milford Cemetery, 41
Mine Run, 202

Minnesota ship, 109
Mississippi River, 177, 302
Mississippi, 236, Mississippi, 237, 253
Monitor and *Merrimac*, 109
Monroe, CT, 63
Monroe, Noah, 166
Moore, B., 253
Morehead City, NC, 84, 101, 106
Morris, Captain, 76
Morris, John Moses, 105, 189, 191
Mount Vernon, VA, 245
Mountain Grove Cemetery, 131, 165, 263, 265, 271
Mt. Ranier, 160
Mud March, 144-6
Muscatine, Iowa, 295
Nansemond River, 151-56
Nanuet, New York, 2
Nashville, TN, 177
National Institute of Health, 170
Naugatuck, CT, 63
Navajo, 183
Nelson, Lord Horatio, 80
Nettleton, Jay, 181, 208
Neuse River, NC, 87, 101
Nevins, Alan, 232
New Bern Civil War Battlefield Park, 88, 89
New Bern National Cemetery, 93-96
New Bern, NC, 8, 84, 87, 88, 90, 91, 93-6, 101, 103-6, 110, 111, 136, 137, 148, 149, 264-267
New Castle, VA, 235, 236
New England Soldier's Relief Association, 5, 243
New Hampshire, 177, 189, 190, 199
New Hampshire Regiments: 10th New Hampshire, 158, 236, 13th New Hampshire, 221
New Haven, CT, 168, 205, 295
New Jersey, 4, 253
New Jersey Regiments: 9th NJ V.I., 74, 75
New Market, MD, 117
New Mexico Territory, 183
New Milford, CT, 246
New Orleans, LA, 61, 178, 270, 271, 302
New Preston, CT, 262
New York City, NY, 3, 5, 47, 263

New York, 1-5, 9, 42, 43, 55, 56, 61, 74, 84, 102 124, 126, 142, 177, 191, 243, 281, 294, 295, 301, 302, 306, 311
New York, ship, 75
New York Regiments: 7th Independent Battery, 56th NY Volunteers, 198, 38th NY, 311, 48th NY, 168, 262, 79th NY, 159, 89th NY, 156, 158, 108th N.Y., 130, 118th New York, 197, 221, 236, 148th New York, 193
Newfield, NJ, 253
Newport News, VA, 84, 107, 109-112, 115, 147, 148, 151
Newport, Rhode Island, 159, 160
Nexsen, Mary Waldron, 6
Nexsen, William, 6
Nichols, Alonzo, 282
Nichols, John (son), 282
Nichols, John B., 23, 277, 282, 283
Nichols, Lizzie, 282
Nichols, Mary, 282
Norfolk, VA, 151, 193-5, 213, 214, 218
North Carolina, 17, 20, 63, 67, 68, 71, 72, 73, 80, 82, 84, 87, 92, 93, 108, 110, 115, 125, 247, 264-67
North Carolina Regiments: 33rd NC V.I., 267, 37th NC, 125
North Star ship, 281, 295
Ogunquit, ME, 13
Old Warren Cemetery, 312
Opelousas and Great Western Railroad, 268
Ople, John, 208
Oregon, 152, 159
Orlean, VA, 135
Overland Campaign, 216, 233, 246
Pamlico Sound, 74
Pamunkey River, 179, 181, 235
Panama, 42
Park Congregational Church, 210, 299
Parke, General John, 81, 87
Parker, George, 310
Parker, Thomas, 266-8
Parkington, George A., 271-3
Peck, General John, 151
Peninsula Campaign, 12, 107, 105, 179
Penn State University, 18, 19
Pennsylvania regiments: 139, 20th PA, 303
Pennsylvania, 18, 19, 178

Perlotto, Kim, 17, 18
Petersburg, VA, 63, 142, 151, 209, 213, 217, 222, 223, 224, 225, 228, 229, 230, 232, 265
Philadelphia National Cemetery., 261
Philadelphia, PA, 69, 195, 243, 244, 261, 306, 307
Philomont, VA, 133
Pitts, Charles, 170
Pitts, William, 170
Platt, Dan, 23, 24, 38-42
Platt, Elisabeth, 40-1
Platt, Emily, 41
Platt, Henry Dwight, 40, 41
Platt, Mary, 41
Pleasant Valley, MD, 133, 134, 136
Plumb, Seth, 157, 181, 248
Plumb, Will, 248
Pocahontas ship, 76
Pocotaligo, SC, 259
Pope, General John, 112, 113
Port Hudson, 269, 303
Port Royal, SC, 259
Port Walthall Junction, VA, 220-23
Portsmouth, VA, 84, 151, 152, 173, 176, 178, 183-7, 189, 190-2, 201, 203, 204, 208, 209, 213, 214, 218
Potomac River, 116, 120, 122, 133, 146
Princeton Theological Seminary, 4
Pulaski, SC, 260, 263
Quebec, Canada, 13
Queen of the West ship, 269
Quinn, Isabella, 171
Quinn, Mary, 171
Raleigh, Sir Walter, 80
Rappahannock River, 112, 115, 137, 138, 142, 145
Regan, Capt. Peter, 197, 198
Reno, General Jesse, 75, 119
Reza, Ygnasia, 285
Rhode Island Regiments: 3rd RI Artillery, 264, 1st RI V.I., 63, 4th RI, 63, 76, 88, 196, 197, 5th RI, 88, 99
Richards, Alonzo, 64
Richmond National Cemetery, 12
Richmond, VA, 12, 37, 105, 107, 110, 111, 114, 136, 137, 140, 145, 176, 178, 181, 182, 193, 195, 216-9, 222, 224, 226, 228, 229, 232, 251, 252, 269, 298
Ricker, Tille, 261

Ridgeville, MD, 117
Riverside Cemetery, 14, 16, 28, 31, 48, 49, 251, 253, 282
Roanoke Island, NC 67, 79-84, 85, 87, 107, 148, 149
Roanoke, VA, 213
Rodanthe, NC, 86
Rodman, Dr., 196, 197
Rodman, General Issac, 121, 125
Rohrbach, Henry, 123
Roys, Harriet, 253
Ruidosa, TX, 284
Sackets Harbor, NY 4
Saint Augustine, FL, 298
San Francisco, CA 282, 295
Sanborn, Lt. Alanson, 193- 200
Sanborn, Thomas and Mary, 199
Santa Fe, New Mexico, 284
Savannah, GA, 260, 263, 264
Save Historic Antietam Foundation, 132
Second Seminole War, 4
Seven Days Battles, 12, 107
Sexton, Henry D., 94, 96
Seymour, Thomas, 148, 150, 155, 270
Shafter, TX, 284, 285, 289
Sharon, CT, 271
Sharpsburg, Maryland, 117, 118, 309
Shelton, Abigail Avis, 166
Shenandoah River, 122
Shenandoah Valley, 94
Shepherdstown, MD, 120
Sheppard, Capt., 197
Sherman, Gen. William, 260
Skowhegan, ME, 142
Small, Major Abner Ralph, 143
Smilie, John H., 90, 265-7
Smith, Chaplain Moses, 8, 237, 238, 243
Smith, Gen. William "Baldy", 217, 232
Smithsonian Institution, 7
Snavely's Ford, 124
Snow, Heman, 98, 99
South Anna River, 182
South Berwick, ME, 277, 278
South Carolina, 183
South Church, 4, 7, 47, 61, 64, 148, 191, 209, 210, 243
South Mills, NC, 84, 184, 187

South Reading, MA, 22, 23, 38, 42, 43, 44, 45, 134, 135, 266, 287, 298, 301, 303, 306
Spanish American War, 63
Spaulding ship, 76
Spring Valley, NY, 55
St. Louis, MO.,118
Staten Island, NY, 4
Staunton, VA, 170
Stepping Stones ship, 156, 158
Stevens, Capt. Hazard, 157-60
Stevens, Isaac Ingalls, 159, 160
Stevens, William, 142
Stocking, Sabin, 169
Stoddard, John, 262
Storm, NG, 277
Strong, Bob, 9, 10, 12-6, 19, 20, 48, 52, 84, 90
Sturgis, General Samuel, 119
Suffolk, VA, 84, 150-3, 157, 159, 161, 162, 165, 168, 169, 173, 213-5
Sutherland, James, 310, 311
Sweetser, Charlotte, 266
Swift Creek, VA, 223-4
Taylor, Frank, 262-4
Taylor, George, 181, 182
Taylor, Rod, 255
Taylor, William, 75
Terrazas, Don Louis, 285
Terry, Gen. Alfred, 217
Texas, 269, 284, 295
Thetford, VT, 199
Thomas Foulks ship, 263
Thomas, Albert H., 223
Thompson, Agnes, 18, 19, 25, 65, 141, 254, 268, 271, 274, 282, 293
Thompson, Captain Alexander, 3, 5, 12
Thompson, Catherine, 6
Thompson, Colonel Alexander, 3, 4
Thompson, Davis, 18
Thompson, Ed and Nancy, 18, 19
Thompson, Margaret, 6
Thompson, Miss Amelia, 6
Thompson, Mrs. Amelia, 5
Thompson, Rev. Alexander, 4, 7, 8, 9, 18, 19, 47, 57, 59, 63, 90, 99, 103, 132, 210, 237, 240, 243, 294, 307, 308
Thompson, William, 4
Tiffany, 261
Tilden, Col. Charles, 143
Tillotson Collegiate and Normal Institute, 295
Tomlinson, John B., 63
Towse, Charlotte, 47
Trafalgar ship, 47
Tredegar Iron Works, 37, 38
Trump, P.B. Van, 160
Tuller, Hattie, 94
Tuller, Isaac, 93-6
Turner's Gap, MD, 118
typhoid, 93-5, 104, 261
U.S. Army Heritage and Education Center, 9
Unionville, CT, 153
United States Marine Corps, 69
United States Naval Academy, 64, 159
USS Gettysburg, 159
Utica (NY) Lunatic Asylum, 198
Vermont, 194, 199
Vermont Regiments: 9th VT, 158
Vicksburg, MS 177, 193, 269
Viele, Gen. Egbert, 193
Virginia Department of Transportation, 214
Virginia, 8, 12, 18, 84, 109, 112, 115, 126, 130, 151, 161-3, 165, 170, 193, 195
Virginia Regiments: 7th VA, 227, 40th VA, 170
Wadhams, Martin, 94, 96
Waite, Stephen Hand, 261
Wakefield, MA 298, 302-6
Waldron, Captain, 143
Wallingford, CT, 205, 208
War of 1812, 177
Ware Bottom Church, VA, 228
Warren, CT, 312
Washington, CT, 50, 297-9
Washington, D.C., 6, 7, 105, 116, 117, 122, 126, 156, 159, 163-68, 173, 174, 201, 202, 243-6, 304, 306
Washington, George, 178, 245
Watertown, CT, 23, 34, 35, 38-40, 298-300, 306-9
Waterville College, 42, 25, 111, 281, 282
Waud, Alfred, 133, 139, 146, 239, 242
Webster, Benjamin, 50
Weitzel, Gen. Godfrey, 269, 270
Weld, Maine, 280

Weldon, NC, 213
Weller, Surgeon, 74, 75
Welles, H. G., The Time Machine, 255
Welles, Thomas, 166
Wellington, Duke Arthur, 74
Wentworth, Jacob, 246-48
West Point, Military Academy, 3-7, 50
West, Daniel J., 259-61
Western Lunatic Asylum, 170
Wheatland, VA, 133
Wheeler & Wilson Manufacturing Co., 38, 42, 260, 265, 272, 298
White House Landing, VA, 62, 84, 176, 180, 229, 233, 234, 238
Whittier, John Greenleaf, 261
Williams, Horace N., 63
Williams, Jonathan, 5
Woolley, Reverend Joseph Judah, 63
Wright, Dr. David, 192-199
Wright, Penelope, 198
Wyman, Ann H., 290, 292
Wyman, Augustine, 290, 293, 295
Yale College, 105
Yale Divinity School, 105, 294
Yorktown, VA, 3, 12, 217-219
Zimmermann, Walter, 2

www.ingramcontent.com/pod-product-compliance
Lightning Source LLC
Chambersburg PA
CBHW030135170426
43199CB00008B/68